Student Teaching
A Process Approach to Reflective Practice

*A Guide for Student, Intern,
and Beginning Teachers*

M. Serra Goethals
Rose A. Howard
Bellarmine College

Foreword by Ken Zeichner

Merrill
an imprint of Prentice Hall

Upper Saddle River, New Jersey   *Columbus, Ohio*

Library of Congress Cataloging-in-Publication Data

Goethals, M. Serra,
    Student teaching : a process approach to reflective practice : a guide for student, intern,
and beginning teachers / M. Serra Goethals, Rose A. Howard ; [editor, Debra A. Stollenwerk].
        p.   cm.
    Includes bibliographical references and index.
    ISBN 0-13-920125-4
    1. Student teaching—Handbooks, manuals, etc.   2. Teachers—Training of—Handbooks,
manuals, etc.   I. Howard, Rose A.   II. Stollenwerk, Debra A.   III. Title.

LB2157.A3 G57 2000
370'.71—dc21

                                                                    99-049272

Editor: Debra A. Stollenwerk
Assistant Editor: Heather Doyle Fraser
Editorial Assistant: Penny S. Burleson
Production Editor: Mary Harlan
Design Coordinator: Diane C. Lorenzo
Text Design and Production Coordination: Carlisle Publishers Services
Cover Design: Tanya Burgess
Cover Photo: ©SuperStock, Inc.
Production Manager: Pamela D. Bennett
Director of Marketing: Kevin Flanagan
Marketing Manager: Meghan Shepherd
Marketing Coordinator: Krista Groshong

This book was set in Palatino by Carlisle Communications, Ltd. and was printed and bound by The Banta Company. The cover was printed by The Banta Company.

©2000 by Prentice-Hall, Inc.
Pearson Education
Upper Saddle River, New Jersey 07458

Printed in the United States of America

10 9 8 7 6 5 4 3 2 1

ISBN: 0-13-920125-4

Prentice-Hall International (UK) Limited, *London*
Prentice-Hall of Australia Pty. Limited, *Sydney*
Prentice-Hall of Canada, Inc., *Toronto*
Prentice-Hall Hispanoamericana, S. A., *Mexico*
Prentice-Hall of India Private Limited, *New Delhi*
Prentice-Hall of Japan, Inc., *Tokyo*
Prentice-Hall (Singapore) Pte. Ltd., *Singapore*
Editora Prentice-Hall do Brasil, Ltda., *Rio de Janeiro*

Foreword

It has not been common for educational planners, administrators, and school officials to view teachers as significant agents in the process of educational reform. On the contrary, the dominant approach has been to "train" teachers to be efficient implementers of policies and practices developed by others who are removed from the classroom. From this perspective, there has been little interest in developing the capabilities of teachers to exercise their judgment about educational matters in or outside of the classroom. Teachers are not taught to acquire the dispositions and self-monitoring skills that will enable them to learn from their practice and become better teachers throughout their teaching careers.

This top-down approach to educational reform has not been very successful in influencing what goes on in classrooms. Announcing changes in schooling, even demanding these, will not change what happens in schools and classrooms if teachers resist and subvert these changes. If one conclusion can be drawn from educational reform efforts over the last 30 years, it is that qualitative changes in classroom practice will only occur when teachers understand them and accept them as their own. During the last decade, a movement has been underway throughout the world to prepare teachers as reflective practitioners who play a much more significant role in determining what goes on in schools (e.g., the purposes and end of their work, the curriculum) and in the process of educational reform. This concept of the teacher as reflective practitioner means that the process of understanding and improving one's teaching must start from reflection on one's own experience. Furthermore, the process of learning to teach continues throughout a teacher's career. The implication of this view is that teacher education programs need to prepare teachers from the very beginning of their education for teaching to aim for this new, more expanded role and to help them acquire the dispositions and skills that will enable them to learn from their practice.

This book focuses on preparing teachers to be the kind of reflective practitioner that has increasingly become the goal in teacher education programs throughout the world. It rejects the limited role of "teacher as technician" who only implements in a passive way what others decide. It argues that teachers also have an important role to play in designing and interpreting curricular and instruction guidelines and educational reforms. An important theme throughout the book is the goal of working for a high quality of education for all children, something that we have not been able to achieve to date in any society in the world. The achievement of an educational system in which the quality of education received is not dependent on one's ethnic background, race, gender, social class, or religion is necessary to the realization in practice of the idea of a democratic and just society.

This book recognizes that the teacher's role is not limited to the classroom and includes attention to such important issues as the broader context of the school and to relations with parents and the community. One of the strengths of this book is that its structure and organization are consistent with its message.

The various activities for prospective teachers that have been built into each chapter encourage a very active and reflective role for those who use it. This consistency between the message and the method is often lacking in teacher education programs, which serves to undermine the achievement of one's goals. The wealth of material in this book will assist prospective teachers to become the kind of educational leaders that are necessary for the 21st century.

Ken Zeichner
Madison, Wisconsin

Preface

Purpose

We have directed seminars and field experiences for undergraduate and graduate student teachers and for more than a dozen years have searched for meaningful activities and processes that engage and guide beginning teachers. The search has focused on the goal to strengthen the link between education courses and the field-based aspects of learning to teach. Furthermore, we want to provide student teachers with opportunities to reflect on their professional knowledge and personal growth—to integrate these understandings into their total experience of being a teacher.

Student Teaching: A Process Approach to Reflective Practice encourages student/intern teachers and those pursuing alternative teacher certification to engage in reflective thinking, reflective practice, and reflective writing. Authentic tasks invite beginning teachers to recall learning acquired through courses in the arts and sciences, content from the teaching major, and all education pedagogy. Expected outcomes and activities in the text take the preservice/intern teacher through the whys and hows of reflective practices by actively involving the teacher in the application of these practices. Beginning teachers are challenged to contemplate current educational paradigms and practices, analyze them, effectuate them, and reflect on their learning experiences in a journal forum. Involving preservice teachers in the application of educational practices promotes ownership and helps them build a professional life on reflective practice. A constructivist learning approach undergirds each chapter and invites beginning teachers to consciously relate all types of learning to new situations and to make meaning from this learning. Student/intern teachers are encouraged to combine their personal investments and experiences of teaching with recognized best practice. Throughout the student/intern teaching experience the beginning teacher is encouraged to develop a positive attitude toward what is observed and practiced at the school level, to look for opportunities for learning, to raise questions, and to seek understanding through reflection. It is our goal that through reflective practice beginning teachers will continue to engage in this process throughout their professional career.

Audience and Intended Uses

We offer a practical guide for reflective practice and provide models of current best practice based on national standards. We encourage beginning teachers to apply this knowledge in their day-to-day teaching in the school. The book can be used in a variety of ways with beginning and/or experienced teachers.

- Undergraduate student teachers will find this process approach to learning helpful throughout their professional placement in the school setting and in the seminar or class accompanying the experience.
- Graduate interns or others interested in pursuing an alternate route in obtaining state licensure will find in this text exemplary reflective teaching practices needed to facilitate learning.

- Experienced teachers desiring to refresh and refine their own reflective teaching practices may review the teaching strategies and application to the national standards.

Organization

Student Teaching: A Process Approach to Reflective Practice calls the student/intern teacher to develop a professional teaching identity through reflective practice. The text is organized around a double focus: personal experience and an application of a recognized best practice of the teaching/learning experience.

Focus One encourages beginning teachers to reflect on their own personal and professional development and the accompanying perceptions, attitudes, and feelings about themselves as persons assuming a new role, that of teacher. Specially designed activities offer opportunities for ongoing personal exploration and evolving professional stories focusing on the goal of becoming a professional teacher. Cooperative learning groups are suggested for this portion of the seminar, along with opportunities for structured dialogue presented to encourage personal and professional growth through shared experience.

Focus Two engages student/intern teachers in reflection about the recognition and use of theories connected with effective teaching and learning. Beginning teachers are asked to review and apply earlier learning strategies recognized as educational best practice. A brief review of selected teaching strategies and knowledge of teaching is provided based on research and national standards. Activities provide opportunities to apply these best practices in classroom instruction. Follow-up questions offer prompts for discussion directing beginning teachers to analyze problems and decisions made in their classrooms.

- The Introduction invites active engagement in the process of reflective learning and provides a road map for using subsequent chapters of the text. This section concludes with suggestions for active involvement in a cooperative learning group. It is intended to enhance teachers' ability to establish and contribute to an atmosphere of professional responsibility within their classrooms and the school.
- Chapters 1 through 3 include observation techniques, designing and planning for instruction, and activities connected with the initial weeks of the beginning teaching experience.
- Chapter 4 reinforces the continued exploration and provision of appropriate instruction that values diversity and promotes student achievement.
- Chapters 5, 6, and 7 refine lesson presentation, address the stimulation of critical thinking through questions, and highlight other key teaching strategies to support the implementation and management of instruction.
- Chapters 8 and 9 are devoted to creating and maintaining the learning climate within the classroom. Included are suggested methods and models of discipline strategies designed to assist the beginning teacher in making connections with observation and practice in the classroom.
- Chapters 10 and 11 focus on the use of multiple assessment instruments for assessing student learning and offers suggestions for communicating the results to students and parents or guardians.
- Chapter 12 emphasizes collaborative efforts with parents, colleagues, and other agencies, with suggested activities for developing a collaborative spirit within the school and community.

- Chapters 13 and 14 focus on refining student/intern teachers' reflection and assessment of their teaching experience and developing a commitment to professional growth.
- Chapter 15 provides suggestions and procedures for pursuing a teaching position.

Special Features

- Organization is logical and motivational, so that beginning teachers can see this book as a framework to assist in refining their teaching strategies and attitude toward teaching, and as a practical resource in a professional education career.
- Affective activities acknowledge and validate the importance of the beginning teachers' personal involvement and ownership in building their professional lives as reflective educators.
- Cooperative learning groups are actively promoted, involving the beginning teacher in the group process.
- Each chapter offers probing discussion questions asking beginning teachers to observe, examine, explain, and discuss their field experiences with peers.
- A learner-centered, reflective, and participatory approach to instructional planning is presented.
- Beginning teachers are encouraged to adopt an inquiring mind with respect to their observations and experiences in schools.
- An introduction to the development of the professional portfolio that beginning teachers can present as clarification and communication of their educational philosophy and growth as a teacher is presented.
- Summaries at the end of the chapter assist the reader in capturing major concepts.
- Technology Tips (Chapters 2, 4, and 11) include ideas for integrating technology in the classroom and present important educational web sites.
- Portfolio Tasks (Chapters 3, 6, 8, 10, 12, and 13) based on national standards can be completed by beginning teachers for professional use in procuring a teaching position.
- Journal entries are presented from secondary, middle, elementary, and special education student teachers responding to their recent experiences.
- Suggested readings and research resources are included at the end of each chapter to give student/intern teachers ample materials to further their exploration or reinforce the concepts presented.

Acknowledgments

In preparing this manuscript we have benefited from the invaluable assistance of a number of creative and reflective colleagues, classroom teachers, school administrators, and friends. We take pleasure in recognizing some of them publicly. We are deeply indebted to our esteemed colleague and friend, Marie Sanders, who offered outstanding editorial contributions, suggestions, and insights strengthening each chapter. We gained much from her enthusiasm and creativity. We are grateful to Maureen Coughlin, friend and esteemed colleague, who made many helpful comments and suggestions from her school placement experiences. From the beginning, John Oppelt, Ph.D., warmly supported this project. A special note of thanks to Ivan and Jean Baugh for computer assistance in the initial draft of the manuscript. We are indebted to Ken Zeichner, Ph.D., a recognized scholar of reflective teaching, who graciously agreed to write the Foreword to this book.

We would also like to acknowledge and extend our appreciation to the many student teachers for their willingness to provide thoughtful response and formative feedback to the text. Special thanks to student teachers whose journal excerpts appear in the book: Susan Brinkhaus, Julie Burke, Danielle Cassady, Jay Ebelhar, Julie E. Hall, Steve Farris, Meri Lou Gonzalez, Rhonda Hedges, Kristin Howard, Debbie Johnson, Kathy Knopf, Amy Maupin, Courtney McMillen, Wendi Nord, Marti Quirk, Stephanie Raia, Jolie Waldridge, and Lisa Washburn.

We extend special appreciation to Merrill, of Prentice Hall: To our editor, Debbie Stollenwerk, for her enthusiastic support from the beginning; to Heather Doyle Fraser, assistant editor, for her persistent and challenging support to produce a quality manuscript; and to our project editor, Kelli Jauron, for her positive support. A special note of thanks to the reviewers who allowed us to engage in our own reflective practice in the revision and editing of this manuscript: Carolyn Babione, Indiana University, Southeast; Terry Carson, University of Alberta; Elaine Chakonas, Dominican University; Allan F. Cook, University of Illinois, Springfield; Sandra L. DiGiaimo, University of Illinois, Springfield; Manina Urgolo Dunn, Seton Hall University; Jeri-Lynn Gatto, Richard Stockton State College; John E. Steinbrink, Oklahoma State University, Stillwater; and Donna Strand, Baruch College.

Brief Contents

Contents

Introducing
the Reflective Approach

"When students and teachers make use of reflection as a tool for learning and assessment, they are creating an opening that allows them to enter into students' work, making sense of their endeavors and accomplishments, and learning how they judge their success."

R. Zessoules & H. Gardner

REFLECTIVE PRACTICES AND YOU

Congratulations! You are entering the most challenging, rewarding, and critical stage of your educational experience. As a practicing professional you are expected to apply all that you've learned thus far about the art and science of teaching. Through practice, discussions, and reflection, you will refine your methodologies and teaching techniques. During this exciting period of reflective learning, your philosophy of education will become grounded in best practice—that is, a compilation of state-of-the-art practices based on national standards and recognized and outlined by learned societies. Zemelman, Daniels, and Hyde (1993) describe best practice as a "shorthand emblem of serious, thoughtful, informed, responsible, state-of-the-art teaching." This critical stage of your experience offers you a number of challenging opportunities for personal and professional growth as an educator.

You are invited to begin this journey of discovery learning by actively engaging in the processes of reflective learning as outlined in this text. *Student Teaching: A Process Approach to Reflective Practice* acts as a unique guide to your student/intern teaching experience. Its interactive format allows you to identify, analyze, reflect, and act upon your personal insights about teaching. Your ideas, discoveries, and understanding of the teacher's role are validated through reflective practices and engaging, thoughtful activities.

Why Do We Say Reflective Practices?

We say *reflective practice* because reflection and the construction of new meaning from new situations, or constructivist learning, are two key factors associated with effective teaching. Reflection is a thoughtful response to either preplanned or spontaneous but conscious decisions and actions. The reflective process asks you to focus continuously on questions such as "What am I doing?" "Why?" "How well are my students learning?" "How do I know?" (Cruickshank, 1987; Fellows & Zimpher, 1988; Valverde, 1982). You are asked to recall the learning acquired through courses in the arts and sciences, content from your teaching major, and the education courses that form your past experiences and understanding. Learning

1

acquired through your previous work with children and adolescents, inside and outside a school setting, enables you to better understand and appreciate the connection between theory and practice. It is through reflective practice that this deeper level of learning occurs.

Constructivist learning asks you to relate consciously all types of learning to new situations and to make meaning from this learning. Your ongoing development depends on a gradual and systematic consideration of what is studied, observed, and discussed. How to integrate your learning into your repertoire of teaching practices becomes the challenge! The seminar format of this text allows you to share and gain from your own experiences and those of your peers. You, as beginning teacher, provide case studies from your own classroom and school experiences for discussion in the seminar. These examples of practical situations allow you to analyze what is happening in the classroom and make professional decisions. Follow-up discussions in the seminar provide you opportunities to act on your insights and your decisions.

How Do We Engage in the Reflective Process?

The chapter activities are designed for your use in collaborating with your supervising teacher, meeting with your college supervisor, and sharing with your colleagues in the seminar setting. We encourage you to become involved in a variety of tasks and to reflect on what you are learning. We have outlined a continuum of opportunities to involve you in activities and situations similar to those you plan for your students.

As manager and director, you are the designer and planner of instruction. Having experience and practice with the activities similar to those you assign students better enables you to ask guiding questions of your students and direct them along the path of meaningful inquiry. Through directions and questions you assist your students in locating and using information and applying concepts to meaningful learning situations. You provide your students with instruction that connects the different disciplines and relate these to real-life situations. Relying on your experience as a learner enhances the learning process for those you teach.

Subsequent chapters focus on such skills as planning, giving directions, questioning, lesson presentation, behavior management, and assessment. Each week you are asked to apply and reflect on one of these skills. Practicing these skills within your classroom helps you to analyze your strengths and note areas for improving your teaching performance.

What Is Focus One?

Each seminar session opens with a **Focus One** activity that allows you to engage in critical dialogue with your peers. This is an opportunity for reflection on the pressing, exciting, and challenging situations you experience in the classroom. Witherell and Noddings (1991) convey that stories and narratives, whether personal or fictional, provide meaning and belonging in our lives. They attach us to others and to our own histories by providing a tapestry rich with threads of time, place, and character. They lead us to discover that which needs doing in our lives!

Focus One activities invite you to explore and to share your stories and experiences as teacher during this period of intense learning. The activities and reflections are designed to guide you in assembling your values and beliefs about teaching, while engaging you in the technicalities associated with everyday classroom life.

Dialogue and 'Teacher Discourse'

Dialogue and "teacher discourse" are recognized means of fostering growth and ongoing development as a teacher. Great teaching grows out of a clear sense of self and often leads to a reinvention of ourselves as teachers (Preskill, 1998; Witherell & Noddings, 1991). Teachers grow and gain insights about teaching by engaging in teacher discourse. Through interactions with peers and discussions about everyday classroom happenings, teachers learn problem-solving techniques and the benefits of questioning classroom practices while gaining insights into the profession of teaching. Teacher discourse encourages listening to others and sharing; as you listen and begin to analyze others' stories, you gain a more holistic view of the profession that leads to your gradual growth in practical and the ethical concerns teachers face everyday.

Simply reading motivational ideas and good teaching practices does not magically transform you into a highly successful and competent teacher. The process of becoming a competent teacher is gained through ongoing practice and a desire to overcome the initial trials associated with teaching. Gradual and steady growth coupled with analytical reflection will aid you in this experience. There are no incantations or chants; only in fairy tales is there instant transformation and triumph (Isenberg, 1994).

Each week you are invited to participate in the activities of **Focus One,** which allot time to absorb the meaning and reflect on the impact of the week's events as you sit quietly for a few minutes and call to mind a specific situation, dilemma, ideal, or conflict from the past week. You are invited to revisit in your mind the place and the persons and to hear what was said. Try to feel the emotions you experienced while in the school. In the discussion that follows **Focus One** activities, you are invited to share stories about your learning and experiences and to listen to others as they contribute their personal narratives. This type of teacher discourse builds a sense of community, links teacher to teacher, and creates the setting in which a rich and critical dialogue can occur.

Discussion Questions

The text allows a number of options for **Focus One** activities. These activities may be done within a seminar, large group, or cooperative learning group structure. Guidelines for using the cooperative learning group approach appear in an appendix at the end of this chapter along with a practice activity and accompanying forms. Other forms and sample responses to **Focus One** activities from subsequent chapters are located in the appendix at the end of the text.

Critical Outcomes

In each chapter **Focus One** enables you to:

- identify your accomplishments as a beginning professional teacher
- analyze your personal response to your successes
- verbalize and plan actions in areas that need strengthening
- engage in critical dialogue with your peers
- discuss concerns about the school setting
- raise questions about assumptions observed at the school level
- build on insights gained from interactions with others
- adopt actions to meet group goals successfully as stated on the action plan (under the cooperative group option).

What Is Focus Two?

While **Focus One** invites you to reflect and discuss your personal experiences and insights about classroom life, **Focus Two** encourages you to look more deeply into the underlying structure of the teaching/learning situation. **Focus Two** introduces you to selected teaching behaviors and skills for best practice. In addition, **Focus Two** involves you in a variety of activities designed to organize your reflective learning and practice. Your mind is whirling with many basic questions about establishing yourself as a professional teacher:

- What is the schedule? How will block scheduling affect me?
- When do I start teaching? How will I know what to teach?
- In what ways do we accommodate for special learners in the class?
- Will the students recognize me as a teacher or another visitor?
- Who decorates the bulletin boards?

Through a reflective process you will not only be able to answer these questions but hundreds of others.

Focus Two challenges you to explore and put into practice:

- your knowledge of content
- your beliefs about teaching
- your understanding of best practice
- your vision of your own teaching

To make **Focus Two** user friendly, an overview of the categories in each chapter with an explanation follows.

Expected Performance

How do we measure performance of these best practices for beginning teachers? State and national standards provide specific criteria for new teacher performance standards. Criteria selected from these standards we label **Expected Performance;** these criteria are included in each chapter. Focusing on several criteria for meeting a new standard each week gives you the opportunity to improve with practice each day. In addition, portfolio tasks are suggested in specific chapters as a means to document what you consider to be best practice within the classroom/s during this time.

Overview: Connecting Focus One and Focus Two

A brief connection is made between Focus One and Focus Two. Reading the brief overview may add a different perspective to your group sharing and allow you to develop more ideas for best practice. Reflecting on **Focus One** and implementing **Focus Two** challenges you and your peers to come to each session charged and excited, eager to share your successes and your stories. Communicating your pride in each other's accomplishments with such expressions as "that's awesome!", "how did you ever?", "how imaginative, creative!" will build a community of learners. This kind of support system and networking is professionally invaluable, especially when you need a new teaching strategy, another way to handle a difficult student, or even affirmation that others have shared your "unique" experience.

Application: Instructional Best Practice

Each chapter focuses on a best practice or teacher behavior to be practiced during your experience. These teacher behaviors or instructional skills have been selected so that you specifically focus on them for a period of time. This does not mean you neglect others of equal importance. On the contrary, your reflection journal will continue to portray your progress in the areas that may be in need of improvement and to document your successes.

Assigned Activities

Organizational skills are a must for effective teaching. Practicing organization and responding to questions and assigned tasks can help you plan, process, and reflect on classes you observe or teach. Even though you may be teaching prior to the actual presentation within the text, the emphasis and treatment of this best practice reinforces and develops it in greater depth. The assigned tasks keep you focused on the continuing development of effective teacher behaviors.

Summary

A brief summary is presented and can be used to recapture the main emphasis of the chapter. The summary can be used the following week with the student/intern teachers as a review of the previous week's best practice.

Follow-Up Questions and Shared Insights

These questions can be used as a follow-up to the assigned activities or as reflective questions in a seminar. They are provided to encourage sharing your application of the best practice. You may want to use your journal and assignment as referents. This may be done with a partner, a small group, or the entire group. Whether you are in a Professional Development School (PDS) or public or private school, each group of learners challenges the beginning teacher in a different way. Sharing with your colleagues contributes to a deeper perspective and understanding of the teacher's role, the students, and the school environment.

Log of Hours

To assist you in recording time you spend in observing, participating, and teaching during this experience, a **log of hours** chart is located in the appendix. Documentation is required in many states as evidence of the specific number of supervised student teaching hours completed. Keeping a careful log and making sure the supervising teacher signs it upon completion of your experience gives you the evidence you may need for your portfolio.

Portfolio Tasks

Beginning with chapter 3, we provide you with opportunities to perform and reflect on your progress under the guidance of supervising teachers and college supervisors. Professional portfolio development tasks are designed and presented to assist you in becoming an excellent teacher candidate who can compile an outstanding/competent teaching portfolio. You will find the rubric with the performance criteria (suggested for use by your college supervisor) in the appendix at the end of the text.

Technology Tips

Technology ideas provide assistance in the integration of technology with the content being taught. In selected chapters you are provided Technology Tips. World Wide Web sites are included as additional resources in planning your lessons.

Journal of Experience

The journal or log of experience is written documentation of your observations and/or reflective response to the teaching methods, classroom organization, and student response to the learning environment relative to your classroom/s.

Journaling or keeping a daily log of your student/intern teaching experiences is an important means of becoming more perceptive about yourself as teacher.

The journal is a valuable instrument toward becoming a more effective teacher. You begin to develop your own style of teaching when observing, reflecting, and documenting your use of best practices. As you plan and implement your own instructional strategies, keep in mind what worked for the supervising teacher and yourself. To reflect and journal your strengths and to plan for improvement after each lesson enables you to focus on specific teaching behaviors for the next lesson.

Your journal is an important opportunity to become a reflective teacher. The format for this student/intern experience is a series of weekly, selected topics for written comments and/or analysis of your observations and experiences. Identifying theories in practice and teaching strategies challenges you to reflect on how you might introduce or plan to incorporate these into your own teaching. You begin to search for different strategies and techniques that will reach all students within your classes. As you gain new perspectives from observing the experienced supervising teacher and reflecting on your own teaching, you are building your own philosophy of education. The following real-life examples provide insights for your journaling:

- You might describe a problematic episode or situation and how the supervising teacher responds to or handles the situation.

  "Ms. A., is acting very low key today because she knows all the students are hyped up for Halloween. This is very effective. She is using lots of walking around the room and touching the children on the shoulder to calm them."

  "Mr. G. is constantly reinforcing student behavior in learning. He uses proximity a lot. He walks over to students who are talking or not paying attention and stands right next to them. That closeness usually 'snaps' the student back to the task."

- You may analyze your feelings and specific behaviors as you step into the role of teacher.

  "Sometimes I think that I go too slowly. I am very cautious of not going too fast, but I think that by doing this, I tend to lose the students who are advanced. I try to keep my pace at one that holds the attention of all the students, but this is very difficult. It is something I definitely need to practice on."

  "The students seem to respond to me very well and seem enthusiastic about my lessons. I feel that my major strengths are my enthusiasm, my use of positive reinforcement, and my use of stimulus variation. I work hard to keep them 'with me' because if they become bored and distracted then they will not learn anything."

- You may describe effective teaching techniques you want to develop or enhance in your own teaching.

  "I noticed that when students gave a quick answer to say what they thought the teacher wanted to hear, she would ask things like, 'why do you think that is,' 'how might that happen,' 'what could make a difference,' or 'what do you think about that?' She never accepts a wrong answer or a quick answer—she wants the students to think about the information."

Your preservice observations equip you with specific skills to analyze and label classroom behavior. Daily practice in identifying and labeling specific teaching skills helps you to become aware of your own classroom behavior and improve your teaching skills. Your observations and written comments may be related to specific aspects of the teaching learning environment listed under **Assigned Activities.**

Journal Excerpts from high school, middle, elementary, and special education student/intern teachers are included. They are selected because they relate to the best practice emphasized in each chapter. These beginning-teacher journal entries may serve as a resource in your own journal writing.

References and Suggested Readings

References provide current research and sources of information. Other sources are suggested for purposes of content review and further understanding of teaching strategies found in the chapter.

Appendix

An appendix is located at the end of the text. You will be alerted when forms, checklists, and other materials appear in the appendix. Guidelines for using a cooperative learning group approach follows this Introduction.

REFERENCES AND SUGGESTED READINGS

Ambach, G. (1996). Standards for teachers: Potential for improving practice. *Phi Delta Kappan, 78*(3), 207–210.

Baloche, L. (1998). *The cooperative classroom: Empowering learning.* Upper Saddle River, NJ: Merrill/Prentice Hall.

Brandt, R. (1989/90). On cooperative learning: A conversation with Spencer Kagan. *Educational Leadership, 47*(4), 8–11.

Brubacher, J. W., Case, C. W., & Reagan, T. G. (1994). *Becoming a reflective educator: How to build a culture of inquiry in the schools.* Thousand Oaks, CA: Corwin Press.

Clark, C. M., & Peterson, P. L. (1986). Teachers' thought processes. In M. Wittrock (Ed.), *Handbook of research on teaching* (pp. 255–296). New York: Macmillan.

Clift, R. T., Houston, W. R., & Pugach, M. C. (1990). *Encouraging reflective practice in education: An analysis of issues and programs.* New York: Teachers College Press.

Cruikshank, D. R. (1987). *Reflective teaching: The preparation of students of teaching.* Reston, VA: Association of Teacher Education.

Darling-Hammond, L., & Falk, B. (1997). Using standards and assessments to support student learning. *Phi Delta Kappan, 79*(3), 190–199.

Dewey, J. (1904). The relation of theory to practice in education. In C. A. McMurray (Ed.), *The third yearbook of the national society for the study of education.* Chicago: University of Chicago Press.

Fellows, K., & Zimpher, N. L. (1988). Reflectivity and the instructional process: A definitional comparison between theory and practice. In H. Waxman et al. (Eds.), *Images of reflection in teacher education.* Reston, VA: Association of Teacher Educators.

Henderson, J. (1996). *Reflective teaching* (2nd ed.) (pp. 18–19). Upper Saddle River, NJ: Merrill/Prentice Hall.

Isenberg, J. (1994). *Going by the book: The role of popular classroom chronicles in the professional development of teachers.* Westport, CT: Bergin & Garvey.

Kagan, S. B. (1989/90). The structural approach to cooperative learning. *Educational Leadership, 47*(4), 12–15.

Preskill, S. (1998). Narratives of teaching and the quest for the second self. *Journal of Teacher Education 49*(5), 344–357.

Schön, D. A. (1983). *The reflective practitioner: How professionals think in action.* New York: Basic Books, Inc.

Slavin, R. L. (1989/90). Research on cooperative learning: Consensus and controversy. *Educational Leadership 47*(4), 42–54.

Valli, L. (Ed.). (1992). *Reflective teacher: Education cases and critiques.* Albany, NY: State University of New York Press.

Valverde, L. (1982). The self-evolving supervisor. In T. Sergiovanni (Ed.) *Supervision of teaching,* (p. 86). Alexandria, VA: Association for Supervision and Curriculum Development.

Wallace, D. K. (Ed.). (1996). *Journey to school reform: Moving from reflection to action through story telling.* Washington, DC: National Education Association.

Witherell, C., and Noddings, N. (1991). *Stories lives tell: Narrative and dialogue in education.* New York: Teachers College Press.

Zemelman, S., Daniels, H., and Hyde, A. (1993). *Best practice: New standards for teaching and learning in America's schools.* Portsmouth, NH: Heinemann.

Zessoules, R., & Gardner, H. (1991). Authentic assessment: Beyond the buzzword and into the classroom. In V. Perrone (Ed.), *Expanding student assessment.* (p. 58). Alexandria, VA: Association for Supervision and Curriculum Development.

Zeicher, K., and Liston, D. (1987). Teaching student teachers to reflect. *Harvard Educational Review, 57*(1), 23–48.

Guidelines for a Cooperative Learning Group Approach
Actively Engaging Seminar Participants

Why Cooperative Groups?

Teaching in the 21st century encourages active learning strategies with students of all ages and across all disciplines. Cooperative learning is recognized as an effective approach to involve learners actively. As a future educator, you will most likely incorporate cooperative learning within your repertoire of instructional strategies. Instructional group strategies designed for teaching academic and social learning continuously evolve through your reflective process. By designing and managing the group structure, you can determine the learning outcome for your students. "Cooperative learning strategies properly structured have proven to be efficient and effective in promoting mastery of knowledge and skills among students of all abilities and ages." (Leighton 1999)

Certain cooperative group structures strengthen social interaction skills and have shown that learning can be individual and quite worthwhile. One of the primary reasons for promoting cooperative learning groups is to teach those skills that contribute to productive working groups. Five basic elements generally associated with effective cooperative learning groups include:

- positive interdependence
- face-to-face promotive interaction
- individual accountability
- interpersonal and small group skills
- group processing (Rhem 1992)

The best way to implement cooperative learning group structures is to engage personally in the process. We invite you to interact weekly with peers in sharing the similar and diverse experiences you encounter. Participating in cooperative learning groups at this time enables you to learn about the attitudes and skills you want to teach students and analyze the concepts and theories about cooperative learning groups. Cooperative learning encourages interdependence and interpersonal interaction and strengthens social skills. As you engage in the process, you will analyze and draw conclusions about the concepts and theories associated with implementing cooperative learning groups.

In achieving group goals, Johnson and Johnson (1989–90) recommend group members practice the following skills:

- getting to know and trust each other
- communicating accurately and unambiguously
- accepting and supporting one another
- resolving conflicts constructively

Teaching social and interpersonal skills to all age learners is fundamental to the cooperative learning process. These skills positively produce student learning. Studies show that when cooperative groups are used, the achievement of these students exceeds that of students taught with other methods (Newman, 1992; Stevens & Slavin, 1995). Practicing these affective skills leads you to a deeper understanding of the foundations of effective group learning. Therefore, we provide a structure that emphasizes interdependence and interpersonal interaction and builds social skills.

From the many cooperative learning structures that are available, we selected Johnson and Johnson's Learning Together Model (1975), which promotes working together to produce a single group product. In face-to-face interactions you are invited to promote positive relationships with your group members and create opportunities for interdependence within your group. The most effective means for individual growth with your group is to acknowledge and genuinely praise one another's accomplishments, including your own! This creates a sense of community and allows meaningful dialogue to occur. In this type of environment you are free to become a risk taker, sharing not only your successes but your questions, mistakes, and fears about teaching. As beginning teachers, identifying and integrating the theories and beliefs that you have about teaching calls for an open forum where discussion encourages you to step freely into the role of teacher. Discussion along with deep reflection allows you to take on that role more freely. You have a built-in support system—your cooperative group!

THE GROUP PROCESS

Cooperative group activities expose you to different perspectives and attitudes. Furthermore, these new perspectives can be very helpful in the development of teaching strategies in the classroom. For this reason, interaction is very important. Your active participation and contributions offer support and encouragement to your peers in ways you might not imagine. We believe that your experiences help to make explicit your implicit theories and beliefs about teaching. Group members should try to share as many insights and experiences as possible. For some, sharing will be easier than for others. If your group creates an open, respectful, and accepting environment, then everyone will share more freely. This in turn will enable all members of the group to benefit from the experiences of others and apply these insights to their classroom practices.

Within your cooperative group, you are also learning about two important components of the Learning Together Model. First, as an individual member of the group, you are accountable for your share of the work and contributions to the groups's success. Individual accountability is the hallmark of successful group process. Second, your input enables your group to put into action a plan that allows each member to grow. Your group's focus for each week is a written action plan that becomes the building block for your personal development as a professional.

Who Participates?

To simulate the collaboration concept observed in schools, each group consists of three to four individuals who work with different ages and content areas. The seminar director, or facilitator, suggests group membership. Each group remains in place for three or four sessions, rotating roles each week. Assuming different roles enables everyone to participate in the group process from a different perspective. Your active involvement in the group allows you not only to experience how cooperative learning groups work, but also to determine how the group process can best be incorporated into your classroom.

What Are the Roles?

Each member of the group will assume a specific role: initiator-reader, encourager, summarizer, or observer.

Initiator-Reader

The initiator-reader is responsible for the group beginning its work promptly and using time productively. Other responsibilities include:

- clarifying the task
- making sure everyone in the group understands the activity and the supplied information
- moving the group toward task completion

Encourager

The encourager promotes positive interpersonal relations through acknowledging the team-building contributions of group members. Other responsibilities are:

- restating group member comments
- connecting the comments of two or more group members
- reminding other members of appropriate social skills when necessary
- assembling and returning all materials that the group uses during the activity (if the group does not have an observer)

Summarizer

The summarizer makes sure the group completes all assigned tasks. Other responsibilities are:

- monitoring time and alerting group members to the time remaining in each session
- restating group member comments
- writing the action plan and the follow-up report to the action plan during the succeeding session
- obtaining group consensus on content of the action plan

Observer

The observer serves as a guide for the group and focuses on the success of the group and its members. Other responsibilities are:

- observing and reminding other members of their roles within the group
- giving reactions to specific behaviors of the group and its members when asked
- assembling and returning all materials that the group uses during the activity

Facilitator

The facilitator teaches the course or seminar and also collects and gives written feedback to each group's action plan and to the individuals' accountability reports. Other responsibilities include:

- providing outside measure of accountability to the group
- commending the group for the quality of its interactions
- providing reinforcement and directions for the cooperative learning group process
- articulating how group members might apply this model of cooperative learning within their classrooms

. . . teachers who receive frequent, systematic feedback based on observations of their performance do a better job of implementing cooperative learning methods.
D. B. Strother

- Organize cooperative learning groups
- Perform tasks assigned the role you assume
- Participate as a group member in practicing the learning together process

PRACTICING THE PROCESS

Now that you have read the information about the cooperative learning groups, you are ready to get involved as a member of a group. This first interaction moves you slowly through a series of steps aimed at helping you learn the process. You are then asked to engage in reflections about your learning, recalling what you did and the outcomes you obtained and comparing these with outcomes expected from the "learning together" group activities. The first activity is an introduction to the cooperative group process.

Step 1: Forming Groups

Your facilitator suggests your group membership. After the groups are formed, the facilitator makes some introductory comments explaining what the activity is, how much time is allotted to complete it, and when the activity will officially begin. Unless otherwise directed, assume your role within the group as soon as the facilitator concludes the opening remarks and the activity begins. Throughout each session, the facilitator is available for any questions about this process. The facilitator also may modify any of the activities or process steps.

Step 2: Choosing Roles

After reading each role description, choose your role and obtain group consensus. Think about the responsibilities of this role.

Step 3: Getting into Action

As the group gathers, the observer (or encourager if there is no observer) obtains a group number and a role marker for each member. (Markers with the group numbers can be made of folder paper and kept in a central location for routine use.) The observer also distributes any other materials needed by the group prior to the task at hand. In addition, the observer designates space for materials. This saves time and allows individuals to fulfill their roles in a timely manner.

Using Discussion Questions

Discussion questions appear in each of the cooperative learning group activities. Each set of questions focuses on different concerns many believe that new teachers experience in adjusting to the teacher role. The questions emphasize the affective aspects you are experiencing. The discussion format invites you to share your personal insights and feelings about becoming a professional teacher. To derive the greatest benefit from the discussion questions, consider the following:

- thoroughly reading the introductory information provided
- clarifying any confusion about what is stated
- responding openly to the initiator-reader's invitation to share
- attending to peers' sharing and feeding back the messages received

Before stating the first discussion point, the initiator-reader checks to see that members of the group understand their roles and are ready to discuss the questions provided. If group members choose, more time can be spent on some questions than on others. The time allotted for each cooperative learning activity is stated at the end of each **Focus One** activity. The initiator-reader confirms this time with the group.

The encourager verbally acknowledges members using positive interdependence, face-to-face interaction, social skills, and group processing. If the interaction among group members strays from the assigned discussion, the encourager reintroduces the topic.

The summarizer keeps the group aware of the time remaining in the session and initiates summary comments that include key ideas shared by group members.

The observer of the group gives the group members some feedback. One approach is to make at least one comment about the performance of the different group roles during this session.

Discussion Questions

1. Have you previously participated in a cooperative learning group? If so, was it a learning together model? What kind of structure did you follow in the group process?
2. As a student/intern teacher, what do you expect to learn from participating in the cooperative learning group?
3. Do you anticipate any difficulties involved in being a group member?
4. Since you will be meeting as a group two to three more times, what would help you work together as a group?

What Is an Action Plan?

The **action plan** is a summary of the group's discussion designed to create a collective goal that guides your thoughts and actions during the coming week. Although stated in practical terms, the plan focuses your thoughts and actions toward the lofty ideals you have about becoming a professional teacher. You and each member of your group needs to contribute to and endorse the plan written by the summarizer. In producing an effective action plan you want to include components such as:

- insights you hear from other members during the session that motivate and inspire you
- ideas and actions you can practice in the school setting during the coming week
- means for remembering to implement the plan during the week (for example, using your journal as a place to write about ways you implement the action plan)

... if I feel I belong, I know I have a place in that group that only I can fill; that I contribute something that is necessary to the group and is valued by other members.
L. Graves

The action plan serves as a means of accountability for your cooperative group. Hence, the action plan is written on the group accountability form. In naming a specific action you will practice for a week, you are naming a short range goal for yourself. You make public your plan by having the facilitator read and comment on the plan. At the following session you review the plan and share with others your experience with carrying out the plan. At the same time you examine the facilitator's comments and in closing write a response that summarizes your group's discussion of personal experiences with implementing the plan. For example, you can state how you might have made the plan more helpful or the ways you found the plan useful in moving you toward a desired goal. At the end of the session each group completes an accountability report action plan, and the observer or encourager returns it to the designated location. The facilitator reads, responds in writing, and returns the action plan to the group the following session.

Group Accountability Report (Sample)
ACTION PLAN

Date _9/21_   Group No. _4_

Action Plan Statement:

This week our group will work on initiating and participating by making our presence known in the classroom. We plan to step up our role, do more in the room such as taking roll or teaching lessons. We will document this in our journals.

Signature of Cooperative Working Group Members:

Initiator-Reader _Marti_   Observer _Corey_

Encourager _Jack_   Summarizer _Latosha_

Facilitator Comments to the Group's Action Plan:

Great plan! You will no doubt be noticed and observed as partner teacher by your students. Assisting the teacher in any capacity will be recognized and appreciated. Good that you make yourselves accountable to one another. Onward!

Group Members' Follow-up Comments to the Action Plan:

Yes, we followed up on our plan. We all got into the thick of things. Each explained the process and actions that s/he took with the students.

What Is the Individual Accountability Report?

Assessing the quality and quantity of your participation as a group member is the purpose for the **individual accountability report.** The report guides you in marking personal progress in performing the different cooperative group roles. Allow yourself the opportunity to grow; do not expect yourself to perform at the highest level at all times and in every role. By stating a specific interpersonal skill you want to strengthen, you are likely to improve this skill in subsequent sessions. Each time you complete the individual accountability report, keep in mind:

- your role in the cooperative group as described in the preceding pages
- the level and degree of your verbal and nonverbal interactions
- the encouragement and support you offer other group members
- your strengths as a group member (or areas needing improvement)
- peer assessments regarding your performance within the group

The rating you give your performance in the group is written on the individual accountability report. You read and sign the report of other group members and they sign yours. Self-assessment is more likely to occur with peer encouragement and support.

Individual Accountability Report (Sample)

Name _Jack Doe_   Date _9/21_   Group No. _4_

Circle your role in the group. Review the tasks associated with your role.

Initiator-Reader   Encourager   Summarizer   Observer

Initiator-Reader
The initiator-reader is responsible for the group beginning its work promptly and using time productively. Other responsibilities:
- clarifies the task
- makes sure everyone in the group understands the activity and the supplied information
- moves the group toward task completion

Encourager
The encourager promotes positive interpersonal relations through acknowledging the team-building contributions of group members. Other responsibilities:
- restates group member comments
- connects the comments of two or more group members
- reminds other members of appropriate social skills when necessary
- assembles and returns all materials that the group uses during the activity (if the group does not have an observer)

Summarizer
The summarizer makes sure the group completes all assigned tasks. Other responsibilities:
- monitors time and alerts group members to the time remaining in each session
- restates group member comments
- obtains consensus from the group on each report
- writes the action plan and the follow-up report to the action plan

Observer
The observer serves as a guide for the group and focuses on the success of the group and its members. Other responsibilities:
- observes and reminds other members of their roles within the group
- gives reactions to specific behaviors of the group and its members when asked
- assembles and returns all materials that the group uses during the activity

---

Individual Accountability Report (Sample)

Communication Rating
(0 indicates Not at All; 5 indicates Highest Quality)

Sent accurate, unambiguous message	0	1	2	3	4	(5)
Actively listened to others:	0	1	2	3	(4)	5
Assisted another with his/her role:	0	1	(2)	3	4	5
Degree of involvement	0	1	2	3	4	(5)

Comment on your performance in the group during this session:

At times I forgot I was the Encourager. Next time I hope to notice the others' role a little better and say supportive type things to them.

Signatures of other group members:

Initiator-Reader ___Marti___   Observer ___Corey___

Encourager ___Jack___   Summarizer ___Latosha___

Facilitator Comments:

Your comments are candid. You will have many opportunities to assume the different roles. You might review the role of Encourager; read the description above and take a few minutes to reflect on what you might say.

Materials Needed

- role markers (5″ × 8″ role identification markers)
- group accountability report (action-plan statement)
- individual accountability report

The observer or encourager collects all materials from the group and deposits these in the designated location.

The total time allotted for this cooperative learning group activity is 25 minutes.

Beginning Time_____   Ending Time_____

- Since the above exercise is a practice of the cooperative group structure, writing an action plan for the coming week is optional.

This first session is a learning time for all group members. You are not only learning about performing a specific role but also learning about the people in your group. Being patient with yourself: allowing time for multifaceted learning to occur is critical to the process.

REFERENCES AND SUGGESTED READINGS

Cooper, J. L. (1991). Cooperative/collaborative learning: Research and practice primarily at the collegiate level. *Journal-of-Staff, Program, & Organization Development, 7,* 143–148.

Graves, L. (1992). Cooperative learning communities: Context for a new vision of education and society. *Journal of Education, 174*(2), 57–69.

Johnson, D. W., and Johnson, R. T. (1999). *Learning together and alone: Cooperation, competition and individualization.* Englewood Cliffs, NJ: Prentice Hall.

Johnson, D. W., and Johnson, R. T. (1989/90). Social skills for successful group work. *Educational Leadership, 47*(4), 29–33.

Leighton, M. S. (1999). Cooperative learning. In J. M. Cooper (Ed.), *Classroom Teaching Skills.* Boston: Houghton Mifflin, 270.

Newman, F. M. (1992). Making small groups productive. Madison, WI: Center on Organization and Restructuring of Schools (Issue Report No. 2).

Rhem, J. (1992). Elements of cooperative learning, *National Teaching & Learning Forum, 2*(1), 3.

Stevens, R. J., and Slavin, R. E. (1995). The cooperative elementary school: Effects on achievement, attitudes, and social relations. *American Educational Research Journal, 32,* 321–351.

Strother, D. B. (1990). Cooperative learning: Fad or foundation for learning? *Phi Delta Kappan, 72*(2), 162.

Observing and Analyzing the Teaching Learning Process

" . . . A process of looking inside, of doing some soul searching, and then using this learning to refocus your vision is purposeful."

Focus One

Expected Performance

- List and examine teacher characteristics you consider most difficult to practice.
- Engage with other seminar participants, sharing your insights about the teacher role.
- Describe contributions you, as student or intern teacher, will make to the students, school, and other teachers.

ಌ

. . . The degree of self-growth depends on your willingness to share, actively listen, and interact with other group members.

ಌ

First Observations

Your head and heart both affect what you say and do in the classroom. **Focus One** provides an opportunity to reflect on some personal awarenesses at this time. The process presented here allows you to identify and analyze your feelings and insights about the role of the professional teacher. Looking inside and doing some soul searching is a meaningful kind of learning. Such powerful learning helps you to refocus your vision of yourself as an educator.

The experiences of your peers are another powerful source for learning. Sharing with one person or within a group allows you to hear your peers describe similar feelings and thoughts about their new experiences and further validates your own experience. As you offer one another support and encouragement, you create a type of bonding that over time strengthens and augments your insights about teaching.

Getting ready for your first teaching assignment brings with it many different thoughts and emotions. Prior to student teaching, earlier portions of your teacher education program provided research-based knowledge on effective teaching. Student and intern teaching offers you extended periods of time for working collaboratively with experienced teachers in applying this knowledge. Donald Schön (1987) calls this practice of the professionals a "core of artistry . . . an exercise of intelligence, a kind of knowing . . . we learn about it by carefully studying the performance of unusually competent performers" (p. 13). Working with an experienced professional in a school setting enables you to reflect on the performance of your supervising teacher and analyze your own ideas of professionalism in terms of your personal performance, background, and expectations of the teacher's role in the classroom.

Being in touch with yourself enables you to better understand where you now are and also contributes to your understanding of what is happening around you. If teachers are to understand and empathize with their students' individual situations, they must have a keen understanding of themselves. During this initial period of student or intern teaching, a variety of activities offer you the opportunity to engage in introspection as you observe what is happening around you. Throughout your journey in becoming and being a teacher, you are encouraged to reflect deeply, to self-assess, and to seek feedback from others. All of these experiences help you learn more about yourself as teacher and directly influence the type of teacher you become (Carter & Doyle, 1996; Cooper, 1999; Jersild, 1955).

Activities within this chapter invite you to address self-development and professional growth opportunities as you engage in teaching tasks and interact with others in various situations. This initial stage of teaching offers rich opportunities for you to observe, pose questions, and write about your learning. As you observe experienced teachers planning curriculum, preparing for a school year, and interacting with administrators and other staff members, you hear teachers voice their plans and concerns. Through your own filter of knowledge, attitudes, beliefs, and values, you process these experiences and reconstruct your own image of the teacher role. In doing so, you are infusing your "personal practical knowledge"—that is, you come to know teaching at the practical level of everyday events. To these immediate and local situations you integrate the formal knowledge you gained from general core and content-specific courses and teacher education courses with your personal aspirations and cumulative experiences (Clandinin & Connelly, 1987; Clandinin, 1989). Your teaching is an integral part of you and is shaped by what you know, practice, and learn.

The discussion questions included here ask you to identify some insights and feelings you have about yourself as a beginning teacher. To these three questions, write your response. Keep in mind that you are writing your personal response. Be spontaneous with your writing and rest assured that your thoughts are the "right answers." You need not show others what you write. Begin with the question that is easiest to answer, then move to another. Leave some space for adding to an earlier response. To save time, write only the number of the question and then your response.

Questions

Teacher Role

1. Recalling your personal goals and knowledge gained from teacher preparation, make a list of teacher characteristics that you believe are most important for you to practice as a teacher.
2. Circle the characteristics that are the most difficult to integrate into your everyday thinking and living as a teacher. Why do you think these are difficult?
3. For some time becoming a teacher has been your goal. As you begin working within this school with these students and teachers, what will you contribute to the students, school, and other teachers?

Task for You

Place your written response in an envelope. Seal the envelope and write your name on the outside. The seminar director collects the sealed envelopes and at a later session returns them to you unopened.

Discussion Questions

1. In answering questions about the teacher role, examine the responses you made. Discuss the reasons some were easier for you to write.
2. Discuss the characteristics you deemed most difficult to incorporate into your daily teaching experiences. Why are these so challenging to you?
3. What difference do you think your presence in the classroom and your team or department membership will make during the coming weeks?

Focus Two

Expected Performance

- Communicate results from using the observation components.
- Focus on learning goals/standards and outcomes.
- Analyze learning experiences that are developmentally appropriate for learners.
- Analyze learning experiences that challenge, motivate, and actively involve the learner.

In Focus One you shared personal experiences identifying your insights and feelings about becoming a teacher. As a beginning teacher you bring your special talents and feelings to the instructional setting. Focus Two gives you the opportunity to review, apply, practice, and reflect on selected instructional best practices. Reflective teaching requires the development of a variety of abilities, attitudes, and knowledge. The best way to gain knowledge about reflective teaching is to observe what is happening within the classroom and talk with teachers about their teaching experiences. Developing skills for conceptualizing what teachers are doing comes with practice. You are about to step into the peak experience of your teacher education program.

Student/intern teaching provides you the experience of working with professionals in the educational setting. You apply the knowledge, skills, attitudes, and values formed throughout your teacher education program to the actual teaching experience. Throughout your entire student/intern teacher experience, self-reflections are made and documented. This reflective process embraces Valverde's (1982) explanation of reflection, a process in which value-laden questions are asked and responses to stored selected data, or memory, are made. Various activities provide opportunities for reflecting on teaching: weekly seminar, journal writing, actual daily practice in teaching, and video and audio recording of teaching. These reflective activities are significant opportunities for integrating all of your teacher education components into the teaching role. The events during this special professional experience focus on the significance of reflection in this integrative process.

APPLICATION: OBSERVING THE TEACHING/LEARNING PROCESS

During the student teacher/internship experience you will be practicing and responding to questions and assigned tasks that help you plan and reflect on your observation or actual teaching. Even though you may be practicing these skills prior to the actual presentation within the text, the emphasis and treatment of this concept during the week reinforce and develop it in greater depth. The assigned tasks for the week ahead continue to keep you focused on a step-by-step development of effective teacher behaviors.

Reflective teaching requires the development of a variety of abilities, attitudes, and knowledge. The best way to gain knowledge about reflective teaching is to observe what is happening within the classroom and talk with teachers about their teaching experiences. Developing skills for conceptualizing what teachers are doing comes with practice. Systematic observations provide detailed and verifiable information that proves to be highly accurate. Becoming a perceptive observer assists you in the development of flexibility and accommodation of instruction and behavior management.

ASSIGNED ACTIVITIES

The following topics serve as guides for your observations. Recording and responding to your observations allow you to reflect upon your understanding of the teaching/learning environment Add any other descriptive information you consider valuable to the observation.

1. Examine the physical features of the classroom used, including: chalkboard space, bulletin board, desk arrangement, lighting, displays, technology, and instructional materials.
   - In what ways are they used to enhance learning in the classroom?
   - How will you plan to use or change the arrangement as you assume the teacher role?
   Note the arrangements made for special learners: equipment, special meetings, classroom seating and floor plan, schedules, and events.
   - In what ways are students' special needs met?
   - What questions do you have concerning these learners?
2. Describe the supervising or team teacher approach and manner with students: personal characteristics, appearance, communication skill, voice, eye contact, facial expression.
   - To what extent do the teacher's characteristics and communication skills make a difference with the learning taking place in the classroom?
3. Observe the classroom management and discipline approach: management strategies, student response to discipline, stated teacher expectations, and classroom rules and consequences for breaking posted rules.
   - How often and in what way does the teacher state expectations?
   - How are teacher expectations met in your classroom setting?
4. Focus on organizational strategies: daily routines, organization of teaching materials, and grouping for instruction techniques.
   - To what degree are organization and routine conducive to student learning?
5. Analyze instructional strategies: learner objectives, motivating techniques, questioning techniques, evaluation of learning, and closure.
   - Identify instructional strategies in which students are actively engaged in learning.
6. Discuss the learner in terms of: interaction with the teacher and peers, individual learning styles, motivation, and following directions (written and verbal).
   - How are the students interacting with the teacher and with one another?
   - Compare and contrast engaged students with disengaged or unmotivated students. Summarize your observation.

SUMMARY

Various activities provide you opportunities for reflecting on teaching: weekly seminar, journal writing, actual daily practice in teaching, and video and audio recording of teaching. These reflective activities are significant opportunities for integrating all of your teacher education components into the teaching role. The events during this special professional experience focus on the significance of reflection in this integrative process.

You have spent considerable time observing all aspects of the teaching/learning process with your classes. Given any teaching/learning environment, a wide range of observations is possible. Your collection of data has significant insights into the instructional and behavioral management of the learners.

FOLLOW-UP QUESTIONS AND SHARED INSIGHTS

Use your observation data, reflections, and journal entries to recall events since the last class meeting and share your response to the following questions:

1. In what ways do the outstanding physical features of the school, classroom, and other areas add to the learning environment?
2. How do the teacher's communication skills, voice, appearance, and personality affect the learning climate in the classroom?
3. What expectations of learner behavior are evident? How are these communicated to the learners?
4. What different instructional strategies modeled by the teacher will you want to incorporate and practice within your own teaching?
5. How were you introduced to the class/es? What was the reaction of the students?
6. What were some of the ways you initiated assisting your partner-teacher?
7. Describe any activities which you directed and any activities in which you interacted with students. How did the learners respond to you? For instance, did the learners refer to you for any questions they had? Did they call you by name?

Additional questions may surface. It will be evident from your participation in the discussion the degree to which your observation skills are becoming more critical.

Technology Tips

The teaching strategies you choose affect student learning. After deciding what you want your students to learn, choosing the strategy to use is another important decision. You can choose from a multitude of teaching strategies. From observing in classrooms, examining texts and teachers' manuals, you are aware of many of these. You also may be aware of the resources available through the use of current technology.

Through the Internet, numerous World Wide Web (WWW) sites provide abundant and quickly assessable sources of information. Many sources contain lesson plans and suggestions for teaching a concept, a skill, or a process. Although the plans are developed by teachers for a different group of learners, you can modify the plans to suit the learning needs of your students and the time frame you have for the course or lesson you are planning. Examine the learner outcomes and objectives of the plan and determine if they match yours.

The sources listed here are some of the available web sites providing unique and creative ideas. These web sites are listed under general and content-specific titles. The general listing includes specific ideas that you can incorporate into your planning. Neither the general listing nor the content-specific web sites are a complete list of available Internet sources, which are continuously developing and changing.

Subsequent chapters of the text provide you with suggestions for integrating technology into your planning. Look for these suggestions under the topic, **Technology Tips.**

General Listing of Content

- Ask ERIC Lesson Plans
  http://ericir.syr.edu/virtual/lessons
- Awesome Library, an educational directory for K–12 educators
  http://www.awesomelibrary.org/teacher.html
- Bascom's Global Resources for Teachers
  http://resources.globalchalk.com/
- Disabilities web site
  http://www.ldonline.org
- Educator Resources, with lesson plans for K–12
  http://mcrel.org/resources/links/lesson.asp
- Integrated curriculum content for K–12 schools
  http://www.educationalstructures.com
- Lesson Stop home page
  http://www.Lessonstop.org
- National Geographic's home page, with live web events
  http://www.nationalgeographic.com/main.html
- NASA's K–12 Internet Initiative
  http://quest.arc.nasa.gov/
- No Sweat, with K–12 homework assistance
  www.Homeworkcentral.com
- Teacher's Edition Online—lesson ideas, teacher tips, and more
  http://www.teachnet.com/
- TeacherNet, an online service for K–8 educators
  http://www.teachnet.com

Content-Specific Sites

- Arts Ed Net, an on-line service for K–12 arts education
  http://www.artsednet.getty.edu
- Discovery Channel School, an on-line service for K–12 science and social studies education
  http://School.discovery.com
- Federal Resource Center for Special Education
  http://www.dssc.org/frc/
- Internet resources for music teachers
  http://www.isd77.K12.mn.us/resources/staffpages/shirk/k12.music.html
- Lesson plans and resources for social studies teachers
  http://www.csun.edu/~hcedu013/index.html
- Math home page for new math teachers
  http://www.clarityconnect.com/webpages/terri/terri.html
- MegaMathematics, offers K–12 math lessons and activities
  http://www.c3.lanl.gov/mega-math/
- Musica, a music and science information computer archive
  http://www.musica.uci.edu/index.html
- Science Learning Network
  http://www.sln.org/
- Social studies lesson plans for K–12 teachers
  www.col-ed.org/cur/social.html

- Stories and activities for K–12 students, presented by Los Alamos National Laboratory
  http://www.c3.lanl.gov/mega-math/
- TeachNet, a science web site focusing on marine life
  teach.com/resources/science.html
- WebQuest, lessons on a variety of subjects such as the Holocost and the Civil War
  http://www.macomb.k12.mi.us/wq/

Journal Excerpts

High School

"Mr. S. introduced me to everyone and they all are so friendly and helpful. I just hope I can remember all of their names! I received my official parking pass and my Faculty Handbook. I read the Handbook and it helped me a great deal. All rules and policies are clearly explained and it is a great quick reference guide. I put paper clips on pages which were particularly important such as schedules, dress codes, school maps, and such. . . . We also had a department meeting. I met all of the teachers as well as the chair of the department. We discussed the curriculum for the upcoming year and Mr. S gave me all the textbooks we are going to be using. It was great to learn about what we are going to be teaching this semester! Native American writings, Cotton Mather, and Edgar Allen Poe to name a few."

"Today I observed various arrangements made for special learners. The most obvious arrangements are made for students with serious skill deficiencies or learning differences. It provides highly individualized instruction in required subject areas. Specialized counseling services are also provided to assist the student in developing interests and abilities, setting goals, making career choices, and solving personal and social problems. . . . Some of the equipment made available are lap top computers and audio tapes of texts in the library. In order to assist with keeping students organized in their schedules, assignments, etc. they use an assignment notebook as a mandatory aspect of the program. A timer is often used to help keep students focused on their tasks. Upon request, weekly "Progress Reports" are issued to the student and the parents."

Middle School

"I am so tired! This is a lot of excitement for one day. Today I felt old. Every now and then I am reminded that I am responsible for a lot of stuff. Today was definitely one of those days. I spent the day helping students find classrooms, collecting strays, passing out forms, and making copies. I sound like I'm complaining, but I'm really not. I loved every minute of the day. I don't have the energy that they do though! I found out that the more time I spent with them, the more peppy I seemed to be."

"Ms. I. gave the students a review of the rules, partly for my benefit. As she's talking, she says a name and continues on. She doesn't even have to wait. Those people off-task know it's time to pay attention. She introduced me much differently than Ms. P. and stressed that I will get respect from all of them. Ms. P. did this as well, but Ms. I. explained my situation and discussed it with them. Ms. P. did not want them to know I was a student."

Elementary

"Ms. W., Ms. K., and I got together to discuss the day and plan a schedule for the next day. There are several special needs students in the class, but there was one who caused us concern. We discussed what worked with him, what didn't and that we would have to watch him carefully and decide on interventions as needed. He was continually off task and seemed to be on another planet most of the time."

"This week has been a whirlwind of information and activity as I prepared to student teach. I have attended a number of faculty meetings to prepare for the coming semester. The first meeting I attended took place on Monday. . . . This meeting was aimed specifically at new teachers. I learned so much at this meeting! I immediately felt very welcome and a little overwhelmed."

"Today was another first for me in this assignment. I was feeling very badly and I realized today just how much energy teaching requires. It was an eye opener. I was exhausted being here just half a day."

Special Education

"Today was my first day and I spent the day getting to know the students, familiarizing myself with the point system, observing some of Mr. D's teaching techniques, and easing myself into the classroom. When the students came in the room they had a writing assignment on the board and got right to work. I was impressed by this. Some of the things I got to be involved in today were working with individual students, playing UNO during their free time, and monitoring their behavior for short periods of time."

"I am continuing to get more involved. The more the students see me do, the more they respect me as a teacher. Although I do not feel completely comfortable with the teacher's style, I am catching on to the way she does things, and trying to do similar things."

"I find that Ms. G. is extremely talented in her planning of interesting lessons for her students. Today the students worked on completing their self portraits that will be hung around the room for open house. She tied the self portraits into the "Art of the Month" and also with a social studies lesson talking about how people are different. The self portraits were just great. I wrote the name of each student on the front of their portrait and then placed the date on the back. I think these works of art will be kept around their homes for a long time."

REFERENCES AND SUGGESTED READINGS

Bennett, D. I., Meyer, C. H., and Meyer, D. E. (1994). *Elementary field experiences.* Albany, NY: Delmar Publishers.

Borich, G. D. (1999). *Observation skills for effective teaching* (3rd ed.). Upper Saddle River, NJ: Merrill/Prentice Hall.

Carter, K., and Doyle, W.(1996). Personal narrative and life history in learning to teach. In J. Sikula (Ed.), *Handbook of research on teacher education* (2nd ed.) (pp. 120–142). New York: Macmillan.

Clandinin, D. J., and Connelly, M. (1987). Teachers' personal knowledge: What counts as 'personal' in studies of the personal. *Journal of Curriculum Studies, 19*(6), 487–500.

Clandinin, D. J. (1989). Developing rhythm in teaching: The narrative study of a beginning teacher's personal practical knowledge of classrooms. *Curriculum Inquiry, 19*(2), 121–141.

Cooper, J. M., (1999). The teacher as a decision maker. In J. M. Cooper (Ed.), *Classroom Teaching Skills* (2nd ed.) (pp. 2–17). Boston: Houghton Mifflin.

Cruikshank, D. R. (1987). *Reflective teaching: The preparation of students of teaching.* Reston, VA: Association of Teacher Education.

Danielson, C. (1996). *Enhancing professional practice: A framework for teaching.* Alexandria, VA: Association for Supervision and Curriculum Development.

Jersild, A. T. (1955). *When teachers face themselves.* New York: Teachers College Press.

Kane, P. R. (Ed.). (1991). *The first year of teaching.* New York: Walker and Co.

Knapp, C. E. (1992). *Lasting lessons: A teacher's guide to reflecting on experience.* Charleston, WV: ERIC Clearinghouse on Rural Education and Small Schools.

McIntyre, D. J., and Byrd, D. M. (Eds.). (1996). *Preparing tomorrow's teachers: The field experience.* Thousand Oaks, CA: Corwin Press.

Posner, G. J. (1996). *Field experience: A guide to reflective teaching* (4th ed.). New York: Longman.

Reed, A. J. S., Bergemann, V. E., and Olson, M. W. (1998). *A guide to observation and participation in the classroom* (3rd ed.). Boston: McGraw-Hill.

Roe, B. D., & Ross, E. P. (1998). *Student teaching and field experiences handbook* (4th ed.). Upper Saddle River, NJ: Merrill/Prentice Hall.

Ross, D. D., Bondy, E., and Kyle D. W. (1993). *Reflective teaching for student empowerment.* New York: Macmillan.

Schön, D. A. (1987). *Educating the reflective practitioner.* San Francisco: Jossey-Bass.

Schön, D. A. (1983). *The reflective practitioner: How professionals think in action.* New York: Basic Books.

Valverde, L. (1982). The self-evolving supervisor. In T. Sergiovanni (Ed.), *Supervision of teaching* (pp. 81–89). Alexandria, VA: Association for Supervision and Curriculum Development.

Wallace, D. K. (Ed.). (1996). *Journey to school reform: Moving from reflection to action through story telling.* Washington, DC: National Education Association.

Wentz, P., & Yarling, J. (1994). *Student teaching casebook for supervising teachers and teaching interns.* New York: Macmillan.

Zeichner, K., & Liston, D. (1987). Teaching student teachers to reflect. *Harvard Educational Review, 57*(1), 23–48.

Developing Instructional Plans

"Becoming a professional teacher engages you in change and experimentation on many different levels and challenges you to initiate action. . ."

Focus One

Expected Performance

- Recall examples and talk with peers about student comments that demonstrate they view you as teacher.
- Examine and describe prior goals that you established for yourself as teacher and describe your current performance toward realizing these goals.

ॐ

. . . A teacher's understanding of others can be only as deep as the wisdom he possesses when he looks inward upon himself.
Jersild, p. 83

ॐ

Am I Initiating?

Change calls for adaptive learning on the part of individuals meeting emerging needs and new situations. Waldron, Collie, and Davies (1999) define adaptive learning as the ability to respond flexibly and proactively to stressful situations and to initiate tasks that challenge these abilities. Being able to adapt provides greater self-control, which in turn allows you to confront or cope by modifying the task or yourself.

Choosing to teach is inevitably accompanied by change and opportunities for adaptive learning. The challenge of teaching, argues Ayers (1993) is deciding what you want to be as teacher, what you care about, what you value, and how you will conduct yourself with students and others in the school. Day by day you are transforming a self-established goal into a reality. In accomplishing this goal you continuously confront new and challenging situations and learn to cope by modifying tasks or your understanding of complex situations. For example, you support educational reform, but you may have to deal with conflicting viewpoints and levels of dedication at the school level. You recognize the need for knowledge and identify the skills necessary to work collaboratively to improve the conditions in the school, and you are willing to share your insights with others (Manouchehri 1998). Interacting with children and adolescents and collaborating with an experienced teacher provide you many opportunities for adaptive learning. Just as you are a unique individual, so are the situations and tasks confronting you and toward which you respond as teacher. Becoming a professional teacher engages you in change and experimentation on many different levels and challenges you to initiate action and "take charge" as the situation demands.

Focus One invites you to assess one aspect of becoming a professional teacher. You are asked to reflect on the levels of your ability to "take charge" and demonstrate initiative in the classroom. During this seminar session, candidly recall and share examples of when and how you practice the taking-charge aspects of teaching.

As you enter the teaching profession, self-assessment takes on new meaning. In reflecting on your performance, compare your teacher behaviors with your philosophy of teaching. Are they compatible? Self-assessment on the part of the teacher begins early in the preparation period and is ongoing. Learning to be "teacher" is a process that extends over months and even years. Immediately after arriving in the classroom and meeting your students, the taking-charge stage of teaching begins. Your first experiences are short activities that may include handing out papers, reading aloud, or locating materials. After working with your supervising teacher and getting to know the students and the school, you will be invited to assume greater responsibilities for student learning. For now, enjoy the process of learning as you prepare to initiate activities.

How do you see yourself as a professional taking charge? Picture yourself within the classroom and recall the verbal and nonverbal exchanges taking place between yourself and the students. The following questions can guide you as you look back over the past week.

- Where are you standing or sitting in the classroom?
- Do you take over and direct an activity when the supervising teacher is interrupted or called from the room?
- Are you working with one student or a group of students?
- What are you saying and/or demonstrating to the students?
- Are you enthusiastic? Knowledgeable?
- What does your tone of voice and facial expression convey about your feelings toward the activity?
- Do students ask you to help them?
- How do students view your role in the classroom?
- How initiating are you?

Discussion Questions

1. How do students describe your presence in their class? Share any comments about yourself that you have heard students make. From these comments, tell how you think students view you as "teacher."
2. Describe some change you think is needed to expand your role from observer to participator or initiator in the classroom. What risks will be involved in making the change?
3. Recall some beliefs you hold about teaching. What tasks have you assumed that indicate you are experimenting with ways for making these beliefs become a part of you as "teacher?"

Focus Two

One of the assigned activities directs you to volunteer giving class directions in this chapter. Ah, to be initiating, to take charge of the students—terrific! This seems like an easy task until you begin. In practicing giving directions, you may struggle with learners asking for clarification in a number of ways. Providing clear directions in both classroom management and instruction are critical to the teaching process. Unclear directions may lead to learner confusion. Have you recognized how essential it is to articulate clearly the directions step by step with the learners? Using "group alert" and gaining all students' attention prior to speaking saves you from repeating directions (Emmer et al., 1997). Using emphasis in your voice gains and retains student attention. Checking for understanding of directions by asking a student to repeat the directions is often beneficial to you, as teacher, and provides clarity for other students.

Expected Performance

- Examine and reflect upon the relationships between learning expectations and daily lesson plans.
- Plan instruction based upon knowledge of subject matter, students, the community, and curriculum goals.
- Provide learning opportunities that support students' intellectual, social, and personal development.
- Incorporate strategies that address physical, social, and cultural diversity and show sensitivity to differences.

Planning effective lessons for a specific group of learners requires demonstrated ability to state academic expectations. You are closely observing your cooperating and team teachers and focusing on the objectives and expectations they hold for the learners. Through your observation and recording of learner outcomes, you are developing deeper insights concerning lesson planning and learner achievement.

APPLICATION: DEVELOPING INSTRUCTIONAL PLANS

Preplanning

Writing a well-developed plan for teaching usually begins with a reflection on the needs of the individual learners within your class/es. Assessing what the learner knows and has demonstrated in previous lessons usually precedes the development of the plan. In addition, formal and informal inventories provide important information about the learners. These may be prepared activity sheets on which students check their interests or a short writing piece describing the student's favorite academic subject, sport, hobbies, music, travel, and books. Taking into account the learning styles of students, using the multiple intelligences enables you, as teacher, to develop your plan with broader perspective.

Learning Styles

According to Shuell (1981), learning styles are "the preferred ways that different individuals have for processing and organizing information and for responding to environmental stimuli." You will be able to perceive the varied learning styles of your students by observing them as they interact within groups and as they explain in writing and speaking what they learned. Effective planning requires that teachers identify the varied learning styles of their students and adapt the instruction to meet student needs.

Multiple Intelligences

Howard Gardner is the chief proponent of the **multiple intelligences** concept. His research portrays eight intelligences possessed by every person to some degree, but many schools may develop only the first two to any extent. Gardner (1995) identifies these intelligences:

linguistic	musical
logical-mathematical	interpersonal
bodily-kinesthetic	naturalist
spatial (visual)	intrapersonal

The goal of the reflective teacher is to provide instruction that will include many of the above eight intelligences. Examples include writing journal entries in the linguistic category, role playing in the bodily-kinesthetic, using the spatial intelligence by creating maps or graphs, creating simulations and completing puzzles in the logical-mathematical, participating in cooperative group activities (interpersonal), performing in a class musical (musical), using the **KWL** method (what I know, what I want to know, and what I learned from this instruction) in the intrapersonal category, or classifying plants, minerals, and animals in the Beta naturalist category. All enrich the diversity of intelligences found in any learner population. Trying to vary your instruction to include the different learning styles and multiple intelligences cannot be done in one lesson. It will take practice and experience to find what benefits your students and helps each to be a successful learner.

Designing and Planning the Lesson

Developing lesson plans for teaching the learners in your class/es gives you direction and focus. You may have been given a particular format or outline for planning your lessons in your methods classes or from an instructor in your orientation for the student teacher/intern experience. Using district, state, or national curriculum standards in designing your plans provides the rationale for your choice of instructional strategies. In addition, the use of state and national standards will more likely guarantee that you are including what is important for learners to know and achieve at a particular level.

Instructional Objectives

Essential to good planning for instruction is the demonstrated ability to write instructional objectives. If you are working toward becoming an effective teacher, it is essential that you know what you want your students to know and accomplish to demonstrate that they have achieved the stated objectives. In other words, when you as teacher have clearly defined goals and objectives or outcomes, learners will know what is expected of them. Gradually, with reinforcement, students will become more self-evaluative and set high expectations for themselves.

The taxonomy developed by Bloom et al. (1956) and Krathwohl, Bloom, and Masia (1964) for classifying objectives identifies three domains for learning:

- **cognitive** ("the recall or recognition of knowledge and the development of intellectual abilities and skills")
- **affective** ("interests, attitudes, and values")
- **psychomotor** ("manipulative and motor skills")

Though each is classified separately, they are essentially interrelated and important in the curriculum. As an example, the learner may develop a piece of writing, recalling information and giving much thought to the topic (cognitive), type the piece of writing on the computer (psychomotor), and become enraptured in the unfolding of the writing piece (affective). Knowledge of Bloom's taxonomy will be helpful in formulating the best objectives for your lesson planning. For those of you who may want to review the taxonomy of the three domains, the chart below, adapted from Bloom et al. (1956) and Krathwohl et al. (1964), may assist you.

Domain and Level	Definition
▲ **Cognitive Domain**	
▲ Knowledge	recalls or recognizes information
▲ Comprehension	understands or knows what is being communicated
▲ Application	transfers learning from one context to another independently
▲ Analysis	breaks down a problem into parts and forms
▲ Synthesis	puts together elements to form a creative whole
▲ Evaluation	makes value judgments using specific criteria

- **Affective Domain**

  - Receiving   directs attention to the stimuli
  - Responding   enjoys an activity or experience
  - Valuing   commits to a belief, view, or idea and can defend or act on behalf of it
  - Organization   develops a system of values and lives by it

- **Psychomotor Domain**

  - Imitation   carries out basic directions for a skill
  - Manipulation   performs a skill independently
  - Precision   performs a skill accurately, efficiently, and meticulously

You may also want to review the components for writing instructional objectives. The following points are adapted from TenBrink (1999):

1. Emphasize the instructional objective is **learner oriented:**
    ex. The *students* will select the main idea from a paragraph provided by the teacher.
    ex. Students will compute solutions to a system of equations using the substitution, addition, and graphing methods.
2. Determine what the learner will accomplish, i.e., **learner outcome** (which should be stated clearly and in observable terms):
    ex. Given a list of organisms found in a particular tropical ecosystem (old lake, inland lake, beach, coral reef) *place the organisms in the order in which they would occur over time, from the pioneer community to the climax community.*
    ex. After practice with first and second Tenors, with Baritone, and with Bass parts, freshmen boys *will sing "Vive L'amour" with accuracy of pitch.*
3. Set the **acceptable criteria** for assessing the level of performance:
    ex. Given five examples students will multiply two-digit numbers by one-digit numbers with *80% accuracy.*
    ex. Using their original drawings, students will: (a) write a description of how the drawing was made, (b) use the proper sequence that would allow another to reproduce the drawing, and (c) complete a rough draft of a descriptive piece of writing *according to the rubric provided by the teacher.*

You may formulate good instructional objectives or outcomes at this time without any additional practice. Some texts include objectives appropriate for a particular grade level, and these may be helpful to you in formulating objectives for your students.

With practice in writing clear, complete, and observable instructional objectives, beginning teachers observing cooperating teachers can recognize what objectives have been selected for a specific lesson taught. Later in this text you will be directed to match the assessment of the lesson with your stated objectives. One of this chapter's assigned activities will give you practice in observing and writing instructional objectives for the learners within your classes.

The following outline of a lesson plan includes all the components you will draw upon to assist you in your teaching. Examples of lesson plans from elementary, middle, and high school and special education can be found in the appendix.

Lesson Plan Guide

Course Level: English 210; Eighth Grade Social Studies; Math, 3rd grade
Period of Day: First 7:50 A.M.; Sixth 1:40 P.M.; 10:15–11:00 A.M.
Type of Lesson: Introductory; Reinforcement of concept; Direct instruction
Reflective Questions: Questions you will ask yourself as you reflect on the contents of your plan.

ex. Can the student perform the tasks I have created for them in this lesson?
ex. Will the students work cooperatively with one another in carrying out the project?
ex. Does the content for this lesson flow from the lesson previously taught?

Objectives: What is it you hope your students will achieve in this lesson?
Materials/Strategies: What specific materials will you need? Will you be using small groups, teacher directed, webbing, KWL charting, or other methods of content delivery?

Procedure

Teacher's Words/Actions Instructional Sequence	Expected Learner Response
A. Lesson initiation (motivation, review, overview): What will you say, show, ask learners to do or say to create and stimulate interest, focus attention, and engage learners in the activity or content?	Write what students are expected to do (i.e., verbal response, listen, journal writing).
B. Lesson development (demonstration, modeling, activities, questions)	
C. Guided practice (examples, illustrations, demonstrations used to accommodate diversity of learner and learning styles)	
D. Independent practice (application of skill/concept, assignment, project): Students demonstrate they can apply and carry out the task themselves.	
E. Assignment: Is there an activity sheet, text page, or project to complete to reinforce the concept, skill, or theme?	
F. Assessment: What means will you select to determine at what level the student has achieved the objectives?	

Performance Criteria/Rubric: You may have a set criteria or rubric that specifies the different levels you as teacher will use in assessing the completed task or project.
Reflective Comments (Self-Assessment): After teaching the lesson, evaluate your teaching. Highlight the strengths and describe areas you want to improve.
Optional: You might want to highlight the following: higher level questioning, real-life application, concrete experience, strategies/considerations for special needs learners, and/or cross-discipline integration.

ASSIGNED ACTIVITIES

1. In your journal list learner objectives you observe for at least one class each day. For the outcomes listed, what activities were planned to provide the teacher written or verbal evidence of meeting this outcome? Describe the techniques you observe or use this week to reach the desired learning outcome (i.e., direct teaching, cooperative learning groups, role playing, problem solving).

Date of Lesson

Subject   Class   Number of learners

Objective or Learner Outcome

Evidence of Learning Outcome

Teaching Techniques

---

2. Select at least two of the above objectives. In conference with your supervising teacher, share your list of objectives and discuss the instructional activities that focused on the objectives.
3. Describe the varied learning styles of the learners in your class/es. What accommodations are made to include varied ways in which students learn?
4. Beginning teachers vary in ability to initiate and participate in instructional tasks within the classroom. Giving directions can be a first step in the process of building your confidence. Determine whether you can detect the difference between students having difficulty following directions and those learners with limited listening skill.

    Volunteer to give directions for at least one class or activity. Respond to the following questions:

   - What are the considerations for stating explicit directions?
   - What were the difficulties you perceived in giving clear directions?
   - What were the difficulties you observed students exhibiting in following directions?

SUMMARY

You are beginning to take a closer look at your students' learning styles and how they best learn. It takes practice to formulate plans for determining the teaching process and selecting materials to be used for the content being presented.

Deciding the means for assessing instruction also takes practice. As you become more perceptive in determining the objectives of the lesson being taught, you begin to see the connection between the objectives of the plan and the appropriate assessment. The selected content and strategies reinforce what you intend learners to achieve from the lesson.

Your cooperating teachers may vary the teaching strategies to assist students who may be more visual or audial. Learners may need more hands-on materials, especially in the teaching of mathematics and science. Visuals, technology, dramatizations, illustrations, and other resources appeal more to some learners and thereby reinforce their learning. Careful observations help you make connections among the different disciplines in the lessons being taught. In addition, the development of lessons that involve multiple intelligences may catch your attention. You may choose to jot down some ideas for future lessons.

FOLLOW-UP QUESTIONS AND SHARED INSIGHTS

Using your journal with the information and insights you have gathered from your observations of the teaching/learning environment, respond to the following:

1. Select one objective or learner outcome you observed and recorded. Describe the strategies used to obtain the desired learner outcome and state whether the observable performance was written or verbal.
2. List the varied teaching techniques used for the different content areas to accommodate special learning styles.
3. Which multiple intelligences (Gardner, 1995) were used in the lessons you observed? What were some noticeable results?
4. Share an example of a cross-disciplinary or integrated lesson plan you have observed.
5. Describe one thinking process or skill presented during a class. Did the learners receive individual or group reinforcement? What instructional materials were used in the presentation?
6. Give an example of directions you stated for learners. What factors helped students in following your directions?
7. When you explained an idea to students and they were confused, how does your rewording of the explanation affect the outcome for the learners?
8. Share one incident which demonstrated your involvement as partner teacher at this time.

Technology Tips

Do you plan to be one of the 2 million new teachers hired during the first decade of the 21st century? As one of these teachers, you are expected to have the skills to integrate technology into instruction. In addition, you are experiencing the "deep impact technology has had on society as a whole: how technology has changed the nature of work, of communications, and the development of knowledge" (Cooper, 1999).

Included in your planning are the considerations of materials and learning tools you will demonstrate and direct students to use. Knowledge of computers and computer software is fundamental to integrating technology into learning experiences. Technology Tips presented here address two aspects for using technology: (a) knowledge of technology hardware and software and (b) strategies for implementing technology into the curriculum. It is helpful to have an introductory course in basic technology applications. In addition, you may seek information from the library and media center personnel in the school to build on your knowledge. Department chairs, team leaders, technology coordinators, and your supervising teacher are resources, too. You will find teachers among this group who are enthusiastic and eager to share their knowledge about available hardware and software. They may make suggestions for using the tools with your specific content.

Technology Hardware and Software

A list of selected technology materials follows. Which of these have you used?

Computer and accompanying peripherals—Laptop model provided each individual student; desktop model in lab setting used by individual student or shared by pairs of students.

Liquid crystal display (LCD) panels—Projection device that displays computer screen images and script.

Graphics calculator—Projection device that displays graphs, equations, and other mathematical expressions.

Laser disc player—Contains images controlled by the teacher in several ways, such as through use of bar code reader or computer driven.

Compact disc read only memory (CD-ROM)—Commercially prepared programs that contain images and text.

Video camera and video cassette player—Camera records activities that are played back, edited by students and groups of students; demonstrations by student or teacher recording in all content areas; commercially prepared recordings are available.

Software as referred to here includes such computer applications as word processing, spreadsheets, and databases. Sources for obtaining commercial electronic media materials are numerous. Quality ratings of these instructional materials can be obtained from the Internet, current books, and educational journals.

As a teacher of the 21st century, you will find the use of the Internet is the fastest growing piece of technology. This "network of networks" connects computers across the world and is accessible through a World Wide Web (WWW) browser (Ryder and Hughes, 1997). Browser software is also available from numerous commercial sources.

Strategies for Implementing Technology into Your Classes

In using any kind of technology, be prepared for Murphy's Law to prevail: anything that can go wrong, will. Thinking ahead, what other strategies will you use if your plan does not work? Including the supervising teacher in the planning provides you a wonderful source of support. Whatever technology you are using, you may want to obtain and practice using the piece of equipment prior to the first class. Helpful strategies are listed below:

1. Review the word processing application that you will be directing students engaged in completing portfolio pieces, poems, and other creative writing activities.
2. Establish an overview of the total task the class will be using the computer to complete.
3. Begin the class by providing an overview of the activity. Post a list to serve as a reference later in the class and for subsequent classes.

4. Explain how students can get help. For example, identify students who are proficient with the task, and put colored cups on the computer to signal that help is needed at this station.
5. Show how graphing calculators require a series of inputs. First, demonstrate the use of inputs. Then provide an example and circulate and monitor to see which students are following the process demonstrated.
6. Monitor the level of challenge commercial software offers individual students. You may make notes that will allow you to prescribe students needing more advanced or less difficult pieces.

Film clips and short excerpts from films are effective means for connecting themes being taught from literary classics and promoting real-life experiences for social studies instruction as an interdisciplinary approach. Before showing the clips, laser disc, or CD, prepare the students for what will be shown. Explain your reason for selecting this specific scene, event, or character. The following are some strategies that communicate to learners specific expectations you have for them.

1. Verbally and/or in writing explain the purpose for showing the video, CD-ROM, or slide.
2. Prior to the audio or visual shown, state learner expectations: to listen, take notice of specific pictures, and/or take notes.
3. As a follow-up to the video or CD-ROM, explain what learners need to identify, describe, or explain?
4. Check for student comprehension of the learning outcome the video intends to further reinforce.
5. Follow up the showing with questions of students, discussion, and clarification of student notes.

Acceptable Use Policy

Students using the Internet present multiple considerations. While this technology allows students to visit far-off museums and view the world from NASA satellite vantage points, there are ever-evolving concerns. In addition to teaching students who are unable to access the Internet, other topics to consider include proper computer etiquette and the Acceptable Use Policy. Locate the Acceptable Use Policy your school or school district has adopted. Familiarize your students with this policy and review it with them periodically.

Teacher Resources

A source for the design of constructivist, cooperative learning projects can be found at:

http://www.ilt.columbia.edu/k12/livetext/topics/search.html

Sources for special education information include:

Federal Resource Center for Special Education
        http://www.dssc.org/frc/
Special Education and Inclusion Issues
        http://www.ndss.org/
Special Education and Technology
        http://glef.org

High School

"One objective from last week was: After listening to the James Thurber story, 'The Night the Bed Fell,' students will identify and use examples of the criteria belonging in an effective personal narrative, i.e., characters, dialogues, etc.). Students are preparing to write personal narratives of their own. They have some study guides to complete as Mr. S. read and explained to them the criteria. We will check student writing sample to make sure that they have included the criteria discussed in class."

"Mr. W's classes are based primarily on a student-centered, cooperative learning approach. His instructional strategies and activities incorporate work in the large group, in cooperative groups of three with designated roles, and also independent practice. He also encourages students to take responsibility for their personal education and growth. He told the students that 'We value that which we learn'. . ."

"I immediately noticed a difference between this class and other English classes. These students need very explicit directions or they will become very confused. For example the supervising teacher told the students to write their paragraphs on every other line of the paper, giving space for teacher comments. It took almost ten minutes of explaining and modeling examples before the students caught on. I feel that teaching this class will teach me so much and help me to be a better educator."

"I think my biggest problem in giving directions is having to state them so many times. Also, students want to ask questions about the directions before you are finished giving them. Oftentimes they just choose not to follow them. . . . It is not an exaggeration to state that I probably give the same information (directions) about 10 times in one class period. My supervising teacher says that this always gets better after the first grading period."

Middle Grades

"I spent the planning period making a lot of copies and reading. We talked about plans. I'm going to plan and teach mini-lessons. I worked on grading papers and labeling our student mailboxes."

"In first period, we had a short team meeting to discuss some dates: field trips, monitoring a basketball game, etc. We also talked about parent-teacher conference day and career testing. It was basically organization of schedules. I just listened, but I am rather impressed by the planning this team does together."

"In fourth period, I went with Ms. P. to the library to discuss a small ordeal with the laptops we've been checking out. I also talked a lot with Ms. P. about my plans for teaching. She gives me a lot of help."

Elementary

"My science class objective was to have learners define work as a force that moves something. The children will explain why specific activities are or are not work. I had the children try to push the wall five inches. I then demonstrated pushing a cotton ball. I pointed out that whoever moved the ball was doing the work, the others were not. I had the children working in groups, trying to move the floor, a pencil, and a cotton ball. They recorded the distance they moved each object and wrote their responses to questions about work on the activity sheet."

"I am still learning about the students' learning styles, but it is obvious through work, words, and actions that they all differ greatly from one another. Many students are difficult to motivate, but we usually do well. Most students may take time, but eventually they get on task. A few initiate the move towards work, sharing, and participating in class. Some students are followers and will join in while others need more encouragement."

"Today I arrived early to discuss the lesson that I will be teaching tomorrow on graphing. I wanted to make sure that my lesson was approved by Mrs. D. The graphing lesson is connected to our reading activities. As a class we will be graphing our favorite zoo animal. Mrs. D. and I discussed my objectives and the best way to present my lesson. I find this very helpful when planning a lesson. The input of Mrs. D. is wonderful and I appreciate all of her experience."

Special Education

"At the end of the day, Mr. D. and I planned for tomorrow. By doing this, I felt more comfortable with the situation, and with my involvement in the classroom. I planned questions regarding the reading assignment for one student and familiarized myself with other material, so that I can get more quickly involved. Mr. D. is giving me a lot more responsibility than I expected and I am glad."

"Over the past few days I have already noted several different learning styles and preferences. Most all of the students seem to assimilate information better if the teacher actually says it verbally and also writes it on the board or hands it out to them. This visual learning style has also been encouraged through video and posters in the room. Some students also participate actively, while others do not join in class discussion."

"Clear and concise directions are key for both of my supervising teachers, because they have so much going on in the classroom. One teacher uses student recapping, the students repeat the directions given, and the other usually writes the directions on the board. Both of them repeat directions several times, and that allows plenty of time for answering any questions and clarifying of any statements! Much emphasis is placed on the individual learning styles and needs of each student."

REFERENCES AND SUGGESTED READINGS

Ayers, W. (1993). *To teach: The journey of a teacher.* New York: Teachers College Press.

Bloom, B., Engelhart, M., Furst, E., Hill, W., and Krathwohl, D. (1956). *Taxonomy of educational objectives: Cognitive domain.* New York: Longman.

Brophy, J. (1998). *Motivating students to learn.* Boston: McGraw-Hill.

Brubacher, J., Case, C., and Reagan, T. (1994). *Becoming a reflective educator: How to build a culture of inquiry in the schools.* Thousand Oaks, CA: Corwin Press.

Campbell, L. (1997). How teachers interpret MI theory. *Educational Leadership, 55*(1), 14–19.

Checkley, K. (1997). "The first seven . . . and the eighth." *Educational Leadership, 55*(1), 8–13.

Cooper, J. (Ed.). (1999). *Classroom teaching skills* (6th ed.). Lexington, MA: D.C. Heath.

Danielson, C. (1996). *Enhancing professional practice: A framework for teaching.* Alexandria, VA: Association for Supervision and Curriculum Development.

Darling-Hammond, L., and Rustique-Forrester, E. (1997). Investing in quality teaching: State-level strategies. *Perspective,* Education Commission of the States.

Dunn, R., Beaudry, J., and Klavas, A. (1989). Survey of research on learning styles. *Educational Leadership, 46*(6), 50–57.

Eby, J. (1996). *Reflective planning, teaching, and evaluation: K–12* (2nd ed.). Upper Saddle River, NJ: Merrill/Prentice Hall.

Emmer, E. T., Evertson, C. M., Clements, B. S., and Worsham, M. E. (1997). *Classroom management for secondary teachers.* Boston: Allyn and Bacon.

Gagne, R. M., et al.(1992). *Principles of instructional design* (4th ed.). San Diego: Harcourt Brace Jovanovich.

Gardner, H. (1993). *Multiple intelligences: The theory in practice.* New York: Basic Books.

Gardner, H. (1995). Reflections on multiple intelligences: Myths and messages. *Phi Delta Kappan, 77*(3), 200–209.

Good, T., and Brophy, J. (1997). *Looking in classrooms* (7th ed.). New York: Longman.

Gronlund, N. E. (1990). *How to write instructional objectives.* New York: Free Press.

Guild, P. B. (1997). Where do the learning theories overlap? *Educational Leadership, 55*(1), 30–31.

Jersild, A. T. (1955). *When teachers face themselves.* New York: Teachers College Press.

Krathwohl, D., Bloom, B., and Masia, B. (1964). *Taxonomy of educational objectives: Handbook II: Affective domain.* New York: David McKay Co.

Mager, R. F. (1984). *Preparing instructional objectives.* Belmont, CA: David S. Lake Publishers.

Manouchehri, A. (1998). Mathematics curriculum reform and teachers: What are the dilemmas? *Journal of Teacher Education, 49*(4), 276–286.

Pool, C. (1997). A new digital literacy: A conversation with Paul Gilster. *Educational Leadership, 55*(3), 6–11.

Ryder, R. J., and Hughes, T. (1997). *Internet for educators.* Upper Saddle River, NJ: Prentice Hall.

Shuell, T. (1981). Dimensions of individual differences. In F. Farley and N. Gordon (Eds.), *Psychology and education: The state of the union.* Berkeley, CA: McCutchan.

Silver, H., Strong, R., and Perini, M. (1997). Integrating learning styles and multiple intelligences. *Educational Leadership, 55*(1), 22–27.

TenBrink, T. D. (1999). Instructional objectives. In Cooper, J. (Ed.), *Classroom Teaching Skills* (6th ed.) (pp. 53–75). Lexington, MA: D.C. Heath.

Waldron, P. W., Collie, T. R., and Davies, C. M. W. (1999). *Telling stories about school: An invitation.* Upper Saddle River, NJ: Merrill/Prentice Hall.

Designing and Planning Instruction

> " . . . by the year 2006, America will provide all students with what should be their educational birthright: access to competent, caring, and qualified teachers."

What Matters Most: Teaching for America's Future

Focus One

Expected Performance

- Recognize, analyze, and share your emotional response to becoming a "competent, caring, qualified teacher."
- Critically listen to your peers' classroom experiences to gain deeper insights into the multifaceted role of teacher.
- Determine which actions or attitudes will strengthen your ability to demonstrate effectively some aspect of the teacher role.

Analyzing Your Emotional Response to Beginning Teaching

Are you feeling a part of the classroom, the team, the school? You now know the routines, the location of supplies, and the names of many students. You are responsible for directing students and planning instruction. You are examining and assessing your performance in some aspects of the teacher role. Away from the classroom and dialoguing with peers who are experiencing similar adjustments and learning, you can now concentrate on your personal development as a teacher.

Many recognize that new teachers feel overwhelmed by the sheer number and seriousness of the decisions and choices they are asked to make. You may question your readiness for so many responsibilities (Eby, 1998; Odell, 1989; Pitton, 1998). During field experiences you became aware of the complex social dynamics of classrooms. Repeatedly you hear about the new ways of teaching and learning promoted by the learned societies and performance standards outlined by national and state reform movements. You are also aware of entering the teaching profession at a time when instruction has become more student centered and learning activities more developmentally appropriate. Teachers are expanding the variety of approaches needed to tailor classroom experiences to the needs of individual learners. In this current high-tech era, teachers establish classrooms of "high touch," that is, a warm and human-oriented place for students (Alley & Jung, 1995; Murphy, 1995) where learning occurs in a caring, creative environment.

Experiencing the multifaceted role of the teacher and engaging in the rapid pace of the classroom, your head may be whirling and your emotions bubbling on the surface. One of the many pieces of your expanding reality is your emotional response to what you are learning and doing. Acknowledging and analyzing your feelings is a critical step toward becoming a professional.

This activity invites you to recognize what you are feeling and understand those emotions as a valid response to certain aspects and demands of the teacher role. You may be saddened by the fact that a number of students do not value learning. You may be outraged to know the neglect and abuse some students experience. You may feel exasperation when a gifted student refuses to use her talents. Feelings are a part of you! They count! They force us to action!

What aspiring and/or experienced teacher does not respond with a rousing "YES" to the quote, ". . . by the year 2006, America will provide all students with what should be their educational birthright: access to competent, caring, and qualified teachers" (National Commission on Teaching and America's Future, 1996). The Commission's description of U.S. educators most likely parallels the vision you have of yourself as a "competent, caring, and qualified" teacher. As you engage in the process of becoming that teacher, you gain a better understanding of the many dimensions of the teacher's role.

Student teaching immerses you into new situations and unfamiliar surroundings. While the classroom is neither new nor unfamiliar to you, being the "teacher" in charge of instruction is different. Through the day-in and day-out routine of teaching, you are meeting the demands of teaching—planning, collaborating, explaining, demonstrating, and managing learner activities. Some of the stardust you felt earlier about being a teacher has settled, and teacher responsibilities seem to extend across the horizon. How many different areas there are to monitor and manage! There is much activity—walking, talking, remembering names, organizing materials, checking, and changing schedules. Much energy and continuous effort is expended. The ideas that seemed logical and well organized in your head may not have played out in what you said or did. Perhaps a class activity did not proceed as you mentally pictured it even though you spent hours planning it! What feelings and emotions are churning inside you as you practice the role of teacher? How do you feel about what you are doing?

Pause here and recall the teacher responsibilities you have assumed and have been given. Recognize and analyze what you are feeling. Are you bewildered? Overwhelmed? Anxious? Take three or four minutes to identify in writing what you feel at this time about the role you are assuming. How have you adapted to this new role? Using affective words, describe your feelings and emotions.

_____

_____

_____

Discussion Questions

1. Using words that convey deep feelings and responses to critical student/teacher issues (i.e., swamped, eager, enthusiastic, anxious, excited, overwhelmed, frustrated, self-conscious, scared, etc.), describe a single incident that moved or challenged you, and analyze your feelings regarding your responsibility or role in the instance.
2. Think about the different roles teachers assume, those engaging the heart and those demanding knowledge and refined teaching techniques. How do your current responsibilities provide you opportunities to integrate what you have learned into your performance as a competent, caring teacher?
3. Telling and listening to stories and others' insights helps you integrate numerous experiences and make sense of them in light of your own. Individuals are often catalysts for helping you recognize and understand your own emotions, while deepening your insights about teaching. What knowledge, attitude, belief, or value have you related to or recalled after hearing others' stories? Explain the effect that hearing these stories had on insights about your own experiences in the classroom.
4. How comfortable are you sharing your feelings with others? To what extent does deep dialogue with others enhance your understanding of how to balance the affective (empathy with students) with the cognitive (understanding of the teacher's role) components of teaching?

Focus Two

Expected Performance

- Identify and design instruction appropriate to learners' stages of development, learning styles, strengths, and needs.

- Incorporate strategies that address physical, social, and cultural diversity and show sensitivity to differences.

- Identify when and how to access appropriate services or resources to meet exceptional learning needs.

- Seek to understand students' families, cultures, and communities, and use this information as a basis for connecting instruction to students' experiences.

- Propose and include learning experiences that challenge, motivate, actively involve learners, and encourage students to be adaptable, flexible, resourceful, and creative.

It is normal to feel overwhelmed. It's okay to be bewildered, feel anxious, tired, or frustrated. Your feelings are part of the process of becoming a competent, caring, qualified teacher. It is reassuring to hear others having similar feelings as you shared experiences with your **Focus One** group. Gaining competence in planning lessons will lessen your sense of being overwhelmed.

Planning for the individual needs of your students can be a difficult process. Coordinating activities that meet the lesson objectives and respond to varied learners within a specified time frame takes organization and planning. Gathering information concerning achievement levels, language abilities, and student interests helps you prepare for the variations and adjustments necessary in planning for individual differences among learners. You have observed a number of teachers who seemed to have the key to effective and efficient planning.

Orlich et al. (1998) suggest four techniques that effective teachers use in their planning process:

1. planning routines to expedite the daily flow of instruction, making sure students know what is expected and arrangements are made to regulate activities beforehand,
2. talking to oneself or using a reflective dialogue about best instructional practices or management techniques to adopt with your class/es,
3. developing interdependent planning levels (long range, unit, and daily), helping to convert long-range goals into daily activities, and
4. collecting a treasury of teaching materials that provide a rich environment for learning.

APPLICATION: DESIGNING AND PLANNING INSTRUCTION

The task of planning for classroom instruction requires knowledge of the planning process and skill in decision making. Selecting a particular framework will aid you in this planning process. In your teacher preparation courses you may have been taught to follow Barak Rosenshine's (1983) six basic teaching functions, Madeline Hunter's (1984) Instructional Theory into Practice, the Sandra Kaplan Matrix (1979), or the James Cooper (1999) planning model when developing your lesson plan format. In this section you will find a suggested framework for planning. Teachers use this framework as they plan for linking the curriculum with assessment. As teacher you are asked to make decisions about curriculum based on data gathered from observation and other assessment sources. As you plan for different grade levels, decisions are made based on reflective insights gained from questions such as those listed under the five categories below. The following questions will enable you to develop a broad perspective as you begin to take on the teacher role.

Diagnosis and assessment of learner needs

1. At what level are students in this class able to read independently?
2. What problem-solving skills do they demonstrate?
3. What works best for this group of learners?

Development of learner expectations

1. What is it that you intend your students to achieve during this class period?
2. What expectations do you have for special learners?
3. What knowledge will your students demonstrate after completing this unit?

Organization of content, resources, and learners

1. What instructional strategies will you use?
2. What technology and other materials will you use to actively engage students?
3. How will you arrange the classroom furniture, technology, and other materials to support the learning environment?

Assessment to determine learner outcomes

1. What criteria or scoring guides do you need to prepare? Does the activity require that a rubric be used for assessing performance?
2. What will focus student attention on what is to be learned and promote student self-assessment?
3. Have you matched the objectives with the assessment instruments you chose?

Practice and follow-up instruction

1. How might you restate, review, and practice skills and content with special needs learners?
2. How often do you ask the students to make connections between today's content and skills with those taught yesterday, last week, or at some earlier time?
3. Based on the results of the assessment, do you need to reteach, reinforce, or move into more challenging content?

Fundamental to lesson preparation is the mastery of the knowledge of the content being taught. Reading a number of outside sources may be required for you to gain a firm understanding of the content. Taking notes and making outlines from the readings may assist you in both short- and long-range planning. These notes may assist you when organizing the concepts and topics to be included in your presentations. Examining texts, curriculum standards, school system guidelines, the Internet, and other supplementary materials available in the school's media center provides additional information needed for teaching.

Communicating with your cooperating teacher/s concerning your plans is also essential. You may want to review grouping patterns, methods for diagnosing learner strengths and weaknesses, and arrangements for special learners within the classroom and school.

Generating varied examples to use in helping students grasp the content being taught would be one of the first steps in the lesson procedure. Choosing your assessment/s to match your objectives is another important step.

After determining from your informal and formal assessment whether you have achieved what you set out to achieve, you may choose to reteach, reinforce the concept, or move on to the next lesson.

ASSIGNED ACTIVITIES

This assignment focuses on preliminary identification of learner ability and examination of instructional resources.

1. Examine the diagnostic and assessment procedures for determining the needs of learners you will teach in your class(es). Look at the following items. Which items can you immediately address? Which items are not

clear at this time? Give examples of any information collected on individual differences of the learner including:

Learner interests

Problem-solving ability

Independent reading ability

Verbal and written language ability

2. Study the varied uses of technology, curriculum guidelines, texts, and other materials used with learners. Briefly describe the use of technology and other materials you and/or the supervising teacher use with students.

3. To what extent have you initiated taking roll, grading papers, designing a seating chart, tutoring, checking homework, or additional responsibilities? Describe your participation.

4. How are decisions made about what and how much content is to be presented during a particular lesson?

SUMMARY

Your application focused on a framework that helped you with organizing your planning. In reflecting, you may have proceeded through the following tasks:

- observing closely the needs of learners
- developing and/or observing the objectives for lessons taught—what you intended that students know and be able to do during a particular class period
- examining materials, including activities that provide students with a positive learning experience
- discussing with the supervising teacher the assessment used with your students
- reflecting on what was accomplished
- planning for review, reinforcement, and/or reteaching the lesson

As you continue reinforcing this process and refining your planning skills, you will discover that there is more to planning for your class than the lesson plan. Even though it is challenging and time-consuming, planning can be exciting and rewarding.

FOLLOW-UP QUESTIONS AND SHARED INSIGHTS

Think back to the very beginning of your experience. Name sources of information you used to help accumulate information concerning learner needs and/or learner differences. Look at your journals and assignments and with the person next to you, locate examples of reflective-type comments. Reflections written soon after observing or teaching describe the real situation and are often more insightful. Decide why your comments were reflective. Now think back over teaching that you did or observed. What were your expectations or those of your supervising teacher? How did you plan for them? What was your rationale for the techniques you planned? List changes you would make and rationale for those changes. Ask yourself these types of questions as you plan day by day:

What is the concept to be taught?

What is my purpose for using this strategy?

How do I approach this concept in a creative way to engage more students?

What can I do with the results of the student assessment?

Do my students need to spend more time on this specific concept?

How will I handle Brittany, Troy, Juan, or Merilou's group?

Journal excerpts cite specific teaching behaviors you tried and your successes or limitations. You may want to relate these experiences to observations or previous knowledge about effective teaching and learning. Finally, note what new ideas, insights, and/or feelings come as a result of your responding in this manner.

Keep in mind all aspects of the planning process as you share your response to the following questions:

1. In what way/s do you assist or direct students throughout the school day (a) during homeroom activities, (b) as students come into the classroom, (c) in the hallway, (d) during assemblies/programs, (e) in cooperative groups?
2. How is the school day organized to schedule special students from your classes? In a collaborating teaching situation, how is teacher time organized to provide additional assistance to learners with special needs?
3. How does the teacher handle "on-task" time when students are leaving during class time?
4. Think about the decisions you are making in planning the content for a lesson. How do you decide the amount of content for a selected lesson?
5. What are your strengths in the planning process? In what areas do you need to improve? You may wish to add a personal action plan for the coming week to reinforce your steps to improve.
6. Take at least two classes and describe the performance expected of the students.
7. Having examined the curriculum, textbooks, technology, and other materials, what are your plans for using these materials in your teaching?
8. What access do teachers have to resources in your school library or media center? Is there a special system for request or checkout?

Portfolio Tasks

Portfolios are increasingly becoming the means of demonstrating the skills, experiences, and accomplishments of the beginning teacher. Portfolio entries are an excellent means for assessing your teaching ability. Standards established by national and state groups are guidelines to assist you in the development of your portfolio. This collection of information may be ongoing throughout your teacher education program. We are providing you with what we call Portfolio Tasks based on national and state new teacher standards that you may complete during your student/intern teacher experience. As you design and perform each portfolio task, you are documenting what you and your students accomplish as a result of your planning and teaching. In addition you engage in reflection about the decisions made as the teacher. This is a major purpose for developing a teaching portfolio, reflecting and documenting your professional growth and competence as a student/intern teacher.

Throughout the student/intern teaching experience you have multiple opportunities to perform and reflect on your growth as a result of the guidance given you by supervising teachers within the university and school settings. These opportunities, together with additional experiences throughout your teacher education program, allow you to make adequate progress toward meeting your goals.

In addition to the teacher education program requirements, many school systems require portfolios for initial teacher candidate interviews based on state and national standards. Three national professional education organizations have developed standards connected to teacher education goals. The National Council for the Accreditation of Teacher Educators (NCATE) accredits teacher education programs based on specific standards. Interstate New Teacher Assessment and Support Consortium (INTASC) developed standards for beginning teachers, whereas the National Board for Professional Teaching Standards

(NBPTS) employs portfolios in the certification of outstanding experienced teachers. Many states have produced their own standards and require that teacher education programs be written according to these standards.

Earlier in your teacher education program you may have developed portfolio entries. Significant additions to your portfolio may be made during your student/intern teacher experience. To assist you with this development, the text presents portfolio tasks that are based on INTASC standards. The appendix contains a copy of both the INTASC standards and standards from one of the states, Kentucky New Teacher Standards for Preparation and Certification. You will find suggested portfolio tasks in chapters under **Focus Two.** A briefcase symbol is used to alert you to the task.

Designs and Plans Instruction

Standards

Your first task is based on the following national standards:

1. The teacher understands the central concepts, tools of inquiry, and structures of the discipline(s) he/she teaches and can create learning experiences that make these aspects of subject matter meaningful for students.
2. The teacher understands how children learn and develop and can provide learning opportunities that support their intellectual, social, and personal development.
3. The teacher understands how students differ in their approaches to learning and creates instructional opportunities that are adapted to diverse learners.

Performance Guidelines

In this first portfolio task, exhibit samples of lesson plans you have designed and planned for the classes you teach. Select six of your best lesson plans for this task. In developing your lesson plans consider such information as learner needs, expectations for learners, the content being taught, strategies to engage the learner, and the assessment to be applied. Using your selected lesson plan format, demonstrate to the portfolio reader that your plan was developed according to the criteria below. You may want to include student work (one or two samples), activity forms that you have developed, pictures of students in group activities, or other artifacts to accompany your plans.

Performance Criteria

The quality of your product will be assessed to the extent that evidence provided:

1. Develops the student's ability to apply knowledge, skills, and thinking processes.
2. Integrates skills, thinking processes, and content across disciplines.
3. Proposes learning experiences that challenge, motivate, and actively involve the learner.
4. Proposes learning experiences that are developmentally appropriate for learners.
5. Incorporates strategies that address physical, social, and cultural diversity and show sensitivity to differences.
6. Establishes physical classroom environments to support the type of teaching and learning that is to occur.
7. Includes creative and appropriate use of technology as a tool to enhance student learning.

8. Includes comprehensive and appropriate school and community resources that support learning.
9. Includes learning experiences that encourage students to be adaptable, flexible, resourceful, and creative.

Caution

As author of your portfolio, all materials in the portfolio should be your own work. When entering student papers, change or delete the names to acknowledge the confidentiality of the students' work. Sample lesson plans that you receive from advisors, supervising or other teachers, or Internet sources must be credited and not considered your work. You may adapt the strategies from these plans to suit the needs and abilities of your students, formatting them in your own words to reflect your teaching style.

Web Sites

The following web sites provide valuable information concerning copyright and multimedia use.

www.clarinet.com/brad/copymyths.html—an attempt to answer common myths about copyright material on the Internet and cover issues related to copyright and USENET/Internet publication.

www.aimnet.com/~carroll/copyright/faq-home.html—site for frequently asked questions on copyright.

www.nlc-bnc.ca/ifla/documents/infopol/copyright/educom.txt—some guidelines on software and copyright.

www.libraries.psu.edu/avs/fairuse/guidelinedoc.html—guidelines for fair use of educational multimedia.

Journal Excerpts

High School

"Over the past few days I have already noted several different learning styles and preferences. Most all of the students seem to assimilate information better if the teacher actually says it verbally and also writes it on the board, or hands it out to them. This visual learning style has also been encouraged through video and posters in the room. Some students also participate actively, while others do not join in class discussion."

"Everything is just great! Today I felt very involved in everything that was going on. First of all, I volunteered to give directions. Then I taught the freshman English class. I wrote up a detailed lesson plan and gave a copy to my supervising teacher to follow as I was teaching. After school we conferenced about the lesson and he gave me so many helpful suggestions! . . . I loved my first teaching experience and I can't wait to do it again."

"Clear and concise directions are key for both of my supervising teachers, because they have so much going on in the classroom. One teacher uses student recapping, the students repeat the directions given, and the other usually writes the directions on the board. Both of them repeat directions several times, and that allows plenty of time for answering any questions and clarifying of any statements! Much emphasis is placed on the individual learning styles and needs of each student."

Middle Grades

"I am still learning about the students' learning styles, but it is obvious through work, words, and actions that they all differ greatly from one another. Many students are difficult to motivate, but we usually do well. Most students may take time, but eventually they get on task. A few initiate the move towards work, sharing, and participating in class. Some students are followers and will join in while others need more encouragement.

"After school I shared tomorrow's lesson plan with Ms. H. She's seen it before. We've been chatting about it all week and sort of sharing ideas. She is really helpful and doesn't mind sharing her ideas and materials with me."

"Many of the students voiced their concerns that the story and study guide was too hard to read and understand. But I stayed with them and encouraged them, giving them ways to find out about the meaning of a story. I showed a lot of empathy, and made sure not to act disgusted with their persistence that it was too hard. I encouraged them and told them I would not have assigned it if I didn't think they could handle it!"

Elementary

"The students in our classroom have many different learning styles. The eight multiple intelligences are evident. The majority of the class learns through visual and auditory instruction. Mrs. H. always writes directions on the board and models what she wants the students to do. This technique is especially helpful when teaching the students to read. They not only hear a word being read, but also see it—either on the board, chart paper, or in a book."

"The reading lesson went well. We did not get as far as I planned, but we can always start up again and continue into next week if they need to."

"There are students in my class that learn better with a hands-on approach, or through movement (kinesthetic learners). My supervising teacher incorporates movement into her lessons. For example, they clap, snap, stomp, etc., when spelling vocabulary words. I plan to do this also when I teach my lesson tomorrow."

Special Education

"I looked at the materials that my supervising teacher uses for math and reading . . . observed where each student was, and worked with several individuals. It seems like we are always teaching two or three lessons at once because the students are on such different levels. . . . This was a shock to my system because I had been used to large group instruction and then working with individuals during the time I gave for independent practice. . . . When they feel that they are learning and are doing well, their behavior improves."

"I've taken the initiative with a number of the students by noting weaknesses and providing special helps in the afternoon homework hustle time. Also, in my lessons I am modifying different activities as needed by the students."

"I actually feel better about myself after my meeting with Dr. M. We closely analyze my lesson and discuss strengths and areas for improvement. Mrs. T. and I had a good talk today after school. Feedback from my supervising teachers and professors really builds my confidence level."

REFERENCES AND SUGGESTED READINGS

Alley, R., and Jung, B. (1995). Preparing teachers for the 21st century. In M. J. O'Hair and S. J. Odell (Eds.), *Educating teachers for leadership and change* (pp. 285–301). Thousand Oaks, CA: Corwin Press.

Borko, H., Michaled, P., Timmons, M., and Siddle, J. (1997). Student teaching portfolios: A tool for promoting reflective practice. *Journal of Teacher Education, 48*(5), 345–357.

Callahan, J., Clark, L., and Kellough, R. (1998). *Teaching in the middle and secondary schools* (6th ed.). Upper Saddle River, NJ: Merrill/Prentice Hall.

Campbell, K., Cignetti, P., Melenyzer, B., Nettles, D., and Wyman, Jr., R. (1997). *How to develop a professional portfolio.* Boston: Allyn and Bacon.

Cooper, J. (Ed.). (1999). *Classroom teaching skills* (6th ed.). Lexington, MA: D.C. Heath.

Darling-Hammond, L. (1997). *Doing what matters most: Investing in quality teaching.* New York: National Commission on Teaching and America's Future.

Eby, J. W. (1998). *Reflective planning, teaching, and evaluation K–12* (2nd ed.). Upper Saddle River, NJ: Merrill/Prentice Hall.

Hunter, M. (1984). Knowing, teaching and supervision. In P. Hosford, (Ed.), *Using what we know about teaching.* Alexandria, VA.: Association for Supervision and Curriculum Development.

Interstate New Teacher Assessment and Support Consortium. (1992). *Model standards for beginning teacher licensing and development: A resource for state dialogue.* Washington, DC: Council of Chief State School Officers.

Jersild, A. (1955). *When teachers face themselves.* New York: Teachers College Press, p. 83.

Kaplan, S. N. (1979). *Inservice training manual: Activities for development of curriculum for the gifted/talented.* Ventura, CA: Ventura County Schools.

Kentucky Education Professional Standards Board. (1994). *New teacher standards for preparation and certification.* (Rev. ed.). Frankfort, KY: Department of Education.

Murphy, J. (1995). Changing role of the teacher. In M. J. O'Hair and S. J. Odell (Eds.), *Educating teachers for leadership and change* (pp. 311–323). Thousand Oaks, CA: Corwin Press.

National Commission on Teaching and America's Future. (1996). *What matters most: Teaching for America's future.* New York: National Commission on Teaching and America's Future.

Odell, S. J. (1989). Developing support programs for beginning teachers. In L. Huling-Austin, S. J. Odell, P. Ishler, et al., *Assisting the beginning teacher.* Reston, VA: Association of Teacher Educators.

Orlich, D., Harder, R., Callahan, R., Kauchak, D., and Gibson, H. (1998). *Teaching strategies: A guide to better instruction.* Lexington, MA: D.C. Heath.

Pitton, D. E. (1998). *Stories of student teaching: A case approach to the student teaching experience.* Upper Saddle River, NJ: Merrill/Prentice Hall.

Rosenshine, B. (1983). Teaching functions in instructional programs. *Elementary School Journal 83,* 335–351.

Wolf, K., Whinery, B., and Hagerty, P. (1995). Teaching portfolios and portfolio conversations for teacher educators and teachers. *Action in Teacher Education, 17*(1), 30–39.

Wolfinger, D., and Stockard, Jr., J. (1997). *Elementary methods: An integrated curriculum.* New York: Longman.

Zubizarreta, J. (1994). Teaching portfolios and the beginning teacher. *Phi Delta Kappan, 76*(4), 323–326.

CHAPTER

Accommodating the Diversity of Learners

> " *. . . If there is anything that we wish to change in the child, we should first examine it and see whether it is not something that could better be changed in ourselves.* "

C. S. Jung

Focus One

Expected Performance

- Identify times when you felt different or isolated from a group.
- Discuss learning activities that generate understanding and acceptance of differences.
- Model inclusive behaviors.

Analyzing the Affective Dimensions of Inclusion

- Do your students look alike?
- Do they like the same music and art?
- Do they hold the same work and family values as you?
- Are there cultural differences among your students and between you and your students?

Because of the many differences that exist among students, schools today are expected to present a multicultural approach to learning. As a teacher you play a significant role in providing such a perspective. In addition to having broad knowledge and an in-depth understanding of multiculturalism, experts in the field emphasize the importance of experiential learning in influencing your attitudes and motivating you to integrate a multicultural perspective into the content of the courses you teach (Banks, 1996; Tamura, Nelson, & Ford-Stevenson, 1996; Moore, 1996). In earlier teacher education courses you most likely encountered multicultural experiences. **Focus One** builds on your prior knowledge and experience and asks you to take advantage of your current classroom setting by incorporating a multicultural awareness into your teaching.

As a student/intern teacher you can expect the whole-life experiences of your students to differ greatly from your own. The quality of your relationship with students from different cultures offers important learning experiences. According to statistical projections, students in the 21st century will be more diverse than ever before. Projected demographics indicate that a higher percentage of students will reflect a variety of cultures and races, represent social classes, claim religious affiliation, and come from family backgrounds that may differ from their teachers. Because of these factors, life for students within your classroom may contrast sharply with the life they experience outside your classroom. It is critical that you recognize and respond to the chasm that may exist between the world views and life experiences held by your students and those held by you—their teacher.

If you have had little exposure or interactions with diverse cultures and ethnic groups, you may encounter student speech patterns and actions that challenge you and leave you feeling ill at ease. Your reaction is normal since language, nonverbal communication, and interaction are among the areas that matter most to teachers (Nelson-Barber & Mitchell, 1992). From your students' perspectives, the way you speak and interact with them may be foreign to their personal experience or conflict with their cultural values. Within such a situation, both you and your students may experience tense moments, especially if students do not feel accepted in the classroom or if fairness becomes an issue. As the teacher you may even feel tense and uneasy about the students as a group! Uncertainty and lack of experience may cause you to focus your attention on the outspoken or inappropriate behaviors of specific students. Does any of this sound familiar?

Take time to examine, understand, and appreciate the differences individually and collectively among the students in your classroom. Get to know those students whose backgrounds, beliefs, and values systems may differ from yours and/or other students'. To accommodate the diversity of learners, you initiate conversations and invite participation from all members of the class. Before meaningful learning can occur, students and teachers must explore diversity within the classroom and set the stage for tolerance where differences are appreciated and similarities are noted. Learning takes place within a social setting and is influenced by the culture and needs of both students and teachers.

Conversations with other teachers help you expand your view of students as unique individuals. You recognize the great potential these young people have for learning and teaching others as a result of their different backgrounds, life experiences, and cultures. Your deeper perspective regarding your students' potential challenges you to explore teaching skills and use strategies that help them make connections, find meaning, and demonstrate understanding. As a result, you increase the amount and frequency of praise and other positive interactions with students that contribute to a healthy classroom climate (Garibaldi, 1992; McDiarmid, 1990; Rust, 1999).

This **Focus One** activity is similar to one involving other student teachers (Tamura, Nelson, & Ford-Stevenson, 1996) and encourages you to become personally involved with your students to gain a sense of what "walking in their shoes" would feel like for you. Begin the activity by recalling your own experiences and feelings about school. Think about a time when you felt different in school, when you felt separate from others because of a real or perceived difference. It may have been when you were in elementary, middle, or high school. It may have happened more recently, while you were working in schools during a teacher preparation course. Did feelings about being different arise from cultural, social, ethnic, or racial remarks or interactions? What happened? Did anyone say or do anything that made you feel different or feel alienated from the group? Did anyone respond to you, help you feel more comfortable? Is there anything someone could have said to you to bring you back into the group? What could someone have done to help you feel included? Taking time to reflect on what you know about diversity, analyze the specifics of the situation. Label the emotions you experienced during the time you felt isolated and apart from the group. In the space below write words, phrases, or sentences describing your feelings.

_____

_____

_____

Using the questions that follow, you are now ready to discuss your experiences and to listen to those of your peers.

Discussion Questions

1. How did you respond to feeling isolated, different from others? If you are comfortable, share your experience and feelings with your peers.
2. How did your reactions affect the way you spoke with your peers, the way you initiated or approached an activity?
3. Think about the students you teach and identify one student whose family background is different from others in the class. What do you notice about that student that sets her/him apart from others? How might you approach this student and learn about her/his experience of school?
4. What do you say and do when students make fun of others who are different?
5. How might you integrate multicultural learning or multicultural issues into your lessons or classes? Give examples of activities that would highlight the diversity in your class and invite discovery and learning about cultural, gender, racial, ethnic, and social differences among the students in your class.

Focus Two

Focusing on the cultural, social, physical, learning, and gender differences of the students within your class/es, you have come face to face with the problems that call for multicultural education. When multicultural education is integrated throughout the school curricula, teachers and students begin to live, learn, and work together in this culturally diverse world. Teachers and students learn to value the diversity that exists in their community. Becoming aware of and affirmed in our own cultural roots is an important first step toward valuing diversity. As we begin to learn about and interact with people from various backgrounds and experiences, we begin to glimpse similarities between ourselves and others and appreciate the differences among us. In becoming more knowledgeable and more sensitive to other cultures, we validate others' experiences, beliefs, values, and customs while affirming our own.

APPLICATION: ACCOMMODATING THE DIVERSITY OF LEARNERS

Increasing your cultural knowledge and examining instructional strategies to prepare students for living in a pluralistic society not only enriches students' personal lives but positively contributes to their school experiences. A wealth of diversity can be explored in literature, art, and music. Stories and poetry can be drawn upon depicting human experiences of poverty, discrimination, and conflict, and liberation, exploration, and justice. As you attempt to enrich the multicultural education of your students, your own class can provide a rich opportunity for community building. Students have diverse backgrounds, a rich mine for exploration, a great place to start.

Realizing and believing that all students can learn is the first step in developing appropriate instruction to accommodate all students in your class/es. Assessing student needs and differences is a significant and important part of the planning process. Thus far in your journals and assigned activities, you have identified and examined differences among students in your classes regarding:

- learning styles
- multiple intelligences
- student interests and life experience

Expected Performance

- Demonstrate consistent sensitivity to individual academic, physical, social, and cultural differences and responds to all students in a caring manner.
- Identify and design instruction appropriate to learners' stages of development, learning styles, strengths, and needs.
- Incorporate strategies that address physical, social, and cultural diversity and show sensitivity to differences.
- Identify when and how to access appropriate services or resources to meet exceptional learning needs.
- Seek to understand students' families, cultures, and communities, and use this information as a basis for connecting instruction to students' experiences.
- Propose and include learning experiences that challenge, motivate, and actively involve learners and encourage students to be adaptable, flexible, resourceful, and creative.
- Demonstrate interpersonal/ team membership skills and responsible caring behavior with students in facilitating instruction.

You have probably recognized that there are additional aspects to diversity and are wondering how you might adapt the instruction to meet all student needs. It can be an overwhelming task to plan for and respond to the ethnic, racial, physical, religious, language, gender, and exceptional differences of students in your classes each day. All students have their own background experiences which give rise to a unique perspective they bring to the classroom. As teacher you are asked to provide developmentally appropriate instruction that values diversity and promotes student achievement. "If we believe that there are not inherent intellectual differences among ethnic, class, and gender groups, then overall academic performance across groups should be similar. The fact that there are differences in academic achievement presents us with the challenge to overcome those differences" (Gollnick, 1992). The challenge facing you is to become knowledgeable, competent, and flexible in selecting and practicing the instructional practices that best suit each individual student. This results in successful learning for every student.

You are not alone in the process of relating to each student as an individual and assuring them of an equal opportunity to succeed. Effective teachers will share their struggles and successes, adapting their plans and instruction to meet the needs of all their students. It takes patient, daily effort to effect successful progress with all learners. One of the first steps is to develop and model good communication skills with learners from all cultures. Being aware of your own verbal and nonverbal behavior increases the possibility of positive interaction with students and others. Another approach is to give step-by-step directions and explanations about how an activity is to be accomplished so that the learner is secure about beginning the task. The following activities provide opportunities to observe, reflect, initiate, communicate, and demonstrate your willingness to promote multicultural education and increase the success rate of all students as they engage in learning activities and performance tasks.

ASSIGNED ACTIVITIES

1. Observe and list the teacher behaviors and attributes that positively support multicultural education in your school this week. How have these behaviors affected the learning environment?
2. Conduct a survey to determine the ethnic, religious, gender, physical, racial, and language differences in your classes. In what ways will you use this information? How might it help sensitize you to the diverse experiences of your students and impact your planning? What activities will you provide that may bring all learners to a better understanding of each other?
3. Choose five students at random from your classes each day. Make a special effort to interact with them positively, if only with a smile, nod of approval, or morning greeting. What was their response?
4. Take special notice of your directions and explanations in at least four classes this week. Have you become more explicit in your instructions, leaving students with fewer procedural questions?
5. How has your own ethnic, racial, and cultural identity shaped your experiences, and how you have interpreted them?
6. Research ideas for teaching strategies that will provide your students with ways to interact effectively and work cooperatively with others who may be culturally, socially, and/or physically different from themselves. Select an instructional approach or teaching strategy that may accomplish the expected outcome you have chosen. Be prepared to share your selection with your colleagues.

"... schools in particular have been the great instruments of assimilation and the great means of forming an American identity. What students are taught in schools affects the way they will thereafter see and treat other Americans, the way they will thereafter conceive the purposes of the republic. The debate about the curriculum is a debate about what it means to be an American."

Arthur Schlesinger

SUMMARY

In our diverse society, students come to school with many cultural backgrounds, and these cultural differences can be a source of misunderstanding and conflict. As a beginning teacher, you want to know and appreciate the cultural background of your students. You will build on your students' strengths and work to eliminate their weaknesses. This challenge includes promoting racial unity and gender equity by creating a positive learning environment, helping all students participate in class activities, maintaining open communication with your students, and providing content, resources, and activities that ensure success for all students. Treating all students with sensitivity and recognizing that students learn in different ways challenges you to observe how your students best learn. Learning experiences designed to accommodate all learners creates an environment where individual needs are met and community is built on differences.

FOLLOW-UP QUESTIONS AND SHARED INSIGHTS

Using the reflections in your journals, the assigned activities, and your background of experiences, share responses to the following questions:

1. How has your own ethnic, racial, and cultural identity shaped your experiences, and how you have interpreted them? What implications does this hold for you as teacher?
2. How can you determine whether you are discriminating against learners based on their gender? What steps can be taken to eliminate gender bias in the classroom?
3. How do you become aware of your cultural and social biases?
4. In what ways does your classroom show evidence of the involvement of both teacher and students learning about various cultures?
5. Describe your own experience in which personal bias or misunderstanding of cultural values or gender or ethnic issues caused you to misrepresent a particular group?
   - What was the result of this misrepresentation?
   - How did the misrepresentation contribute to conflict?
   - How could the situation have been handled more constructively?
6. Identify teacher behaviors and characteristics that would demonstrate support and commitment to multicultural education.

Technology Tips

With the introduction of the World Wide Web in 1991, a multitude of continuously expanding resources became available. The web provides color, graphics, and pictures on topics as extensive as any library. Teachers in primary through 12th grades can access different web sites and search out instructional ideas and other information about teaching.

Extending the emphasis on multiculturalism in this chapter, the Technology Tips encourage you to use the web as a teaching resource. Some consider the World Wide Web a possible means for making the interaction and communication that uses the transcultural technologies while respecting the local culture and institutions (Collis & Remmers, 1997; Willis & Dickinson, 1997). Think about ways you might use the web as another source of ideas for integrating a multicultural perspective into your instruction. With the rapid proliferation of web sites, continual changes and expansions occur and new sites appear. You may know other web sites and access these for information and teaching suggestions. The following list of selected web sites provides gender inclusive activities and suggestions for teaching students about other cultures, races, and ethnic groups. The grade level and content area of these lesson plans are indicated.

World Wide Web Sites

- Lesson plans and curriculum ideas developed for elementary and secondary levels. Presents an inquiry-based approach to art education: http://www.artsednet.getty.edu/ArtsEdNet/Resources/Erickson/Place/index.html
- Six elementary level lesson plans designed to integrate diversity into mathematics and social studies content: http://www.census.gov/ftp/pub/edu/diversity/
- Five junior/senior high lesson plans emphasizing diversity and connected with mathematical and social studies concepts: http://www.census.gov/ftp/pub/edu/diversity/
- Student activities using Internet for investigating special populations (suitable for upper elementary and high school students): http://edweb.sdsu.edu/people/cmathison/truths/truths.html
- Activities for high school students integrating the World Wide Web and video conferencing on the topic of African American history: http://www.kn.pacbell.com/wired/BHM/AfroAm.html
- Lesson plans designed by GirlTECH teachers for teaching mathematics, science, social studies, and computer literacy. The list provides numerous plans for grades 7–12 that can be adapted for grades 4–6: http://ww.crpc.rice.edu/CRPC/Women/GirlTECH/Lessons/
- Unit and lesson plans for elementary level:
  Celebrations: Resource Guide for Elementary Teachers
  Community Unit
  http://www.teacherlink.usu.edu/resources/ed_lesson_plans/index.html
- Social studies lesson plans and activities for all grade levels:
  AskAsia Lesson Plans
  Latin America—Lesson Plans
  Japan Lessons K–12
  http://www.mcrel.org/connect/sslessons.html
- Information center for accommodations necessary for life-experience differences, i.e., disability, language, aging, location, culture, etc.: http://www.itpolicy.gsa.gov/coca/index.html
- Curriculum Design for Excellence OnLine presents an inderdisciplinary approach to K–12 education: www.Rogertaylor.com

Journal Excerpts

High School

"I am surprised at the variety of students within each class. This is truly a multi-cultural group. In second period alone there are students with Italian, Native American, Latin, African American, and Asian backgrounds. Today the students were asked to write about their names, how they got them, and where they came from. The students were asked to switch notebooks with another student. Each student then introduced the student whose notebook they had. This assignment was not only helpful to Mrs. M. and me, but also to the students for a number of reasons. It helps students learn the names and realize how different each of us really is and yet we're all friends. I think in some ways for a number of students it may have helped break down the walls of some stereotypes we hold."

"I spend time at the beginning of class teaching students the basic skill of organization. With freshmen especially I insist that they write the homework in their assignment book. I remind the sophomores about their assignment, but with the freshmen classes I spend more time teaching them techniques for organizing the different tasks. I tell them when they need to write down notes. I also either write on the board or on the overhead the notes they need to copy. At times they also work in groups and read to each other the notes they have taken. This seems to help them use their notes and to improve their thinking about the information given."

"I have some special needs learners whom I had to keep a pretty steady pace when I explained the use of computers. I had to watch every student making sure she or he was on the correct screen. But I couldn't take too much time because I'd lose the other students who had more expertise. It helps to have a small number of students so that I can arrange to work one-on-one to make sure they all have the information needed."

Middle School

"I was taken aback today when our notoriously loud and non-focused sixth period class performed so well. Normally they get one or two lectures about behavior and respect everyday. However, today for some reason, they focused beautifully, read well, acted out the words in an interesting manner. It was a pleasant way to end the day because it reaffirmed my belief that all students are capable of focusing on learning and succeeding!"

"I circulated each period and gave advice on revisions (mainly on the form of the paper and on following directions and being concise). I found it rewarding for me to spend quality time helping those students who really wanted to be better writers and sought my advice on how to make their pieces better. I feel honored to help them and I can also sympathize with them because there have been times in my own life when I've felt like, no matter how hard I worked at something, I just couldn't get it. I am pleased that I've been able to offer good suggestions and praise for their effort."

"Even though I feel this placement has been tougher than some of the other places I could have gone, I wouldn't change it. I think this is right where I needed to be in terms of students. There are so many of them and they are so different—so many different backgrounds. I was a little intimidated at first, but not any more. I love it, and I think that I am really gaining a deeper level of understanding for these differences and I rejoice in them."

Elementary

"I circulated around the room and helped the students generate and brainstorm clues for a Math lesson. Some students needed more help than others. It's always amazing to me how diverse the learners are. Some students thought of more than three clues, others couldn't even get one clue written down without assistance."

"During our examination of the Kindergarten newspaper, we encountered a section on differences. At this point I stated the question, "How are we alike?" The learner who responded related the question to himself and one neighbor, but not the whole class. I had to clarify what I was asking and restate the question as, "What is one thing that we all share in common that makes us all alike?" This new question helped the students understand that I was searching for a similarity among all of us, not just pairs."

"Something I've been pondering for awhile is the "self-fulfilling prophecy" item. I think it is so scary that you can shape someone's performance by developing preconceived notions about them. I have to be very careful about being judgmental both socially and academically with a number of students. Today two or three seemingly below average students surprised me very pleasantly by catching on quickly to the pattern concept."

Special Education

"Although I was not teaching during this time, I can tell that M. believes all of her students can learn. She varies who she calls on due to the abilities of each of her learners. She called on *all* of her students whether they volunteered or not."

"Ms. L. engages poorly motivated learners by utilizing positive praise toward students behaving on-task and/or by rewarding good behavior with treats. Yesterday she repeatedly praised those on-task until the behavior of the targeted pupil improved. Today, she specifically called a pupil out and emphasized any positive contributions he made."

"I worked with two students at the same time which was a big mistake. The academic difference between these two is remarkable. They have similar behavior problems, but J. has a much easier time focusing on tasks—if he wants to! On the other hand, M. gets very frustrated and loses it behaviorally. It is all very interesting! The one thing I have learned with M. is that you have to be extremely patient with him."

References and Suggested Reading

American Association of University Women. (1996). *Growing smart: What's working for girls in schools.* Washington, DC: American Association of University Women.

Arnow, J. (1995). *Teaching peace: How to raise children to live in harmony: Without fear, without prejudice, without violence.* New York: The Berkley Publishing Group.

Banks, J. A. (1996). *Multicultural education: Transformative knowledge and action.* New York: Teachers College Press.

Banks, J. A. (1994). *Multi-ethnic education: Theory and practice* (3rd ed.). Needham Heights, MA: Allyn & Bacon.

Byrd, D., & McIntyre, D. J. (Eds.). (1997). *Research on the education of our nation's teachers: Teacher education yearbook V.* Thousand Oaks, CA: Corwin Press.

Collis, B. & Remmers, E. (1997). The worldwide web in education: Issues related to cross-cultural communication and interaction. In B. H. Khan (Ed.), *Web-Based Instruction.* Englewood Cliffs, NJ: Educational Technology Publications.

Cooper, J. M. (1997). Integrating technology into teacher preparation. *Quality Teaching, The Newsletter of the National Council for Accreditation of Teacher Education, 7*(1), 1.

Delpit, L. (1994). *Other peoples' children: Cultural conflict in the classroom.* New York: New Press.

Dilworth, M. (Ed.). (1992). *Diversity in teacher education: New expectations.* San Francisco: Jossey-Bass.

Garcia, E. (1994). *Understanding and meeting the challenge of student cultural diversity.* Boston: Houghton Mifflin.

Garibaldi, A. M. (1992). Preparing teachers for culturally diverse classrooms. In M. E. Dilworth (Ed.), *Diversity in teacher education: New expectations.* San Francisco: Jossey-Bass.

Glickman, D. D. (1998). *Revolutionizing America's schools.* San Francisco: Jossey-Bass.

Goodlad, J. I. (1997). *In praise of education.* New York: Teachers College Press.

Gollnick, D. M. (1992). Understanding the dynamics of race, class, and gender. In M. E. Dilworth (Ed.), *Diversity in teacher education: New expectations.* San Francisco: Jossey-Bass.

Gollnick, D. M., and Chinn, P. (1998). *Multicultural education in a pluralistic society* (5th ed.). Upper Saddle River, NJ: Merrill/Prentice Hall.

Irvine, J. J., & Foster, M. (Eds.). (1996). *Growing up African American in Catholic schools.* New York: Teachers College Press.

Kozol, J. (1991). *Savage inequalities: Children in America's schools.* New York: Crown Publishers.

Ladson-Billings, G. (1995). Multicultural teacher education: Research, practice, and policy. In J. A. Banks & C. A. Banks (Eds.), *Handbook of research on multicultural education* (pp. 747–761). New York: Macmillan.

Ladson-Billings, G. (1994). *The dream keepers: Successful teachers of African American children.* San Francisco: Jossey-Bass.

McDiarmid, G. W. (1990). Challenging prospective teachers' beliefs during early field experience: A quixotic understanding? *Journal of Teacher Education, 41*(3), 12–20.

Moore, J. A. (1996). Empowering student teachers to teach from a multicultural perspective. Presentation at American Association of Colleges for Teacher Education (Chicago, Feb. 21–24, 1996) (ERIC Document ED 394979).

Nelson-Barber, S. S., & Mitchell, J. (1992). Restructuring for diversity: five regional portraits. In M. E. Dilworth (Ed.), *Diversity in teacher education: New expectations.* San Francisco: Jossey-Bass.

O'Hair, M. J., & Odell, S. J. (1993). *Diversity and teaching: Teacher education yearbook I.* Fort Worth, TX: Harcourt Brace Jovanovich.

Pai, Y., & Adler, S. (1997). *Cultural foundations of education* (2nd ed.). Upper Saddle River, NJ: Merrill/Prentice Hall.

Pang, V. O. (1994). Why do we need this class? Multicultural education for teachers. *Phi Delta Kappan, 76*(4), 289–292.

Putnam, J. (1997). *Cooperative learning in diverse classrooms.* Upper Saddle River, NJ: Merrill/Prentice Hall.

Ryder, R. J. (1997). *Internet for educators.* Upper Saddle River, NJ: Merrill/Prentice Hall.

Rust, F. O. (1999). Professional Conversations: New teachers explore teaching through conversation, story, and narrative. *Teaching and Teacher Education.* (In press).

Spring, J. (1997). *Deculturalization and the struggle for equality* (2nd ed.). New York: McGraw-Hill.

Tamura, L., Nelson, P., & Ford-Stevenson, T. (1996). Preparing teachers to recognize multiple perspectives. Presentation at American Association of Colleges for Teacher Education (Chicago, Feb. 21–24, 1996) (ERIC Document ED 399235).

The National Commission on Teaching & America's Future. (1996). *What matters most: Teaching for America's future.* New York: National Commission on Teaching & America's Future.

Tiedt, P. L., & Tiedt, I. M. (1995). *Multicultural teaching* (4th ed.). Needham Heights, MA: Allyn & Bacon.

Villa, R. A., & Thousand, J. S. (Eds.). (1995). *Creating an inclusive school.* Alexandria, VA: Association for Supervision and Curriculum Development.

Wetzel, K., Zambo, R., Buss, R., & Arbaugh, N. (1996). Innovations in integrating technology into student teaching experiences. *Journal of Research on Computing in Education, 29*(2), 196–214.

Willis, B., & Dickinson, J. (1997). Distance education and the world wide web. In B. H. Khan (Ed.), *Web-based instruction.* Englewood Cliffs, NJ: Educational Technology Publications.

5 Practicing Lesson Presentation Strategies

> " *. . . Teaching is communicating. Learners' success depends on the teacher's ability to communicate clearly essential content, information, and skills and to explain and demonstrate learning processes.* "

Expected Performance

- Participate in drawing activity.
- Consider your personal preference for receiving verbal communication.
- Discuss how student discourse contributes to the communication process.
- Explore ways for strengthening your communication as a teacher.

What Am I Saying? What Am I Hearing?

You are initiating more and assuming greater instructional responsibilities. Consequently, you decide what information students receive and choose the means you will use for sending information to students. How clear is your communication with students? With your supervising teacher? Are you discovering that the message sent is not always the message received? How do your verbal communication skills contribute to instructional practices?

In a study of classroom discourse Cazden (1986) maintains that spoken language is the medium by which much teaching takes place and in which students demonstrate much of what they have learned. Whatever teaching approach you choose—whether it be direct teaching, problem-based instruction, or cooperative learning—you use verbal language in helping students acquire knowledge. For example, if you are teaching students to write a process essay or to find the longitude lines on a map, you give directions and present information for the purpose of acquiring a specific outcome. You refer to the textbook and supplement the content to facilitate students' comprehension and use of the information. You are the "vehicle of instruction" (Good & Brophy, 1994). In your role as teacher you communicate using spoken language to direct students' attention and engage them in discourse.

The thoroughness of your communication affects student participation and, consequently, student achievement. Once you send students a clear and unambiguous message, do you take for granted they "get it"? Can you recall quickly moving through an explanation to the total class and asking students to apply the newly learned information to a task? Can you recall being so excited about the learning activity and concept you taught that you failed to consider the task from the learner's perspective? Forgot to check students' understanding or clarify your expectations of them? This kind of one-way communication is often the basis for teacher and student frustration (Harris & Bessent, 1969). Giving directions for an activity without checking to see if students understand what you expect of them is only one part of the communication process. An initial step in direct instruction (Arends, 1998, 1999) or active learning (Good & Brophy, 1994) is gaining student attention, explaining, and giving directions. Checking for understanding and getting feedback from students is necessary to the communication process.

Seminar Leader's Tasks

- Name one person to be Sender.
- Provide Sender copies of Communication diagram numbers 1 and 2 located in the appendix.
- Allow time for Sender to prepare directions.
- Provide two sheets of paper per person.
- Record the time used for each drawing activity.
- Collect and score drawings and return to participants (during/following the group activity).

Effective teaching depends on accurate communication between teacher and student and between student and student. Inviting students to talk about their understanding allows you a window into their thinking and an opportunity to provide corrective feedback when you observe faulty, incomplete understanding (Arends, 1998). Lesson clarity depends on two-way communication (Borich, 1999; Good & Brophy, 1994; Harris, Bessent, & McIntyre, 1969). An interactive communication process invites dialogue and clarification and helps ensure the message sent is the message received. You understand the importance of two-way communication when you see quizzical looks, dejected faces, blank stares, and other signs of distress on your students' faces! Taking time to read and respond to these visible signs of miscommunication eliminates discouragement and confusion for the students and the teacher. Engaging in a two-way communication process helps you become a more astute decision maker.

The **Focus One** activity for this seminar session emphasizes the importance of verbal communication in the teaching/learning process. You are asked to examine your personal experience with two different ways for sending and receiving verbal communication. One is an uninterrupted, step-by-step message, while the other offers an opportunity for questions and interaction as the communication progresses. As you participate in the activity, keep in mind the following three points about receiving verbal communication:

- your preferred style of communication
- your peers' preferred style of communication
- the communication style preferred by students in your classroom

This activity consists of two parts. First, you are asked to complete individually an activity demonstrating one-way communication followed by a similar task demonstrating two-way communication. Each activity asks you to draw a diagram. During each activity reflect on your personal experiences with different styles of communication. After completing the drawing portion of each activity, you are invited to discuss with other seminar members your experiences with each style of communication. The Discussion Questions will guide your discourse and guide you to apply what you are learning toward improving the quality of communication in your classroom.

Prior to beginning the activity, the seminar leader invites someone from the group to be the Sender and provides this person with the diagrams to be used in each exercise. The diagrams and directions needed by the Sender are located in the appendix of this text. The Receivers, all other participants, are seated in one large group and have paper and pencils ready for drawing.

Directions for One-Way Communication Process

You as the Sender verbally direct the group in drawing Communication Diagram #1 found in the appendix of the text. Take a position where all Participants can hear clearly but not see either you or the diagram. Perhaps you will stand behind the group or behind a screen. Before beginning the activity, you will want to study the diagram. Being unable to see the Participants drawings may cause you to feel uncomfortable. Give your best effort to the following tasks:

- state directions using specific, understandable terms.
- repeat directions you think are needed.
- emphasize parts of the exercise you judge helpful.
- pace moderately your speaking of directions.
- allow lag-time between diagrams.
- decide when the activity is completed and ask for participants' papers.

(Communication Diagram #1 is found in the appendix of this text.)

Directions for Two-Way Communication Process

Before beginning the two-way communication process, you may take whatever position in the room seems helpful for communicating with all members of the large group. Participants do not see Communication Diagram #2 that they are to draw. You speak the directions they are to follow for drawing the different figures. Throughout the time keep in mind the following:

- answer all questions.
- look at group members but not their diagrams.
- repeat directions at any time.
- interact verbally with group members.
- refrain from pointing, tracing in the air, showing pictures, and all other nonverbal clues.
- collect participants' papers after checking to see that drawings are complete.

(Communication Diagram #2 is found in the appendix of this text.)

Discussion Questions

1. With which type of directions were you more comfortable? With which type were you more accurate? How does your preference compare with that of your peers?
2. When would you use one-way communication in the classroom? For what reason?
3. Give examples of two-way communication from the classroom. Analyze what you learned from students talking and "thinking aloud," interacting with you and one another in the communication process.
4. After examining your use of communication, what are some ways you could strengthen your one-way and two-way communication in the classroom?

Optional Activity: Total Group Discussion of Process

A discussion of the activity as experienced by different participants provides a variety of insights and perspectives. The Sender's insights and experiences vary from those of the Receivers, and the Seminar Leader provides another perspective.

The Sender may be dissatisfied with the performance and feel put on the line. You can support your peer's willingness to take a risk by applauding and encouraging such personal learning.

As Receivers you can compare your level of performance on the two drawings. Sharing the comfort level you experienced while making the drawings allows you to compare your experience with peers. Listening to others helps you recognize the variety of your strengths and limitations as a verbal learner and provides insight into the students' preferred communication styles. Such information further expands your understanding of the complexity inherent in verbal communication.

The Seminar Leader's comments about observations made during the demonstration can be informative. The Leader might describe the participants' nonverbal responses while drawing the diagrams and also note the time differences between the two styles of communication.

Focus Two

Expected Performance

- Identify and design instruction appropriate to students' stages of development, learning styles, strengths, and needs.
- Create a learning community in which individual differences are respected.
- Model or demonstrate the skills, concepts, attributes, and/or thinking processes to be learned.
- Use teaching approaches that are sensitive to the multiple experiences of learners and that address different learning and performance modes.
- Include creative and appropriate use of technology as a tool to enhance student learning.

Specific teacher behaviors are critical to student achievement. You recognize that communication is essential. **Focus One** emphasizes the importance of two-way communication. You are aware of the significance of effective communication to the introduction and the flow of a lesson. It sets the stage for students' engagement in an activity whether you expect them to listen actively or take notes. Perhaps you observed an effective teacher using multimedia, the chalkboard, or an overhead projector in an overview of the lesson content. How amazed you were that the students seemed to be attentive to the teacher! Observing how the motivation or initial activity engages the students and prepares them for the lesson content is stimulating. You decide to use a motivating activity to grab the attention of the students at the beginning of each lesson you plan.

APPLICATION: PRACTICING LESSON PRESENTATION STRATEGIES

The instructional strategies vary with your plans for accommodating learners within your class/es. Capturing students' attention, maintaining the flow of the lesson, helping students retain the material or finding solutions to problems, and assessing the outcomes are essential teacher behaviors. Most learning theorists and teachers use their own variation of lesson presentation strategies.

PRESENTATION STRATEGIES

Introduction to the lesson, sometimes referred to as **advance organizer** (Ausubel, 1978), **anticipatory set** (Hunter, 1982), or **motivation** (DeCecco, 1968); **explanation and reinforcement** to achieve and retain learning; and **closure** techniques to emphasize major points in a lesson are the most frequently researched skills and are recognized as best practice (Shostak, 1994).

Focusing and keeping the learners' attention on the lesson content takes creativity and planning. Providing an overview of what the lesson will include, perhaps a short movie clip or brief outline on the chalkboard, may strongly encourage students' willingness to engage in the lesson and recall what was emphasized initially. For example, before continuing to work with students on their narrative writing project, the teacher may begin the class with the following orientation adapted from Barry Lane's *After the End:*

> "Class, today you will use your vocabulary cards for lesson number three and review vocabulary words with a partner. I will provide the phonetic spelling to help you with syllables and pronunciation of the words. Next, with a group of three you will move to five different stations that emphasize the use of five senses as a means for expanding the use of descriptions in your writing. After this, I will show you how to use this detail and description to create a real special moment in your narratives. I call this, 'exploding the moment.' Finally, you will have time to work on the story you are writing and to find an event in which you can 'explode the moment.' "

Varying the presentation and maintaining a high level of learner participation requires knowledge of the content and skill in the use of various interaction techniques. Interacting with students throughout the presentation, clarifying learner questions, handling any miscommunication, and/or emphasizing main ideas are teacher behaviors that aid student engagement in the learning process. Using your voice for emphasis, perhaps becoming a bit dramatic for effect, adds spice to a lesson. Varying the type of lessons by using large group response, group or individual research, Internet searches, paired debates, problem solving, case study, and games such as Jeopardy keep students excited and motivated.

Helping learners summarize the content presented takes careful planning and time management. Consider the following examples as **closure** for your lessons:

- Student/s explain the key points they have learned during the class.
- The teacher or a student gives a wrap-up or brief summary during the last few minutes of the class period.
- In self-contained classrooms the teachers summarize the outcomes from the morning session or in the afternoon before dismissal.
- Students write a summary statement or steps to be taken to proceed with an individual assignment or group project. You may want to design a special form for this purpose.
- Student briefly explains the process they or the group used for completing an assigned task.

Using a specific closure strategy can help you transition from one instructional activity or lesson to the next. For example, a student summarizes ideas discovered from reading about a science experiment. Next you give directions for performing the science experiment. Upon completion of the experiment, you ask the students to give a verbal or written summary of the results.

As closure for this Application activity, let's review the presentation strategies you will be practicing this week:

Introductory—advance organizers, set induction, anticipatory set, motivating activity, overview.
Explaining behaviors—definitions, examples, non-examples.
Reinforcing techniques—practice, repeating, emphasizing.
Closure activities—summary, culminating or concluding activity, wrap-up session.

ASSIGNED ACTIVITIES

The following assignment affords you the opportunity to observe and practice your presentation strategies. Respond to the following using your observations and experiences:

1. Each day choose a class to observe and record an example of the following:

Date	Class	Teacher
Introduction		
Explaining behaviors		
Reinforcement techniques		
Closure methods		

2. In what ways do you help students focus or engage their attention:
   - during a lesson overview?
   - during group activities or discussion?
   - during a lecture or presentation by teacher, visitor, student?

3. To what extent do you practice the following:
   - Circulating around the classroom and monitoring learner activities?
   - Reviewing and making connections with the major idea or concept being taught?
   - Providing variety and challenge in practice and drill?
   - Keeping learners alert and focused on the task at hand?
   - Maintaining a moderate pace in lesson presentations?
   - Reviewing major points during a teacher-directed lesson?
   - Leading students to extend knowledge gained from the lesson?
4. Observe your supervising or another teacher using cooperative learning. Perhaps you also plan and use this instructional strategy.
   - How were the students prepared for the tasks to be accomplished?
   - In what ways were the students held accountable for the completion of the task?
   - Write in your journal any questions or reservations you have about cooperative learning at this time.

Summary

Once you engage the learners, you realize the importance of carrying through the instruction. Instruction may take the form of a mini-lecture, a discovery activity, a writing project, or a problem-solving activity for an individual or a cooperative group. You want to make sure your explanations are clear whether emphasizing key points in an outline, reviewing vocabulary, or asking students to demonstrate their understanding of a concept through verbal or written response. Reinforcing the ideas, skills, and concepts through group projects or individual practice helps students retain basic information. Perhaps the most difficult portion of instruction is concluding the activity or lesson. To include a summary at the end of the lesson or unit, ask students to verbalize or write in their journal their reflections of what they have learned. Managing your time for using closure strategies takes practice. You will develop and practice these and other instructional behaviors throughout your teaching career.

Follow–Up Questions and Shared Insights

Using the following questions, share your observations and/or successes and difficulties you faced in practicing the introduction, explanation, reinforcement, and closure techniques in your lessons.

1. Relate an introductory exercise you observed or used that motivated and involved students with the content being presented. Tell how voice, technology or instructional aids, thinking strategies, and/or lesson review/overview were used to capture the learners' attention.
2. In what way was the introductory activity used later in the lesson to: (a) elicit further information, (b) make applications, and/or (c) make comparisons?
3. What types of quick recall, reinforcement, review, and/or emphasis using voice or chalk/dryboard were used in a lesson? Which techniques did you consider effective in attaining the outcomes set forth for the activity?
4. Give one example you used in helping learners organize their ideas, themes, and activities this past week.
5. What explaining behaviors have you used in lessons taught? Were there times when you called on one of the students for an explanation or

example or when you observed group members explaining a concept or making a connection for other members?

6. Share the different closure techniques you observed or used in lessons this week. Describe how closure helped the learner organize and retain learning.

Journal Excerpts

High School

"Before a lesson is planned, I meet with both of my supervising teachers to decide what needs to be taught, the level and diversity of learners, and what prior knowledge these students have. For example, when I taught the "Leads" lesson to sophomores, I knew that they had learned something about leads already and that this would be more of a review lesson. I also knew that I needed to incorporate movement into the lesson, because the students would have been sitting doing procedural kinds of things for the first 15–20 minutes of class. Along with this, I needed to cue my learners with special needs in the class—using lots of visuals and cooperative groups."

"With the freshman, we are beginning The Process Essay or "How To" paper. After notes were completed, the students were paired up. Each pair was given two cups of milk and four Oreo cookies. The partners had loose leaf paper and a pen to take notes. Each person was to explain How to Best Eat an Oreo Cookie, while the partner took notes on the steps they used. These were collected and then the class (as a group) brainstormed for topics for a How To paper."

"I am learning not to immediately call on a student the minute he raises his hand. Today I had not gotten two words out of my mouth before a student raised his hand. Instead of immediately calling on him, I said '_____ please put your hand down and listen. If you are afraid you will forget your question, jot it down.' He put down his hand and after I finished explaining, he still asked his question."

Middle School

"Ms. H. used this advance organizer at the beginning of fifth period. 'Remember, these are the things that you have to have included with your final draft . . .' She lists on the overhead: web, rough draft, list of new lead questions, web of snapshot, final draft—in ink. 'If you need help, raise your hand and either Ms. C. or I will come help you.' "

"An example of explaining skills I used this week is from a language arts class. I told the class that we are going to be reading a story this week as a class; but before we can do that, we need to know some words and their meaning. I wrote the words on the board. Then, I separated the tables of students into Guessers and Checkers. The Guessers write down their guess of what the word means while the Checkers actually look up the word. Then we compare answers. The Guessers typically used context clues to gain meaning, but occasionally meanings were gained through root words. By having the meaning and pronunciation of words repeated, I reinforced the vocabulary for the story. For closure to this part of the lesson, I asked the class to explain what we were doing and why they needed to know the vocabulary words in a story."

Elementary

"In second and third periods, we read a story in play format. It was fun, but like their other skills, reading seemed difficult for them. They had no idea about using expression even after we explained it and gave examples."

"I did a reading lesson using the book, *Corduroy.* Then, I wanted to do a sequencing lesson for reinforcement of what we did last week. We finished the story map, but the students had to finish the sequencing activity sheet after lunch. Nearly every student did perfect work on this assignment. They placed all of the pictures in the correct order. It's so pleasing to watch them learn."

"Today students were to begin working on their world maps and flags. I saw some very creative maps but I found myself reexplaining the directions about drawing the lines of latitude and longitude on the maps. I was a bit confused about why they weren't doing as my instructions asked them. We even discussed the directions together before we started. I asked about questions they had. I'm anxious to see how the maps turn out at the end of the activity."

Special Education

"Today I noticed how easy it is to lose the students. If you let them sit for even two minutes, then you lose them for an additional five. Anytime that I'm walking to get a marker, I try at least to keep talking to the students so I can fill the space and keep them from talking."

"During centers Melissa became very upset and complained that she couldn't complete her 'I can' paper. I gave her different suggestions which she disliked. However, we finally settled on 'I can read.' I had to work with her step-by-step until she finally completed the project. The only thing that I regret is that she took all of my attention away from the other students."

"I noticed that Ms. M. used familiar sentences in her spelling test. I think this is a good modification. As I see it, she is dedicated to doing whatever it is that will help our students to learn better. After school while the students are waiting for their buses, I have started the routine of working with all of the students on their multiplication facts. I love the resource room with two teachers because it allows for so much individualization."

REFERENCES AND SUGGESTED READINGS

Arends, R. I. (1999). *Classroom instruction and management.* Boston: McGraw-Hill, p. 63–67.

Arends, R. I. (1998). *Learning to teach.* Boston: McGraw-Hill, p. 380–381.

Ausubel, D. P. (1978). In defense of advanced organizers: A reply to the critics, *Review of Educational Research,* 48, pp. 251–257.

Banks, J. A. (1991). Teaching multicultural literacy to teachers, *Teacher education,* 4(1), 135–144.

Borich, G. D. (1999). *Observation skills for effective teaching.* Upper Saddle River, NJ: Merrill/Prentice Hall, p. 26.

Cazden, C. B. (1986). Classroom discourse. In M. C. Wittrock (Ed.), *Handbook of research on teaching* (p. 432). New York: Macmillan.

Collis, B., & Remmers, E. (1997). The world wide web in education: Issues related to cross-cultural communication and interaction. In B. H. Khan (Ed.), *Web-Based Instruction.* Englewood Cliffs, NJ: Educational Technology Publications.

Darling-Hammond, L. (1997). *The right to learn: A blueprint for reform.* San Francisco: Jossey-Bass.

DeCecco, J. P. (1968). *The psychology of learning and instruction: In Educational psychology.* Englewood Cliffs, NJ: Prentice Hall.

Frieberg, H. J., & Driscoll, A. (1996). *Universal teaching strategies* (3rd ed.). Boston: Allyn & Bacon.

Gage, N. L., & Berliner, D. C. (1992). *Educational psychology* (5th ed.). Boston: Houghton Mifflin.

Good, T. L., & Brophy, J. E. (1994). *Looking in classrooms.* New York: Harper Collins College Publishers, pp. 26–82, 373–410.

Harris, B. M., Bessent, W., & McIntyre, K. E. (1969). *In-Service education: A guide to better practice.* Englewood Cliffs, NJ: Prentice Hall, pp. 202–204.

Hunter, M. (1982). *Mastery teaching.* El Segundo, CA: TIP Publications.

Joyce, B., & Weil, M. (1996). *Models of teaching* (5th ed.). Needham Heights, MA: Allyn & Bacon.

Lane, B. (1993). *After the end: Teaching and learning creative revision.* Portsmouth, NH: Heinemann.

Ornstein, A. C. (1995). *Strategies for effective teaching* (2nd ed.). Madison, WI: Brown & Benchmark.

Shostak, R. (1999). "Involving students in learning." In J. Cooper, (Gen. Ed.), *Classroom teaching skills* (6th ed.). Boston: Houghton Mifflin Company. Heath.

6 Stimulating Critical Thinking: Questioning Strategies

> *"For student teachers, the opportunity to talk about their actions, their thinking, their beliefs, and their feelings, is part of the process of learning to be a reflective teacher."*
>
> A. E. Richert (p. 191)

Focus One

Expected Performance

- Examine current experiences that celebrate your accomplishments.
- Identify and share feelings about your progress as a student/intern teacher.
- Explore the connection between personal/ professional success and motivation.

The Teacher's Story: A Process

Think back to your initial teacher education courses. What mental picture did you have of the teacher you wanted to be? How has this image changed? Expanded? As you are working with students and your supervising teacher, observing and implementing best practices, your image of the ideal teacher becomes clearer. You better understand who that ideal teacher is, and you have a broader and more in-depth expectation of how that person performs as teacher. How does what you know about yourself match the image of the teacher you carry around in your head and cherish in your heart? Are your actions and speech what you want them to be? When you compare your real self with your ideal self, you may feel discouraged that you don't measure up. Recognizing and acknowledging the difference between the ideal and the real teacher can contribute to your personal and professional growth. Allow yourself to consider your progress and accomplishments, and look forward to the image of the practicing professional you now envision.

You have completed the initial weeks as a beginning teacher. You have moved from being on "cloud nine" to feeling "I'm so tired, I don't think I can put one foot in front of the other!" You have felt elated, anxious, eager, afraid, frustrated, sorry for yourself, worried, put upon, put out, let down, and a litany of other emotions. But how you have grown! You are organized. You know routines and student names. You observe, plan, and direct instruction. You give clear directions and model effective communication skills. You name classroom management practices you intend to improve. You use a firm voice when reminding students of expected behavior. Planning takes less time even though you are now teaching more classes. You are learning much and feeling more and more like a teacher.

Take another look at your ideal teacher and what you intend to be. Ayers (1995) describes teaching as intellectual and ethical work that when done well, requires wide-awake inquiry and critical and caring people. Although there is always more to learn and know as teacher, at the heart of teaching is a passionate regard for students. The ideal teacher works to see each student as capable of learning and creates an environment that nurtures and challenges the wide range of students in the class.

For more than a dozen years you have observed teachers, and to some degree you may have internalized their values, beliefs, and practices. Only now as a student or intern teacher are the values inherent in teaching taking root: your value system, rooted in personal values, may also be heavily influenced by the values of your supervising teacher, the school, and others within that school (O'Hair & O'Hair, 1996; Zeichner & Gore, 1990). Identifying and understanding your personal and professional values points you in the direction of becoming that ideal teacher you envision.

Wanting to help children and adolescents may have motivated you to choose teaching. Perhaps your interest in teaching a certain subject, coupled with a desire to work with youth and contribute to the betterment of society, motivated you to become a teacher. You may have elected to leave another line of work to enroll in teacher education courses to meet a personal goal. You now have the opportunity to incorporate what you learned in these courses into your current classroom experiences. Perhaps you take initiative in using different strategies to teach reading or take time to prepare and introduce supplemental materials and activities into a unit you are teaching. Perhaps you engage the learners by helping them connect new learning to old concepts and generate active learning. How does what you practice in the classroom connect with the teacher you dreamed of becoming?

Trying to connect what we make of ourselves with what we strive to accomplish in the lives of students is risky business (Green, 1995). Sometimes when we see our students engaged in instructional activities, our level of caring is elevated. In turn, students often respond to us with a bit more trust. At other times we acknowledge the painful fact that things can go badly in the classroom. Your journey toward becoming that ideal teacher is indeed a growth process. During this student or intern teaching experience you have moved beyond the fantasy of becoming a teacher and stepped into the role of teacher; your backpack is stuffed with experiences! Looking back helps you get your bearings in this journey, set goals, and define markers of progress along the way.

This activity invites you to identify and share at least one accomplishment you associate with becoming the ideal teacher you envision. The incident or example you choose to share is important because it is the representative of you becoming a professional teacher. Sharing your experiences generates valuable insights for others having similar experiences. Sharing and having others listen to your accomplishments can energize you and other group members. It allows you to imagine many ways for becoming the ideal of a "competent, caring, effective teacher." Sharing our experiences invites us to examine and perhaps reveal our personal insights about the process necessary to becoming a teacher.

Before sharing with the group, take time to recall a successful teaching experience. Think about a specific teacher attitude or practice you demonstrated. For example, you remained calm while feeling pulled in 20 different directions, or you praised a student for suggesting another way to think about the character in a story. Maybe you clearly stated what you expected of students and they responded to what you asked them to do! You may have written in your journal about a number of successful situations. What insights into teaching do you have as you reflect on these experiences? Describe how you felt using specific feeling words. In the space below, name at least one success story, then write words, phrases, or sentences that capture the emotions and feelings embedded within the teaching experience.

_____

_____

_____

Analyze the experiences you named. Did you include teacher characteristics and practices? Do you see a connection between this list and the image you have of the teacher you want to be? How does analyzing this list of descriptors give you insights about yourself as a practicing professional?

Discussion Questions

1. Analyze and describe for others the insights and feelings about yourself as teacher at this point in your journey.
2. Compare and contrast your teaching accomplishments with your image of the ideal teacher. Summarize and share your findings.
3. Now that you are teaching, your perception of teachers may have changed. What most surprises or challenges your current perception of the teacher's role? What do you still question or wonder about this profession?

Focus Two

Expected Performance

- Elicit samples of student thinking and stimulate student reflection on their own ideas and those of others.
- Demonstrate appropriate questioning strategies to engage students' cognitive processes and stimulate critical thinking.
- Develop a variety of clear, accurate presentations and representations of concepts, using alternative explanations to assist students' understanding and presenting diverse perspectives to encourage critical thinking.
- Integrate skills, thinking processes, and content across disciplines.
- Guide students to express, examine, and explain alternative responses and their associated consequences relative to moral, ethical, or social issues.

Sharing your teaching experiences with peers during **Focus One** boosts your overall confidence and renews your energy for getting students to think on higher levels. You are practicing skillful questioning and problem-solving techniques that require learners to perform at higher cognitive levels. Higher-order thinking is complex and challenges you to develop creative and adaptable questions.

Elevating students' understanding requires more from you than just telling them about a new idea, concept, or problem. To get them to think about specific content you must guide students' thinking from one level to the next. Once you identify the variety of cognitive levels at which students are operating, you can better assist all learners in moving to higher levels of thinking.

The process of inquiry, discovery, and problem solving relies heavily on student involvement. The constructivist philosophy actively engages the learner in the problem-solving approach to learning. Writing and asking meaningful questions is crucial to student learning and challenges them to operate and think more critically.

APPLICATION: STIMULATING CRITICAL THINKING WITH QUESTIONING STRATEGIES

Skillful questioning techniques in classroom instruction increase opportunities for learning. John Dewey (1910) considered the questioning process as the very art of teaching. Effective teachers are skillful in balancing factual and critical thinking questions. Selecting just the right question to emphasize a major point or to stimulate lively discussion takes practice.

Questions serve different purposes and can be separated into specific categories:

1. To give instructions to your students
2. To review and remind students of classroom procedures
3. To gather information
4. To determine student understanding of the concept or material
5. To discover student interests or experiences
6. To guide student thinking and learning

(adapted from Callahan, Clark, & Kellough, 1998)

The art of questioning requires that you provide questions that are clear, purposeful, brief, natural, & adapted to the level of the class, sequenced, and thought-provoking (Good & Brophy, 1994). Allowing sufficient wait or think time after asking a question gives the students confidence to respond. Your response to the student affects subsequent teacher-learner interaction during a class. You might rephrase or amplify student responses. At other times you may correct, clarify, or redirect student responses by inviting other learner ideas to be given. By expanding on student responses or asking another question, you may lead students to begin thinking on a higher level.

You may find the following guidelines helpful for refining your skills of questioning:

- Ask questions that are clear.
- Ask questions that are stimulating.
- Ask questions that are relevant to learners.
- Vary the length and difficulty of questions.
- Allow sufficient time for thinking.
- Follow up on incorrect responses.
- Encourage learners to ask questions of each other and to make appropriate comments.
- Ask questions that are suitable to all learner ability levels.
- Distribute questions about the class fairly.
- Ask questions that match lesson expectations.
- Call on volunteers, nonvolunteers, and disruptive learners.
- Listen carefully to learner response.
  (adapted from Ornstein, 1995)

Formulating questions to stimulate thinking and appropriate responding demands an understanding of the cognitive levels of development. The taxonomy of Bloom et al. (1956) provides a framework for developing the types of questions you will want to include as you plan and analyze your questions according to your instructional objectives. The levels of cognitive development and examples of questions in each level are presented for your review.

Levels of Cognitive Development and Examples of Questions

Level 1: *Knowledge* (recalls or recognizes information)
   Ex: What is closure?
   Using your text, list the major steps for solving a math problem.
Level 2: *Comprehension* (understands or knows what is being communicated)
   Ex: Discuss some differences between the cultures of India and the
      United States. (Materials have been read.)
   Compare the Republican and Democratic platforms.
Level 3: *Application* (transfers learning from one context to another
   independently)
   Ex. Study the picture on page __. Indicate what you would do to
      determine in what country this picture was taken.
   Mrs. Bell is purchasing a new home. She needs linoleum for her
      20′ × 20′ kitchen. How much linoleum will she need to purchase?
   At $12 per square foot, what is her total cost?
Level 4: *Analysis* (breaks down a problem into parts and forms)
   Ex: After completing the science experiment, what do you conclude is
      the name of the gas in the unlabeled test tube?
   What information can you use to support the statement: President
      Lincoln was a friend to the slaves?
Level 5: *Synthesis* (putting together elements to form a creative whole)
   Ex: Create a new instructional activity for a listening skill.
   How can we raise money for the Crusade for Exceptional Children?

Level 6: *Evaluation* (makes value judgments using specific criteria)
>   Ex: Which of these pictures do you like best?
>   Do you think the asteroid F 97 will touch the earth?

You may want to practice your understanding and recognition of the different levels of questions. Locating questions from teacher guides to determine the different levels is a good start. A number of researchers have found that a disproportionate high percentage of lower-level (recall or knowledge level) questions are found in teacher guides and student activity books. It is therefore essential that you develop activities to raise student thinking to higher levels. Here are some suggestions as you design your plans for incorporating and encouraging critical thinking in your classroom:

- Ask higher cognitive level questions prior to textbook reading, during your review, or as a part of your advance organizer.
- Increase the number of higher-level questions asked of your students as the school year progresses.
- Discuss the cognitive levels of questions with students.
- Ask students to develop questions from textbook reading or other material.

Highlighting higher-level questions on your lesson plan at this time alerts you to their importance and ensures using these questions throughout the lesson.

As a reflective teacher, you want to model and encourage critical thinking in your students. Students develop thinking skills at different rates and through a variety of approaches. You, as teacher, will sometimes use discovery learning and inquiry teaching strategies with your students. Posing problems and asking probing questions encourages students' growth in their thinking process. Problem solving engages students in a process that begins with identifying the problem and concludes with proposing solutions. Students are more actively involved in seeking and discovering knowledge with problems that are real and connect to their life experiences.

At other times students will need a more direct teaching approach. Teaching them to classify, compare, sequence, infer, and predict is challenging. These are, however, the baseline skills students need to apply, interpret, and use information to solve problems, discover new ideas, and respond to higher-level questions.

Myriad resources can help students become critical thinkers. You may want to try one of these activities, "Twenty Questions" (Orlich et al., 1998), an activity in which participants ask questions to identify some problem or concept. Another resource that supports **problem-based learning,** an instructional method that uses a real-world problem as the context for an in-depth investigation of core content, is the PBL Network. You can ask questions, share methods and materials, and learn more about problem-based learning from other interested professionals through a mailing list server and an electronic interactive forum on the Association for Supervision and Curriculum Development web site at: <http://www.ascd.org>.

Encouraging your students to ask probing questions and solve difficult problems challenges them in developing critical thinking. How exciting for you as teacher when students ask higher-level questions and explore creative solutions to real-life problems!

Assigned Activities

1. Journal the levels and the effectiveness of the questions asked in at least four classes you observed or taught this week.

Class	Teacher	Date
Question		
Level		
In what ways were the questions effective?		

2. Journal an analysis of the diverse levels of questions found in a teacher's guide you use.
3. Journal examples of teacher responses to learners that you observe and make while interacting with learners.
4. To what extent do you guide learners in their response? Journal three examples.
5. Relate how student responses to questions caused you to rephrase and clarify what was said.
6. In what ways do you encourage student questions?

SUMMARY

Formulating a variety of good questions, listening carefully to student responses, and responding in ways that will build student confidence takes daily reflective practice. The design and manner in which you phrase your questions and responses influences the quality of learning within the classroom. Students often transition to new and more complex ideas through teacher or peer responses. Using probing questions to help students expand on their initial response, allowing students enough wait time to make a response, and positively reinforcing them for creative and critical thinking builds student self-confidence.

This week you observed the types of questions used by your supervising teacher/s. You are aware of your questions and the effect questions and responses have on learning in the classroom. Becoming "question-conscious" may lead to improving your questioning skills. Just think, you may be instrumental in creating real critical thinkers among your students. Isn't this the heart of teaching, the very process of reflection—getting students to question, to probe, to investigate, to solve problems, to discover that thinking is essential to learning?

FOLLOW-UP QUESTIONS AND SHARED INSIGHTS

Reflecting on your observations and/or teaching, assigned activities, and journal entries, respond to the following questions:

1. What effect did the questions you prepared for your lesson plan have on student responses?
2. Describe an incident or situation wherein student response caused you to clarify or rephrase your questions?
3. How did your use of different cognitive level questions help expand your understanding of how students think?

4. What kinds of questions do students ask? Share examples of new insights you gained from student questions?
5. Share examples of oral and written questions observed or used in your classes. You may give the context in which the questions were asked. As others share examples of the questions asked of their students you may use the chart in Figure 6.1 for keeping a record of the variety of examples given by your peers. After everyone has the opportunity to share, check to see if you categorized the questions the same as your peers. Discuss any differences in your categorization with them.

FIGURE 6.1 *Questions Chart*

Questions	Knowledge	Comprehension	Application	Analysis	Synthesis	Evaluation

Portfolio Tasks

Implementing and Managing Instruction
Standards
- The teacher understands and uses a variety of instructional strategies to encourage students' development of critical thinking, problem solving, and performance skills.
- The teacher uses an understanding of individual and group motivation and behavior to create a learning environment that encourages positive social interaction, active engagement in learning, and self-motivation.
- The teacher uses knowledge of effective verbal, nonverbal, and media communication techniques to foster active inquiry, collaboration, and supportive interaction in the classroom.

Performance Guidelines

You are to provide evidence of your ability to motivate, support, and encourage group and individual reflective inquiry in the specific content area you teach. How do you organize and manage the group process? Reflective inquiry means that students are actively involved in an in-depth investigation of questions related to the content being taught. Your evidence should include strategies that address physical, social, and cultural diversity and describe the experiences for multiple levels of complexity to accommodate students at different levels of performance. Evidence needs to show student work over an extended period and should include the following:

1. A brief narrative outlining:
   a. the ways in which inquiry is used with learners in your class
   b. how each piece of evidence promotes inquiry
   c. the specific academic expectations toward which the inquiry is directed
   d. the specific group management techniques used
   e. a description of the class, any special needs students, and adaptations of the instructional task for this particular class
   f. the preventive disciplinary approaches used with the class
2. Samples of student inquiry-related work, either individual or small group, showing a variety of different media, for example:
   a. use of written sources
   b. student written work
   c. databases and computer simulations
   d. student-produced artwork, music, and projects
   e. videotapes of student activity

Performance Criteria

The quality of your work will be assessed to the extent that the evidence provided:

1. Demonstrates that communication with students is challenging, positive, and supporting.
2. Establishes and maintains a standard of mutually respectful classroom interactions.
3. Incorporates strategies that address physical, social, and cultural diversity and describes experiences for multiple levels of complexity to accommodate students at different levels of performance.
4. Selects content and organizes materials, equipment, and technology appropriately and accurately to create a media-rich environment.
5. Demonstrates ability to use and manage individual and group inquiry.

Journal Excerpts

High School

"I asked, 'What is the literal and figurative meaning of the story?' After I got blank stares, I realized that the students needed to review the meaning of figurative and literal. I had taken for granted that students would remember. After they heard the definition, students were able to answer the question."

"The interaction of student responses to questions and my rephrasing and clarification are quite evident to me. For example the nonverbal responses to my directions or instructions often result in my rephrasing. When students' responses contain the general idea that I wanted the students to explain, I probe the student for a fuller response and then rephrase the more specific answer in my own words. Several times I ask a student to give the class a general definition and then I will write the more technical one on the board by incorporating the student's answer with my own clarification of the term."

"Sometimes student responses alert me to the fact that my question was not quite clear. They might ask, 'Do you mean . . .?' or 'What do you mean by . . .?' This obvious confusion helps me to be more clear in rephrasing and then follow up to make sure I was successful."

"I have encouraged the sophomores to be aware of their thinking process through the writing of a persuasive paper. They are required to submit brainstorming, outline, bibliography, copies of sources, and a first draft. I provided numerous comments to encourage them to be aware of their planning, organization, etc. On Friday they will bring their drafts to a peer review session and then submit a final draft. This activity allows them to analyze a piece of writing and obtain an objective opinion about their own overall thinking, writing, and planning process."

Middle School

"Knowledge level questions are very good for verbally quizzing students. In teaching a poetry lesson, I used higher levels of questions. A particular poem written by a child living in the projects is a very moving and quiet poem that uses lots of descriptive language. Many of my students can relate to this situation. One student responded, 'He doesn't like it.' I asked, 'Why don't you think he likes it?' Then the student started giving examples from the poem. I like this questioning because it leads the student in many different directions. The discussion took a unique form and shape based on one student's answer to this question."

"I try very hard not to give the class the answer. First I might restate the question. Sometimes I will give examples of what I'm looking for in the answer. Often, I will ask other students if they can explain the question. If everyone seems lost, I start giving hints."

"We have many ESL students on our team. Because of this, I find myself rephrasing often. I rephrase based on the look on their faces more often than their verbal responses. I can tell when they're puzzled. I might repeat or use hand gestures to help clarify a question."

"The hardest kinds of questions for this class to answer are the ones that ask them what they think. For example, 'Why do you think this author wrote this poem?' When they stated, 'I guess he likes poetry, I don't know.' I further probed by asking 'What was his purpose for writing it?' This question got a better response."

Elementary

"I asked several questions during reading/language arts lesson today. The questions I asked were clearly phrased and matched the learning expectations I had stated. Some children had difficulty answering them. If a student got two events out of order, I helped them by saying, 'Are you sure that happened next?' "

"Before the grandparents came, Mrs. H. did a chart with the students and had them generate questions that they would like to ask the grandparents. For example, 'What is one question that you would like to ask the grandparents?' This was a good way for assessing who could think logically and ask questions. Most of the students thought of good questions with only a few silly ones offered."

"Mrs. P. had the students do a problem-solving activity. She gave each table some Cheez-its and told them to work cooperatively and divide the crackers evenly to each person. After every table had finished, she had them discuss what strategy they used to solve the problem. They did extremely well with this activity."

Special Education

"Character Education curriculum involves the class in a values lesson each morning. I have enjoyed watching the responses the students have to such lessons as honesty. The new word for the month is honesty, so Mrs. C. led a class discussion on honesty. She webbed out what the students thought honesty meant. It was interesting to see how they defined honesty."

"This week when the students were asked what was the main idea of *Yertle the Turtle*, the response they gave was not what I was looking for. Thus, I worked with the students and rephrased my question incorporating a term that I thought they could better relate to."

"After breakfast we played a Jeopardy-type game with the children using questions from the senses. This was neat because the students could get a lot of points by working as a team with their partner, and by staying quiet while others were answering. Getting the correct answer also gave them points. They seemed to like this and they worked well together."

REFERENCES AND SUGGESTED READINGS

Ayers, W. (1995). Thinking and teaching. In W. Ayers (Ed.), *To become a teacher* (pp. 59–64). New York: Teachers College Press.

Beyer, B. K. (1995). *Critical thinking.* Bloomington, IN: Phi Delta Kappa Educational Foundation, Fastback No. 385.

Bloom, F., Engelhart, M., Furst, E., Hill, W., and Krathwohl, D. (1956). *Taxonomy of educational objectives: Cognitive domain.* New York: Longman.

Checkley, K. (1997). Problem-based learning: The search for solutions to life's messy problems. *Curriculum update.* Alexandria, VA: Association for Supervision and Curriculum Development.

Ciardiello, A. V. (1993) Training students to ask reflective questions. *The Clearing House, 66*(5), 312–314.

Commeyras, M. (1995). What can we learn from students' questions? *Theory into Practice, 34*(2), 101–106.

Dewey, J. (1910). *How we think.* Lexington, MA: Heath.

Dillon, J. (Ed.). (1990). *The practice of questioning.* New York: Routledge.

Duckworth, E. (1987). *The having of wonderful ideas and other essays on teaching and learning.* New York: Teachers College Press.

Eby, J. W. (1998). *Reflective planning, teaching, and evaluation K–12* (2nd ed.). Upper Saddle River, NJ: Merrill/Prentice Hall.

Freedman, R. L. H. (1994). *Open-ended questioning: A handbook for educators.* Menlo Park, CA: Addison-Wesley.

Good, T. L., & Brophy, J. E. (1994). *Looking in classrooms.* (6th ed.) New York: Harper Collins.

Goodlad, J. I. (1984). *A place called school.* New York: McGraw-Hill.

Green, M. (1995). Choosing a past and inventing a future: The becoming of a teacher. In W. Ayers (Ed.), *To become a teacher* (pp. 65–77). New York: Teachers College Press.

Guyton, E., & McIntyre, D. J. (1990). Student teaching and school experiences. In W. R. Houston (Ed.), *Handbook of research on teacher education* (pp. 514–534). New York: Macmillan.

Hunkins, F. P. (1994). *Effective questions, effective teaching* (2nd ed.). Needham Heights, MA: Gordon Publishers.

Hyman, R. T. (1979). *Strategic questioning.* Englewood Cliffs, NJ: Prentice Hall.

Jacobsen, D., Eggen, P., & Kauchak, D. (1999). *Methods for teaching: Promoting student learning* (5th ed.). Upper Saddle River, NJ: Merrill/Prentice Hall.

Meyers, C. (1986). *Teaching students to think critically.* San Francisco: Jossey-Bass.

O'Hair, D., & O'Hair, M. J. (1996). Communication: Reflections and implications. In D. J. McIntyre & D. M. Byrd (Eds.), *Preparing tomorrow's teachers: The field experience* (pp. 211–218). Thousand Oaks, CA: Corwin Press.

Orlich, D. C., Harder, R. J., Callahan, R. C., & Gibson, H. W. (1998). *Teaching strategies: A guide to better instruction* (5th ed.). Boston: Houghton Mifflin.

Ornstein, A. C. (1995). *Strategies for effective teaching* (2nd ed.). Madison, WI: Brown and Benchmark.

Paul, R. (1995). *Critical thinking: How to prepare students for a rapidly changing world.* Santa Rosa, CA: Foundation for Critical Thinking.

Raths, L., Wassermann, S., Jonas, A., & Rothstein, A. (1986). *Teaching for thinking.* New York: Teachers College Press.

Richert, A. E. (1992). Voice and power in teaching and learning to teach. In L. Valli (Ed.), *Reflective teacher education cases and critiques* (pp. 187–197). Albany: State University of New York Press.

Sanders, N. M. (1966). *Classroom questions: What kinds?* New York: Harper & Row.

Wassermann, S. (1992). *Asking the right question: The essence of teaching.* Bloomington, IN: Phi Delta Kappa Educational Foundation, Fastback No. 343.

Wilen, W. W. (1991). *Questioning skills for teachers* (3rd ed.). Washington, DC: National Education Association.

Wilen, W. W. (Ed.). (1990). *Teaching and learning through discussions: The theory, research, and practice of the discussion method.* Springfield, IL: Charles C. Thomas.

Zeichner, K. M., & Gore, J. M. (1990). Teacher socialization. In W. R. Houston (Ed.), *Handbook of research on teacher education* (pp. 329–348). New York: Macmillan.

Varying Instructional Strategies

> *"There must be links, above all, between what we are trying to make of ourselves and what we are striving to make possible in the lives of those we teach. . ."*

Maxine Green (p. 65)

Focus One

Expected Performance

- State characteristics and practices of the ideal teacher you now see.

- Compare and contrast your current perceptions of the ideal teacher with that of six weeks ago.

- Discuss accomplishments you recognize and influences that motivate you to change.

What Do I Now See?

Thinking back to your first days of teaching makes you aware of the many ways your perceptions about teaching have changed. These changes are the result of your experiences in the school, your reflective practice, and the sharing of your insights with others. Student teachers tell us they have never learned so much in such a short period of time! How does reflection contribute to and impact learning so deeply?

Reflection is an active process through which you critically examine what you do in the classroom: your thinking and acting patterns, your questions and emotions, and your teaching methods and philosophy of education. True reflection engages you in a process that encourages growth. While reflection is an internal process, it is assisted by external processes such as journaling, exchanging stories, dialoguing, and interacting with others. To encourage your growth as a professional, you engage in these intellectual pursuits to develop your potential as a reflective learner, one who is able to give.

The reflective process provides you opportunities to refine your educational beliefs continually and develop professional skills that demonstrate your heightened understanding of teaching and learning as processes. You analyze your teaching strategies, the students' responses, and the educational climate you create. You assume increased responsibility for yourself as teacher and learner while expanding your influence with students and others in the school setting. Implementing a reflective process approach to teaching allows you to stand back and gain a new, deeper perspective on what you are doing in the classroom and how it affects teaching and learning, your own as well as that of your students (Calderhead, 1992; Zeichner, 1992; Schön, 1987). As Richert (1992) points out:

> Voice is a necessary part of reflective teaching as it is an instrument of self consciousness that allows teachers to examine their beliefs and experiences. By talking about what they do, believe, feel, or think teachers raise to a level of consciousness the complex matters of their work. (p. 190)

Through discussion you identify the affective characteristics associated with the role of the teacher. Through journal writing, dialogue with peers, and conferences with supervisors, you assess your progress daily. Because of these reflective interchanges you redirect your actions and refocus your thinking week by week. You live the life of the teacher, and your diverse experiences work to transform your understanding into personal learning about the teacher role.

Conversations about past and present perceptions of the teacher role allow you to examine the purpose and consequences of that role from your own experiences of becoming a teacher. In the initial stage of student teaching, you responded to questions about the teacher role. You are now performing many teaching tasks and your experiences during the past weeks affect how you think and feel about the teacher role. Your reflections lead you to think about your work and question its purpose and the consequences of what you do. With your peers, supervising teacher, and college supervisor, you raise new questions and share insights about the profession of teaching. According to Richert (1992), you "come to know" in a way that enables you to enter and participate in the social and intellectual life of the professional teacher. This "coming to know" is your elevated awareness of the teacher role as you examine and analyze the numerous dimensions of teaching.

When you read the words *teacher role*, what's the first thing that comes to mind? More than likely you have mastered the everyday activities associated with teaching. Lunch count, attendance, and homework concerns seem routine. You are more fully involved in the lives of your students and understand their individual needs. You collaborate and network with other teachers, and you reflect on your classroom experiences. This deeper connection to the role of teaching helps you to focus on different aspects of what being a teacher means for you.

We realize that your growth during student teaching is mammoth and occurs at an unbelievably rapid pace. One way of helping you become more conscious of your growth and understanding is by asking you to examine and compare your earlier reflections about teaching to your present considerations.

This **Focus One** activity asks you to look once more at your perceptions about the teacher role. You are asked to revisit the same questions you answered before you became fully involved in the lives of learners and with other teacher-related activities. As the result of your ongoing experiences, the previous responses are likely to differ from what you now name as the expectations and duties of a teacher. You may describe new and deeper elements associated with teaching, and your response may indicate a more critical understanding of what is expected of teachers.

Read the three teacher role questions and write a response to each. When responding it is not necessary to recall what you wrote earlier. In fact, we prefer that you be spontaneous and write what comes to mind! Unless you choose to share with others, you are the only reader of your responses. To save time write only the number of each question and your initial thoughts.

Questions

Teacher Role

1. Recalling your personal goals and knowledge gained from teacher preparation, make a list of teacher characteristics that you believe are most important for you to practice as a teacher.

2. Circle the characteristics that are the most difficult to integrate into your everyday thinking and living as a teacher. Why do you think these are difficult?
3. For some time becoming a teacher has been your goal. As you begin working within this school, with these students and teachers, what will you contribute to the students, the school, and other teachers?

Seminar Leader Tasks

For this activity the following are suggested:
- Paper and pencils
- Envelopes collected from chapter 1 Focus One activity

While student/intern teachers are writing, the seminar leader distributes the envelopes and asks students to respond to all questions before opening their envelope.

After you finish writing, open the envelope given you by the seminar leader. Beginning with the first question, carefully examine what you wrote earlier in the semester and what you just completed writing. Compare the first response with your current one.

- What is common to both responses? Circle similar words and phrases.
- How is today's response different from the one written earlier? Make rectangular boxes around different aspects of the teacher role that you just wrote.
- Which responses express a deeper understanding of the teacher role? Place an asterisk by responses that indicate a deeper understanding and new learning about the teacher role.

Discussion Questions

1. How are today's responses to the questions similar to those you wrote earlier? In what ways are they different?
2. Now that you are teaching, what surprises you about being the teacher? What motivates you to be a "good" teacher? What delights you most about teaching?
3. Think about your earlier images of the teacher you hope to become. Which teacher responsibilities and expectations are easiest to assume? What is your reaction when your own or others' efforts do not meet these expectations?
4. After careful consideration, what would you like to change about your image of the ideal teacher? Why? How might you do this?

Focus Two

In **Focus One** you shared your perceptions of the teacher role after several weeks of actual daily experience in the classroom. You may not have had a clue as to all that teaching involves! Teachers today have a greater responsibility than ever for making solid decisions that affect curriculum. By focusing on what students know and are able to do, teachers believe that all students can learn at reasonably high levels. In a study by Emmer, Evertson, and Anderson (1980) involving experienced and inexperienced teachers, experienced teachers who are flexible and vary their instructional strategies are found to be more interesting to students than inexperienced teachers who have no knowledge of alternative teaching strategies. This is a time for you to learn and practice varied instructional strategies. Soon students will number you among the more interesting teachers they have known!

APPLICATION: VARYING INSTRUCTIONAL STRATEGIES

To engage learners from diverse cultural and socioeconomic backgrounds and with varied learning styles, teachers use many different instructional strategies. Using a variety of teaching strategies to help learners assimilate knowledge, assess the degree of learning taking place, and determine whether learners have transferred the strategies into personal learning tools is part of the teaching/learning process. Varied strategies can take students from basic recall of information to higher levels of thinking and learning. Inquiry, discovery, and/or exploratory learning are highly motivating strategies for both teacher and student. Selecting the instructional strategies that best suit your students requires that you examine, practice, and revise a variety of strategies before making the choice.

Arends (1998) suggests a model of four cognitive strategies (rehearsal, elaboration, organization, and metacognition) that help learners act on new information and connect it to prior information. Using this model as an introduction, Table 7.1 categorizes key instructional strategies from classroom practice into five groups:

1. **cognitive** strategies that move from basic memory techniques to self-assessment thinking techniques
2. **collaborative** strategies that involve teacher and student/s in a cooperative approach to learning
3. **community-based** strategies that take teacher and student outside of the classroom to a broader learning environment
4. **organizational** strategies that give the teacher specific techniques to guide student learning in structured or logical format
5. **problem-solving** strategies divided into both process and product.

Consider the purpose and examples summarized in Table 7.1. We suggest that you review those unfamiliar strategies from teacher preparation texts and materials referenced in this chapter.

Effective teachers use different strategies to achieve their learning outcomes as they prepare instruction. A strategy that is growing rapidly in its use within the classroom is cooperative learning. Your seminar may be organized in a cooperative learning format. Good and Brophy (1994) provide a broad summary of classroom research on cooperative learning and offer certain qualifications to teachers when using this strategy.

1. Cooperative learning is not a wholesale replacement of whole-class instruction by the teacher but an adaptation in which follow-up activities are accomplished through group cooperation.
2. Cooperative learning approaches may be more effective in certain classes than in others.
3. There may be optimal levels of the use of cooperative learning groups within courses or across the school day or year.
4. Cooperative learning emphasizes cooperation and deemphasizes competition.
5. Modeling, demonstrating, and practicing the cooperative learning approaches (sharing, listening, integrating ideas of others, and handling disagreements) is essential. Collaboratively, teachers and students participate in evaluating behaviors within the groups.
6. Cooperative learning activities engage the learner in the content currently being taught.

Perhaps the strategy that is most familiar to you and one that you experienced most often in your own education is the lecture method. Use of the

TABLE 7.1 *Key Instructional Strategies*

Strategy	Purpose	Example
Cognitive		
rehearsal	to commit materials to memory	repeating phrases, underlining key words
elaboration	to create associations and connections between new information and prior knowledge	note taking, using analogies
organization	to cluster ideas and identify key ideas or facts from large amounts of information	outlining, webbing, mapping
metacognition	to think about thinking, to select, use, and monitor learning strategies	ask students to reflect verbally or in writing an explanation of their solution
Collaborative		
cooperative learning	to encourage academic achievement, acceptance of diversity, and social skill development	assign specific roles and tasks to group members
peer or cross-age tutoring	to encourage peer acceptance, academic achievement, and social skill development	student helping another with a difficult concept
reciprocal teaching	to teach students strategies to improve subject matter and reading comprehension	teacher models, then students learn to perform on their own
Community-Based		
field studies	to give students an opportunity to solve problems in the real world	science project that requires samples of soil
mentoring/ apprenticeship/co-op	to provide opportunities for students to acquire skill from experts in a particular area	pair students with business individual
service learning	to encourage volunteerism among youth	students assist the elderly in a nursing facility
Organizational		
advance	to help students bridge new learning materials to prior knowledge	teacher or students review or summarize previous lesson
compare/contrast Venn diagrams, flowcharts, sequence chains, time lines, task analysis	to help students identify similarities and differences, to show specific information in logical form and relate it to the big picture	(draw Venn diagram) give students an overview of the lesson or task to complete
graphic representations	to highlight critical attributes of a concept	visual or media aid
KWL	to help students retrieve relevant background knowledge and learn with awareness of purpose and accomplishment	learners write what they know, what they want to learn, and what they have learned about a topic
PQ4R	to preview, question, read, recite, review	reading assignment
mapping, webbing	to outline or analyze a concept	attributes ← lake → definition / ↓ examples / non-examples
note taking	to listen or read and take notes on what was said or read	have students take notes during an oral presentation
storyboard	to relate a story or procedure by means of pictures attached to a canvas or board	depict the three branches of government

TABLE 7.1 *Continued*

Strategy	Purpose	Example
story map	to elicit meaning from a text or story	title → central events / central ideas
mnemonics	to assist the memory by developing association between new materials and familiar patterns	devise a pattern of letters to recall important information or processes
scaffolding	to reduce complex tasks to manageable steps	help students concentrate on one step of the task at a time
learning centers	to provide opportunities to practice decision making and new skills, use resources, and review or reinforce learned material	create a measurement center for practice or enrichment

Problem Solving
A. Process

Strategy	Purpose	Example
brainstorming	to elicit numerous imaginative ideas, solutions, or responses to open-ended question or problem	ask students to generate descriptive language for an item
discussion	to share opinions to clarify issues, relate new knowledge to prior experience	teacher facilitates interactive exchange with students
heuristics	to assist learners in conceptualizing problems and organizing their solutions	given verbal problems, students come up with alternate solutions
inquiry, discovery	to lead students toward a previously determined solution or conclusion	lead students through questioning to arrive at the concept mountain
questioning	to stimulate critical and creative thinking	see Chapter 6

B. Product

Strategy	Purpose	Example
debate	to add competition and create excitement to instruction	debate use of the World Wide Web as an educational tool
interviews	to relate writing tasks to real life	to develop questions for use interviewing person who experienced the Great Depression
research	to direct students in locating and using primary and secondary resources	assigning students to locate print and nonprint resources on space exploration
role play	to enable students to think, feel and act as other persons	choose character from history or story to portray
simulations	to represent reality as closely as possible	use computer simulations (Oregon Trail) or develop one suitable for grade level

lecture, if well planned, can stimulate student interest and engagement in the subject matter. Rather than use an entire class period for lectures, many teachers are using mini-lectures and mini-lessons (10 to 20 minutes of direct instruction) to emphasize material and engage students in the learning process. A number of strategies can be used to get students involved in the material emphasized: advance organizers, outlining, note taking, mapping or webbing, KWL (what you know, what you want to know, and what you have learned), graphic model, questioning, and discussion. Your enthusiasm will only further ignite the students' interest!

Discussion, when well planned and directed, leads students to think beyond the textbook. Facilitating a discussion requires that you know the subject matter and can emphasize the connections of ideas or opinions expressed, elicit responses from the students, clarify or expand on the topic, and, finally, summarize and bring to closure the response to the topic.

Other instructional strategies you might try are:

- verbally walking the student step by step through a conceptual map or web
- identifying and defining a problem with the students, verbalizing the approach to take, subdividing the problem being investigated, deciding on an approach and listing alternate approaches, checking on the progress of the investigation, and assessing strategies used in the process
- demonstrating and modeling note taking, outlining, and storyboarding
- using a Venn diagram to picture the use of compare and contrast or fact and opinion, and summarize student responses
- providing multimedia approaches that connects content with the outside world

Instructional strategies can be used in many other ways:

- implementing resource or thematic units,
- cultivating critical reading,
- developing writing across the curriculum, or
- reinforcing skill-based learning.

As you vary your teaching strategies your students begin to think about complex issues from various points of view. Providing multiple approaches leads students to apply and increase their thinking in a wholistic manner.

ASSIGNED ACTIVITIES

1. Observe your supervising teacher as he/she uses cooperative learning. If you planned and used this instructional strategy, reflect on its effectiveness. How were the students prepared for the tasks to be accomplished? In what ways were the students held accountable for the completion of the task? Journal the questions and/or reservations you have about using cooperative learning at this time.
2. Select an instructional strategy you have not yet practiced. Outline how you plan to use it in your teaching and tell what learner outcomes you expect to achieve.
3. Develop a web or concept map that contains key concepts of at least one lesson you are teaching this week.

SUMMARY

At the beginning of the school year your supervising teacher initiated and now continues to practice techniques contributing to the classroom environment. In addition to observing these practices your involvement with students requires that you make these strategies your own. The assignment activities asked you to take an in-depth look at what you observed and did, and to examine the reasons behind your actions. You reflected on teacher attitudes and characteristics that motivate students, communicating clear expectations, using different means for relating to students from a diverse population, promoting positive working relationships among students, and arranging a learner-friendly physical environment.

Identifying instructional activities to take students beyond rote learning into discovery and exploration is challenging! You note that instructional strategies help your students meet the outcomes selected in the planning phase of instruction. Trying several new strategies may have been a struggle at first, but realizing that "Rome was not built in a day," you begin to reflect on your daily progress. Students seem to be engaged (well, most of them), and you are beginning to see results in their assignments and assessments. You are gaining confidence in your teaching and even find that working with your supervising teacher has allowed specific strategies to come alive for you. Because of your success and determination, you are willing to try new instructional strategies that motivate and challenge your students to think more critically.

FOLLOW-UP QUESTIONS AND SHARED INSIGHTS

You have identified a variety of teaching strategies in your experiences working with learners. From your journal and school experiences as a beginning teacher, share your responses to the following:

1. Identify four different instructional strategies you most often use with your classes.
2. Discuss how the use of these strategies encourage students to be actively engaged in the learning process.
3. Discuss the difficulties and successes you recognize when using these strategies within your classroom.
4. Describe how each strategy you selected affects student learning.
5. Which of the strategies you observe or practice enables you to connect the subject matter with the students' prior knowledge?
6. Describe a strategy you have implemented that required a team effort between you and your supervising teacher.

Journal Excerpts

High School

"After watching the movie, *Bernice Bobs Her Hair,* an F. Scott Fitzgerald story, the students used their movie study guides (which they completed during the movie) for discussion within the small groups. Students presented their group response to the guided questions. After the first group presented, I clapped and told them they did a good job and asked a couple of questions to begin a discussion. The class responded positively to this verbal and nonverbal behavior and others began to point out the strong points that were reported by the groups."

"The students are writing oral histories. They picked a person to interview last Friday. I assigned the actual interview over the weekend. Following the book's suggestion, I asked the students to write notes from their interview on index cards. This will help to keep them organized."

"I am still struggling a little with the group discussions. It is hard to find a balance of discussion in the large group. They either make too many irrelevant comments or don't participate much. I'm trying to find a balance by monitoring the room, proximity control, engaging questions, asking students to cite where the group is finding the answers, etc. Most of my responses simply involve encouragement and guidance."

Middle School

"For this week, we prepared the students quite a bit because of the number of field trips. A couple of strategies that I use often are graphic organizers and brainstorming. Most of the time I use them in conjunction with one another. I am a big fan of webbing and use it in nearly every subject. I think it's not only a great way to organize thoughts but also helps students learn how to take notes.

"In second period, the algebra class used a balance and manipulatives to work 'Hands-on Equations.' The teacher prepared an actual model, but the students had a laminated paper drawing for their use. Everyone has the same set of materials to work the equation. They really enjoy this and it helps them to SEE how to find the answer."

"Ms. I. and I taped an enlarged number line to the floor. Students walked it as a model for adding and subtracting in one-step equations. It was really neat."

"Some classes haven't finished reading *Anne Frank* yet; however, Ms. A. wanted to get a feel for what they thought about the story thus far. She led them in a discussion about the feelings they have. She asked them if they could sympathize with Anne's feelings of loneliness and isolation from the outside world. Students seem to respond to discussion more openly than they do when they are assigned a learning log entry which is written. I see the value in both discussion and writing."

Elementary

"Today I read the poem 'Johnny Appleseed' to the class. I had the students do an activity sheet on sequencing the order of the growth of the apple tree. I also had the students do a writing assignment with cut-out apples and an apple stencil. They were to write a sentence describing their cut-out apple and on the back of the same paper they were to write a sentence using one directional word. For example, 'I see a worm inside my apple.' These writings were super!"

"One thing which Mrs. L. does (which I found excellent) is allow the children to bring closure to the lesson. She has one child come to the front of the room and explain what they did in that lesson for the day. Not only does this bring closure to the lesson, but it also presents the information and ideas in a way that may be different from the way the teacher actually presented the idea. After all, children understand each other better than they understand an adult. This may be an excellent way to make sure you include closure in a lesson and assess that the class knows what is going on."

"I have become rather brave, and I plan to allow the children to make sand paintings both today and tomorrow. I hope this will go over okay. Mrs. D. seemed rather surprised to see me undertake such a messy project, but she said she would be there to help me throughout the project. I had no idea I was taking on such a big project. The children are extremely excited about painting. I had this dream that sand was going to be everywhere and that the children would run haywire through the school. Gladly, I was wrong. The children worked wonderfully on this project and created some of the neatest sand paintings I have ever seen.

Special Education

"G. and C. are now mainstreamed for math every morning. During this time we do calendar, DOL, journals, daily questions, states and capitals, and magic sentences. C. and L. are still able to draw pictures for their journal while J. must write his. J. has a difficult time staying on task during this time. I decided that I would set a timer for him to finish DOL and the journal. I explained to him that I was giving him fifteen minutes to finish each assignment. It should only take J. this long if he would stay on task. It worked!!! Wonderful!"

"Today we had computer. After the normal computer class Mr. D. demonstrated 'Wiggle Works' to the students. Soon they will start using it. Most of the students did well even though the demonstration made the class last longer than usual."

"I had assigned a page for math with problems of greater than and less than. The students were to choose which item was greater. So I made an alligator from construction paper and explained to the students that the alligator only ate the greater numbers. I then used the wipe off board to show the numbers presented in pictures. The students then placed the alligator eating the larger number. This activity went well."

REFERENCES AND SUGGESTED READINGS

Anderson, L. (1989). Learners and learning. In M. Reynolds (Ed.), *Knowledge bases for beginning teachers*. Englewood Cliffs, NJ: Prentice Hall.

Arends, R. I. (1998). *Learning to teach* (4th ed.). Boston: McGraw-Hill.

Barell, J. (1995). *Teaching for thoughtfulness: Classroom strategies to enhance intellectual development* (2nd ed.). White Plains, NY: Longman.

Brooks, J. G., & Brooks, M. G. (1993). *In search of understanding: The case for constructivist classrooms*. Alexandria, VA: Association for Supervision and Curriculum Development.

Brophy, J. (1998), *Motivating students to learn*. Boston: McGraw-Hill.

Calderhead, J. (1992). The role of reflection in learning to teach. In L. Valli (Ed.), *Reflective teacher education cases and critiques* (pp. 139–146). Albany: State University of New York Press.

Callahan, J. F., Clark, L. H., & Kellough, R. D. (1998). *Teaching in the middle and secondary schools* (6th ed.). Upper Saddle River, NJ: Merrill/Prentice Hall.

Clark, L. H., & Starr, I. S. (1996). *Secondary and middle school teaching methods* (7th ed.). Upper Saddle River, NJ: Merrill/Prentice Hall.

Cruickshank, D., & Metcalf, K. (1994). Explaining. In T. Husen and T. N. Postlewaite (Eds.), *International encyclopedia of education* (2nd ed.). Oxford: Pergamon Press.

Dewey, J. (1916). *Democracy and education: An introduction to the philosophy of education*. New York: Macmillan.

Eby, J. W. (1998). *Reflective planning, teaching, and evaluation K–12* (2nd ed.). Upper Saddle River, NJ: Merrill/Prentice Hall.

Eggen, P. D., & Kauchak, D. P. (1996). *Strategies for teachers: Teaching content and thinking skills* (3rd ed.). Boston: Allyn and Bacon.

Emmer, E. T., Evertson, C. M., & Anderson, L. M. (1980). Effective classroom management at the beginning of the school year. *The Elementary School Journal, 80*, 219–231.

Evertson, C. M., Emmer, E. T., Clements, B. S., & Worsham, M. E. (1997). *Classroom management for elementary teachers* (4th ed.). Boston: Allyn and Bacon.

Freiberg, H. J. (1996). *Universal teaching strategies* (2nd ed.). Boston: Allyn and Bacon.

Gagne, E. D., Yekovick, C. W., & Yekovick, F. R. (1993). *The cognitive psychology of school learning* (2nd ed.). New York: Harper Collins.

Giordano, G. (1992). Heuristic strategies: An aid for solving verbal mathematical problems. *Intervention in School and Clinic, 28* (2), 88–96.

Good, T. L., & Brophy, J. E. (1994). *Looking in classrooms* (6th ed.). New York: Harper Collins.

Green, M. (1995). Choosing a past and inventing a future: The becoming of a teacher. In W. Ayers (Ed.), *To become a teacher*. New York: Teachers College, Columbia University.

Harmin, M. (1994). *Inspiring active learning: A handbook for teachers.* Alexandria, VA: Association for Supervision and Curriculum Development.

Henderson, J. G. (1996). *Reflective teaching: The study of your constructivist practices* (2nd ed.). Upper Saddle River, NJ: Merrill/Prentice Hall.

Hunter, M. (1982). *Mastery teaching.* El Segundo, CA: TIP.

Jacobs, H. H. (1989). *Interdisciplinary curriculum: Design and implementation.* Alexandria, VA: Association for Supervision and Curriculum Development.

Jacobsen, D., Eggen, P., & Kauchak, D. (1999). *Methods for teaching: A skills approach* (4th ed.). Upper Saddle River, NJ: Merrill/Prentice Hall.

Johnson, D. W., & Johnson, R. T. (1991). *Learning together and alone: Cooperation, competition, and individualization* (3rd ed.). Englewood Cliffs, NJ: Prentice Hall.

Kameenui, E. J., & Carnine, D. W. (1998). *Effective teaching strategies that accommodate diverse learners.* Upper Saddle River, NJ: Merrill/Prentice Hall.

Lovitt, T. C. (1995). *Tactics for teaching* (2nd ed.). Upper Saddle River, NJ: Merrill/Prentice Hall.

Moore, K. C. (1998). *Classroom teaching skills* (4th ed.). New York: McGraw-Hill.

Newman, F., & Wehlage, G. (1993). Five standards of authentic instruction. *Educational Leadership, 50* (7), 8–12.

Orlich, D. C., Harder, R. J., Callahan, R. C., & Gibson, H. W. (1998). *Teaching strategies: A guide to better instruction* (5th ed.). Boston: Houghton Mifflin.

Ornstein, A. C. (1995). *Strategies for effective teaching* (2nd ed.). Madison, WI: Brown and Benchmark.

Post, T. R., Ellis, A. K., Humphreys, A. H., & Buggey, L. J. (1997). *Interdisciplinary approaches to curriculum.* Upper Saddle River, NJ: Merrill/Prentice Hall.

Richert, A. E. (1992) Voice and power in teaching and learning to teach. In L. Valli (Ed.), *Reflective teacher education cases and critiques* (pp. 187–197). Albany: State University of New York Press.

Rosenberg, M. S., O'Shea, L., & O'Shea, D. J. (1998). *Student teacher to master teacher: A practical guide for educating students with special needs* (2nd ed.). Upper Saddle River, NJ: Merrill/Prentice Hall.

Ross, D. D., Bondy, E., & Kyle, D. W. (1993). *Reflective teaching for teacher empowerment: Elementary curriculum and methods.* New York: Macmillan.

Schön, D. A. (1987). *Educating the reflective practitioner* (pp. 12–17). San Francisco: Jossey-Bass.

Slavin, R. (1995). *Cooperative learning* (2nd ed.). New York: Longman.

Wolfinger, D. M., & Stockard, J. W. Jr. (1997). *Elementary methods: An integrated curriculum.* New York: Longman.

Zeichner, K. M. (1992). Conceptions of reflective teaching in contemporary U.S. teacher education program reforms. In L. Valli (Ed.), *Reflective teacher education cases and critiques* (pp. 161–186). Albany: State University of New York Press.

CHAPTER

Creating a Learning Climate

> *"People who serve as models of behavior usually are admirable ... or more competent than the learner or observer."*

Zabel and Zabel (p. 91)

Focus One

Expected Performance

- Identify examples of modeling used to teach appropriate attitudes and behaviors.
- Analyze modeling and other strategies for teaching character education.
- Discuss the complexities teachers and schools encounter with moral education.

Teacher as Role Model

Learning to teach is an ongoing process and one that suggests you are always continuing the journey to become a teacher. This process of becoming entails examining specific goals of teaching while keeping in mind the total, complex act of teaching. Reflective teaching asks that you as teacher also engage in moral deliberation as you face head on the difficult questions about good reasons for educational actions in your classroom and the demands society makes of public education (Zeichner, 1990).

Among the current and frequently cited societal needs from American schools is character education. Lickona (1999) describes character education as "the deliberate effort to cultivate virtue" and says "character education has three goals: good people, good schools, and good society" (p. 78). Popular press and professional journals advocate the role of the school as that of fostering good character in youth. That the school needs to play a unique moral role in a democratic society has wide public support, and character education is being emphasized in teacher preparation (Berkowitz, 1999; DeVries, 1999; Lickona, 1999). Jones, Ryan, and Bohlin (1999) insist that teachers must be able to model those character qualities that students need to develop. Modeling is a powerful means for nonverbally communicating the positive attitudes and actions you want your students to learn and practice. Consider how you can use modeling in the classroom.

Just as your university professors and supervisors are urged to be models for you, so you are urged to act and deliberate on what it means to exemplify moral character for your students (Zeichner, 1990). The respect and cooperation shown you may have been powerful motivators for reexamining your current performance and may have challenged you to search for ways to develop and model attitudes and behaviors children or adolescents need to learn. DeVries (1999) maintains that fostering the construction of good character demands a certain kind of interpersonal context, the creation of an interpersonal atmosphere composed of the entire network of interpersonal relations that make up the learner's school experience. These interpersonal relationships are the context for the learner's construction of the self, of others, and of subject matter knowledge. These conditions promote both character and intellectual development, and the teacher-learner relationship is an important component of these conditions. The behaviors you model are but one portion of teaching the values that promote mutual respect; the children and adolescents experiencing this interpersonal atmosphere also receive a powerful foundation for learning.

Being a reflective teacher calls for an active, persistent, and careful consideration of your beliefs in light of your background and educational experiences (Zeichner & Liston, 1987). Because teaching offers opportunities to influence students' thinking about value-related issues and activities, it is laden with ethical and moral responsibilities and consequences. Your personal experiences are influenced and molded by your values and principles. Perhaps you have chosen to do service learning and upon reflection you are amazed at your personal growth and the change in your world view. These broadened attitudes are now a part of you, and as teacher you model behaviors and use language to promote an atmosphere of mutual respect. Your students are likely to intuit or learn consistently modeled behaviors reinforced in a "good" school and useful in a "good" society. Your growing experience and competency encourages and invites your students' admiration, and interactions between you and your students reinforce values (Zabel & Zabel, 1996). Examining the quality of your interactions with students is an important step in determining the interpersonal atmosphere your words and actions promote within the classroom setting.

Young people observe adult behavior and search for images that contribute to the development of their values and attitudes. Think about what you want students to observe about you as their teacher. Since you value learning and working in an environment characterized by respect and concern for others, you model for your students those attitudes. You want students to be interested and enthusiastic about learning. It's important that your students respect and care about themselves, each other, and you.

From their daily interactions with you, students learn what you know and value about others and how important learning is. A student reaches to pick up an object falling from a peers' desk, and you pause to say "Thank you, Devon." You interrupt someone who is speaking with, "Excuse me, Nicole. . . ." The tone and expression of your voice communicate a gentle, caring spirit of helpfulness. You encourage students to think critically for themselves rather than querying you for answers by saying to them, "That's a wonderful question. Now how are you going to find that answer?" You put the responsibility and initiative back into their hands. You are very conscious of what you do and say in the classroom; you realize that your students watch and listen to you, absorb every nuance. You are modeling for students the behaviors you want to see in their actions and speech in the classroom. Do your interactions and conversations with students invite them to adopt the behaviors you model?

This activity asks you to recall a time during the past week when you consciously used modeling to teach students, where you used verbal or nonverbal communication to relay a single message. Pause to recall a specific classroom event (one in which students were involved). Use the space below for writing what you did and/or said to students.

_____

_____

_____

_____

Discussion Questions

1. Appraise and describe a situation in which you used modeling to teach students. How has modeling been effective in establishing mutual respect among the students in your class?
2. Summarize what modeling requires of you as a teacher. To what extent are you comfortable in seeing yourself as a model for your students?
3. In response to the public's call for schools to teach children and adolescents moral character, how prepared do you feel to teach values? What teaching strategies would you use? Discuss with the group the issues you would want to avoid and why.

Focus Two

The interactive activity in **Focus One** asked you to examine ways you use modeling to teach students appropriate behaviors. Your focus during the past week has been on clearly communicating your expectations. Modeling is an approach for teaching students appropriate behavior. In addition, taking advantage of modeling opportunities strengthens your current emphasis in establishing a classroom environment.

APPLICATION: CREATING A LEARNING CLIMATE

Classroom management and instructional strategies are inseparable. Everyday you practice multiple strategies and reflect on the effectiveness of your practice. As a student teacher you are keenly aware of managing student behavior and your concerns about classroom management are normal. Classroom management is a priority for experienced teachers, and tops their list of concerns about teaching. By identifying, discussing, and reflecting on the different aspects of managing behavior, you are building confidence and improving ways for creating a learning environment.

The topics reviewed and practiced in this chapter are considered preventive classroom management techniques. In using preventive techniques you work to create a positive learning climate and reduce or eliminate a number of misbehavior from occurring. Preventive discipline techniques, furthermore, promote and build student self-control and motivation. How does this happen? How do effective teachers prevent misbehavior from occurring? Five effective techniques for creating a learning climate are listed below. Which are used by teachers you observe? Which do you intend to practice?

- Exhibits positive attitudes and characteristics
- Communicates clear verbal and nonverbal expectations
- Relates to diverse students populations
- Promotes working relationships among students
- Arranges positive physical environment

Expected Performance

- Use an understanding of individual and group motivation and behavior to create a learning climate that encourages positive social interaction, active engagement in learning, and self-motivation.
- Communicate with and challenge students in a positive and supportive manner.
- Establish and maintain standards of mutually respectful classroom interaction by establishing the importance of shared expectations during individual and group responsibilities.
- Demonstrate flexibility and modify classroom processes and instructional procedure as the situation demands.

Exhibits Positive Attitudes and Characteristics

Beliefs and attitudes teachers hold about themselves, about learners, and about their role powerfully impact their interactions with students. As a professional teacher, you are the primary instrument when describing the learning climate in the classroom. What teacher attitudes and characteristics do you possess that contribute positively to the learning environment? Do you observe and model attitudes such as "I feel lucky to be here!" "I like what I'm doing!" "I believe in you!"? Students receiving these kinds of messages from you are likely to think learning is worthwhile and school can be exciting.

How do you communicate to students the importance of a task? Planning appropriate, challenging activities and enabling students to succeed boosts their confidence. Expect to assist students repeatedly and insist they complete tasks. Students who experience success feel more positive about themselves and you as the teacher. Your belief that students can learn, your positive words and actions, and confidence in your teaching ability nurture a prevailing can-do spirit that permeates your class. Reflecting on how you perceive and respond to your role as leader and manager of the teaching/learning setting contributes to a productive learning climate.

Communicates Clear Verbal and Nonverbal Expectations

Activities connected with rules and procedures require the teacher's most salient verbal and nonverbal communication skills. Stating and posting rules and consequences, procedures, and clear directions communicate to students your expectations concerning classroom behavior. In monitoring students you "catch" them behaving appropriately and reinforce them for doing so.

You are observing and learning the impact nonverbal communication has on an uninterrupted flow of instruction. Your gestures, eye contact, facial expressions, and pointing to lists of rules communicate to students approval and reminders about your expectations. Continuously sending verbal and nonverbal messages keeps students mindful of the purpose for their involvement. These messages help create a rich learning environment.

Rules and procedures relate to both managing instruction and behavior. The list of classroom rules is generally short, not exceeding four or six, and addresses broad areas of behavior. Teachers often involve students in making and explaining rules while emphasizing the importance of clearly understanding what behavior is expected in the classroom. Involving students in the process of rule making promotes a sense of ownership and builds a community of learners. Current practice recommends that class rules be clearly and prominently posted.

Daily procedures address more specific routines and tell students what is expected of them at the beginning/ending of class/school day. Outlining and practicing procedures help students to meet expected behaviors when joining the reading group, in obtaining and returning class supplies, and in responding to interruptions. New procedures may be introduced and others replaced as the year progresses. The process varies according to learners' age, instructional period, and student needs.

The supervising teacher may plan and conduct the rule-making process and invite you to give input. If you were not present for the rule-making process, the supervising teacher may review the classroom rules as a reinforcement for students and/or as a part of introducing you to the class. This introduction and discussion of rules with the supervising teacher allows you to gain a deeper understanding of the rules and procedures of your particular setting. Furthermore, it initiates you into the authority role, as you monitor the rules and remind students what you expect of them. Student teaching allows you the opportunity to apply prior knowledge about rules and procedures and to construct a deeper understanding about their importance in creating an environment that is respectful, tolerant, and fair to all.

How comfortable are you with having power and authority? If student teaching is the first time you are responsible for others' behavior, you may feel apprehensive and hesitant about speaking and acting in ways you recently identified as being "the establishment." If you teach high school, you may be just a few years older than your students, and you both know you are new to teaching! At the same time, you realize the responsibility and authority accompanying the teacher role; you believe that students need to respond to you as teacher. Clearly communicating your expectations (verbally and nonverbally) is the preventive stage of classroom management.

Your weekly seminar offers an opportunity to share your questions and concerns openly about communicating your expectations and about the learning climate in your classes. Take advantage of your peers' suggestions, and during later sessions share management strategies you used that positively impacted on student behavior in your classes.

Relates to Diverse Student Populations

Earlier you examined and identified examples of differences that exist among the learners in your classes. Being sensitive to and informed about the varied cultural, social, and ethnic backgrounds of students, you can plan instructional activities that connect with their life experiences. Have you included resources and activities highlighting different cultures into the content? Did you observe student response to information about a specific culture, race, special learner needs, or ethnic group? By integrating student experiences and prior knowledge into instruction you take advantage of the diversity existing among your students. In doing so you help your students feel they belong to the group and you create an opportunity for deeper understanding and tolerance among your learners.

You may be engaged in cooperative learning groups during part of the seminar. You can talk more often and decide how you will perform a task within a given time frame. This experience allows you to think about how it feels to work within a group. During student/intern teaching your reflection on the use of cooperative groups is one means for meeting student needs. Students claim they work harder and enjoy participating in cooperative groups because they are socializing as they work (Glasser, 1990).

Group work is a favorite learning strategy for some (but not all) students. You can help students understand the process and reward those individuals and groups following the process outlined for them. We encourage you to consider how group instruction allows you to give greater attention to specific student needs as compared with using only a direct teaching approach. In assigning students to groups, you provide an opportunity for peer teaching and allow students to develop and strengthen social skills in performing different roles within a group. Well-planned and well-managed group activities positively contribute to the learning climate.

Promotes Working Relationships among Students

Connected with the ability to work in groups are skills for resolving conflict nonviolently. Conflicts are natural and normal occurrences among persons working together (Bodine & Crawford, 1998). You may have already witnessed conflicts erupting into violent outbreaks among students in your school. Because of the increasing number of violent incidents occurring, many schools now offer students peer mediation training and other conflict resolution programs. While incorporating the total conflict resolution process into instruction may not be practical, you can model and directly teach the skills included in conflict resolution. For example, you may teach students to listen sensitively, work together, trust, help each other, express feelings of anger and frustration in nonaggressive ways, and respond creatively to conflict (Girard & Koch, 1996). You realize that attaining these goals requires you to teach, model, and practice the skills. Look for opportunities to reward students using these skills in their daily interactions with peers. Teaching students to view conflicts as situations they have the ability and choice to resolve allows you more academic class time. A successful learning environment increases the chances that the instructional activities you plan will interest and engage students in the content areas.

Arranges Positive Physical Environment

Organizing and arranging the physical features of the classroom occurs as school begins and continues throughout the year. **Assigned Activities** in chapter 1 asked you to observe physical characteristics and to get involved with arranging the classroom in preparation for students. Planning instruction includes thinking ahead and anticipating learner movement and use of space and is therefore included among the preventive actions you want to consider in creating a learning environment.

The physical arrangement of the classroom suggests the type of interaction between you and your students (Weinstein & Mignano, 1997). Deciding how to arrange desks, tables, and other classroom furniture accompanies your decisions about whether you use teacher-directed or student groups during your instructional activities. You may have student desks or tables in rows and later rearrange them into groups, thus providing flexibility during a single period of extended instruction.

Classroom displays convey messages about the students and your interests and values. Teachers often choose an array of action posters, motivational quotes, and assorted hangings to express their values and vision about school and learning (Weinstein, 1996). Messages selected and displayed on the walls and bulletin boards can energize and motivate you and your students. Displays of varied student work communicates to observers that you promote and value the varied talents of many students. While displays of student work are more plentiful in elementary classrooms, we also see student work and informational materials displayed in most high school classrooms. Other messages about students appear, for example, in student writing samples, art work, and other creative projects. What you exhibit in your classroom helps to show students the quality of work you expect, and most are thrilled to have their work publicly acclaimed. Creating a learning environment that encourages positive social interaction, active learning, and self-motivation challenges any teacher and is especially challenging for beginning teachers.

ASSIGNED ACTIVITIES

This week's assignment asks you to reflect on what you are observing and doing to create a learning environment in your classes.

1. Observe your supervising teacher during two teacher-directed classes or parts of classes. Using Figure 8.1, modify the rows and columns to show the seating arrangement of students in your class. Tally each time the supervising teacher interacts with a student. After a day or so repeat the activity using a different colored pen to show the separate markings. Place

FIGURE 8.1 *Seating Chart*

1	2	3	4	5
6	7	8	9	10
11	12	13	14	15
16	17	18	19	20
21	22	23	24	25
26	27	28	29	30
31	32	33	34	35

an (X) marking the supervising teacher's location during the class. In your journal respond to the following questions:
- In what part of the room does the chart show the most frequent interactions?
- For which section of the room are there fewer tallies?
- After examining the chart what new insights do you have about teacher/student interactions?

2. In your journal describe how the teacher uses verbal and nonverbal communication to encourage, motivate, and involve students. Give specific examples, one from each day, and explain what the supervising teacher said/did. Describe how student behavior changed as a result of the supervising teacher's communication.

3. If you were not present when class rules were established, talk with your supervising teacher about **when, how,** and **by whom** rules and procedures are established. Describe how you monitored and reviewed rules and procedures with students this week.

4. Describe in your journal some cultural, social, or ethnic information or experience you have had during student teaching. What did you learn that helps you to teach students from diverse backgrounds?

5. Ask the supervising teacher to observe you during two classes and use Figure 8.2 for tallying your interactive behaviors. We suggest that you not know when the observations are made.

FIGURE 8.2 *Verbal and Nonverbal Teacher Behaviors*

Eye Contact ex. Looks at students while teaching them, Eye range includes all learners		
Facial Expression ex. Matches verbal expression, Pleasant, smiling, listening		
Posture ex. Alert and attentive to learner participants, Confident		
Gestures ex. Nodding in agreement, shaking head in disagreement, Placing hand on shoulder Pointing to charts, diagrams, etc.		
Voice ex. Clear articulate, Changes inflection, volume, and rate		
Position to Learner ex. Moves about the classroom to view all learners		

After conferencing with your supervising teacher and examining Figure 8.2, write your reflections in your journal. Include comments on the strengths you demonstrated and areas you want to improve. You may want to consider the following:

- In what ways would you change the nonverbal communication indicated by the tallies?
- How would the changes improve the interactions you have with students?
- What do the tallies indicate about your attitude toward students and what you are teaching?

SUMMARY

Misbehavior affects you and your students and can destroy the learning environment of your classroom. When students behave inappropriately, the teaching/learning time is shortchanged and teachers become frustrated and discouraged. Learning to anticipate, plan, and manage the complexities of teaching, including maintaining a learning environment, is a critical area that you and other student/intern teachers are eager to master.

FOLLOW-UP QUESTIONS AND SHARED INSIGHTS

From observations described in your journals, share with others your experiences based on the following questions.

1. After reflecting on verbal and nonverbal communication used by the teacher(s) you observed, what communication techniques are important for competent teachers?
2. In this chapter you read that teacher attitudes toward students are communicated in a variety of ways. Describe examples of teacher expressions, signs displaying values and beliefs, or activities that evoked a positive response from students.
3. Name some successful approaches you used to engage students who have different backgrounds and learning styles.
4. Share with the group examples of learner behavior that you have promoted:
   - Listening to each other—Describe how you encouraged learners to listen to each other.
   - Working as a group on a joint project—What are some examples of directions that were specifically given?
   - Learner response to mistakes made—What did you say or do to teach the class an appropriate response to others' mistakes?
5. If you were in the class when rules were established, share what you now think are important components of the rule-making process. Share at least one significant insight you now have about the importance of establishing rules and consequences and outlining classroom procedures. Tell how this contributes to creating a learning environment.
6. After examining Table 8.2 completed by your supervising teacher, tell how you plan to sharpen your interaction with learners. What strengths did you demonstrate in teaching? What areas need improvement?

Portfolio Tasks

Creating and Maintaining the Learning Climate

Standards

- The teacher uses an understanding of individual and group motivation and behavior to create a learning environment that encourages positive social interaction, active engagement in learning, and self-motivation.
- The teacher communicates high expectations and challenges students in a positive and supportive manner.
- The teacher establishes and maintains standards of mutually respectful classroom interaction.
- The teacher uses classroom management techniques that foster self-control and self-discipline.

Performance Guidelines

1. You are to provide evidence of your ability to establish a climate that:
   a. promotes and maintains learning in your classroom
   b. shows how you teach, monitor, and follow up rules and procedures
   c. demonstrates sensitivity to individual differences
   d. shows flexibility and modifies instructional techniques
   e. uses media to enrich the teaching/learning process

2. Samples may include and not be limited to the following:
    a. list of your classroom rules, consequences, and procedures
    b. discipline strategies most often practiced
    c. brief narrative outlining a description of your class and how instructional tasks were adapted for this class
    d. pictures and/or videotape of your learning environment that include students engaged in multimedia projects, oral presentations, art, music, research, or lab activities

Performance Criteria

The quality of your entry will be assessed to the extent that evidence provided:

- demonstrates that communication with students is challenging, positive, and supporting
- establishes and maintains a standard of mutually respectful classroom interactions
- uses classroom management techniques that foster self-control and self-discipline
- encourages responsibility to self and to others
- demonstrates ability to use and manage individual and group inquiry

Journal Excerpts

High School

"Expectations of student behavior were made clear on the first couple days of class. The students were allowed to ask questions so I think expectations were clear. Students know that they are to enter the classroom prepared for learning tasks. The teachers begin class with a review of previous material and/or summary of learning tasks for the day . . . gets students focused on the class."

"J., my supervising teacher, is very outgoing and enthusiastic. She likes for her students to be 'pumped up' about everything and she often uses a 'cheerleader' type of approach! With freshmen, this seems to work particularly well, because they are already excited just to be in high school and they really want it to be fun. She tells them why she does everything and this really seems to help them comprehend why they are being encouraged to do certain activities! She uses a strong, loud voice that is full of enthusiasm. Still, it can be very firm when needed. Her eye contact is also very dominant. She really looks at her students when she is teaching or they are talking. She is obviously reading their comprehension levels and showing them her full attention. . . . She praises a lot and smiles a lot, but she also uses her 'looks' to get her point across."

"Mrs. P. put a poster on the board with the name of a song and a sort of practical connection alongside it! She explained that she had made a musical tape with a mixture of songs that describe things about herself and the feelings of the year. She began with a classical piece to explain that everyone find time to 'nourish the spirit' by reflecting. Next she played Aretha Franklin's 'R-E-S-P-E-C-T' and she wrote on the poster 'What everyone needs'—this allowed her to subtly introduce classroom expectations. Next, she played 'Ain't too Proud to Beg' and wrote on the poster, 'What I want you to be . . .'—this was explained that she wanted the students to never be afraid to ask for her help. Finally she played 'Why Walk When You Can Fly,' a country song stressing the importance of always having a positive attitude. In this way Mrs. P. introduced herself, addressed different learning styles, and suggested some of her expectations from the students."

"Today I had to talk to a student after school about his attitude. He has consistently turned in poor work and does not take any of the assignments seriously. I am nervous about talking to this student, so Mr. G. and I talked about it. He gave me great advice (as usual), and I think that I handled the situation well. I sat down and pulled a desk up next to me. I did not want to make it confrontational. I was honest with him about how I was feeling and I let him speak too. I hope that this little talk will help the student improve in the class. Only time will tell!"

Middle School

"I have to say that all of the students in this eighth grade class do perform what's expected of them. Mrs. D. is very effective this way. If they have trouble, then they get help, but all do experience success in the end. The students show consideration to one another by keeping silent while their classmates are talking. They try to help each other within cooperative group settings. One thing that I thought was kind of funny was that while they had time in class to work on their homework, they were extremely conscientious about the noise level."

"Some nonverbal interactions that I have witnessed would be the use of peer editing and editing marks. I know K. uses these marks quite a bit when grading their writing. She also uses them during their Daily Oral Language activity. They have picked up on these and use them frequently themselves. Another is that when the students are asked to read another student's work, they read the entire story, essay, etc., entirely through once before commenting on it. Now, I know that this is also a behavior that K. exhibits. I don't blame them—I want to be like her too!"

"The skills I learned in peer mediation will be very beneficial to me in the future. Conflict (peaceful) resolution is an ability we all need to have. I think it is encouraging that these middle schoolers care enough to be a part of the solution to the problem of violence in schools."

"When students come in, my supervising teacher handles business briefly and jumps into action. The students know then, it's time to get serious. With each lesson, she briefly states her plan and goals and usually reminds students of the lessons' purpose during and after it as well. She told them she never assigns busy work and believes all work should be beneficial, so she makes her objectives clear. Her attitude is also encouraging."

Elementary

"I have become very aware of how effective various forms of discipline can be in maintaining a creative learning environment. Mrs. W. and I have been implementing a new behavior management technique with the students this week. The students are very aware of their responsibilities using this method of record keeping. The students lose a letter from the word *celebrate* if their behavior is inappropriate. I like this method very much. As a teacher I can quickly walk over to a student and *x* out a letter when that student is not on task. I do not have to say a word to the student in order to gain his/her attention. The other students are very aware of my actions, but I do not have to say a word. This method is making students responsible for their own behavior and/or actions."

"We began the day with a class meeting. I think such meetings are necessary and are a wonderful way to get students involved in *their* classroom. It also equips the students with a sense of responsibility. Each class meeting begins with compliments. Each student compliments another. Next, they talk about "happenings" within the classroom, whether good or bad. It is a time to review rules, especially those being broken most often. It is also a time to discuss positives."

"Ms. P's ability to communicate well can be attributed to her clear voice. She speaks so that all the students can understand her. She never raises her voice 'as a rule,' and she doesn't need to. She also maintains eye contact with the entire class during instruction. This keeps the students on task because they realize that she is aware of their behavior at all times. She almost always has a smile on her face and her enthusiasm is 'catching' for the students. Her expressions are very motivating for these first graders!

Special Education

"I have a child who is mute. I have been using reinforcement when he responds to a question with verbal cues from an adult or peer. I also conned M. into eating his lunch. I sat by him and teased with him that I love all the things on his tray and if he wasn't going to eat them he could give them to me. He would eat them and it became a game. All the children at the table began to join in my game and by the end of lunch M. was laughing with the other students. I really think he will talk with time and intervention. Something is wrong, but what it is, is a mystery!"

"The rules were established at the beginning of the year through discussion and role play. She made sure the students understood that they were everyone's rules. There is a list of rules posted. I monitor, review and reinforce adopted rules by modeling (giving cues), adding visuals (pointing to list) and verbal reminders to instruction, and reinforcing good behavior through stickers."

"I have been thinking about the effectiveness of the class helpers. While I think the helper positions are an excellent way to teach students responsibility, sometimes I become frustrated because I know I could do their jobs much more efficiently by myself. Yet, this is a preoccupation that I must overcome not only in teaching but in every aspect of my life."

REFERENCES AND SUGGESTED READINGS

Berkowitz, M. (1999). Obstacles to teacher training in character education. *Action in Teacher Education, 20*(4), 1–10.

Bodine, R. J., & Crawford, D. K. (1998). *The handbook of conflict resolution education*. San Francisco: Jossey-Bass.

Deutsch, M. (1992). Typical responses to conflict. *Educational Leadership, 50*(1), 16.

DeVries, R. (1999). Implications of Piaget's constructivist theory for character education. *Action in Teacher Education, 20*(4), 39–47.

Duttweiler, P. C. (1995). *Effective strategies for education students in at-risk situations*. National Dropout Prevention Center. Clemson, SC: Clemson University.

Edwards, C. H. (1993). *Classroom discipline and management*. New York: Macmillan.

Emmer, E. T., Evertson, C. M., Clements, B. S., & Worsham, M. E. (1997). *Classroom management for secondary teachers* (4th ed.). Boston: Allyn and Bacon.

Emmer, E. T., & Hickman, J. (1991). Teacher efficacy in classroom management and discipline. *Educational & Psychological Measurement, 51*(3), 755–766.

Evertson, C. M., Emmer, E. T., Clements, B. S., & Worsham, M. E. (1997). *Classroom management for elementary teachers* (4th ed.). Boston: Allyn and Bacon.

Girard, K., & Koch, S. J. (1996). *Conflict resolution in the schools*. San Francisco: Jossey-Bass.

Glasser, W. (1990). *The quality school.* New York: Harper & Row.

Gordon, T. (1974). *Teacher effectiveness training.* New York: David McKay.

Hogelucht, K. S. B., & Geist, P. (1997). Discipline in the classroom: Communicative strategies for negotiating order. *Western Journal of Communication, 61*(1), 1–34.

Johnson, D. W., & Johnson, R. T. (1996). Conflict resolution and peer mediation programs in elementary and secondary schools: A review of the research. *Review of Educational Research, 66*(4), 459–509.

Johnson, D. W., Johnson, R. T., Dudley, B., & Burnett, R. (1992). Teaching students to be peer mediators. *Educational Leadership, 50*(1), 10–15.

Jones, E. N., Ryan, K., & Bohlin, K. (1999). Character education and teacher education. *Action in Teacher Education, 20*(4), 11–28.

Jones, V. F., & Jones, L. S. (1998). *Comprehensive classroom management: Creating communities of support and solving problems* (5th ed.). Boston: Allyn and Bacon.

Kreidler, W. J. (1984). *Creative conflict resolution.* Glenview, IL: Scott, Foresman.

Kohn, A. (1996). *Beyond discipline: From compliance to community.* Alexandria, VA: Association for Supervision and Curriculum Development.

Lickona, T. (1999). Character education: Seven crucial issues. *Action in Teacher Education, 20*(4), 77–84.

McCarthy, C. (1992). Why must we teach peace. *Educational Leadership, 50*(1), 6–9.

Nimmo, D. (1997). Judicious discipline in the music classroom. *Music Educators Journal, 83*(4), 27–33.

Richert, A. E. (1992). Voice and power in teaching and learning to teach. In L. Valli (Ed.), *Reflective teacher education: Cases and critiques.* Albany: State University of New York Press.

Savage, T. V. (1991). *Discipline for self control.* Englewood Cliffs, NJ: Prentice Hall.

Thayer-Bacon, B. J., & Bacon, C. S. (1998). *Philosophy applied to education: Nurturing a democratic community in the classroom.* Upper Saddle River, NJ: Merrill/Prentice Hall.

Weinstein, C. S., & Mignano, A. J. (1997). *Elementary classroom management: Lessons from research and practice* (2nd ed.). New York: McGraw-Hill.

Weinstein, C. S. (1996). *Secondary classroom management: Lessons from research and practice.* New York: McGraw-Hill.

Zabel, R. H., & Zabel, M. K. (1996). *Classroom management in context: Orchestrating positive learning environments.* Boston: Houghton Mifflin.

Zeichner, K. M. (1990). Educational and social commitments in reflective teacher education programs. *Proceedings, Fourth National Forum, Association of Independent Liberal Arts Colleges for Teacher Education* (pp. 55–60).

Zeichner, K. M., & Liston, D. P. (1987). Teaching student teachers to reflect. *Harvard Educational Review, 57*(1), 23–48.

Maintaining the Learning Climate

> *"... We need nothing less than clear thinking, careful planning, excellent communication skills, and an overriding concern for the well being of students. Combining these skills with our current knowledge on effective practice will surely result in more efficient and more effective ... practices."*

> T. R. Guskey

Monumental Design

Why are you becoming a teacher? Do you want to work with youth? Do you like sharing knowledge with children? Do you enjoy working for youth's best interest? Are you hoping to help students learn how to care for themselves, each other, and the global community? How do you feel about working with teachers as colleagues? From watching and working with others who embody professional teacher characteristics, why do you feel drawn to teaching?

Teaching is a service-oriented profession. This means that people who choose teaching as a profession expect to derive job satisfaction from working with and for the well-being of others. Job satisfaction is evident in your enthusiasm for teaching and your positive mind-set toward the events and people within the school.

As you approach being inducted into the teaching profession, you see more clearly critical aspects of the teacher role. Your desire to work with youth now causes you to look at classroom policy and practices that are good for your students. You are concerned about their intellectual growth and are aware of your need to help them learn ways to interact with and contribute to the global community. You understand what being of service to others means in the daily routine of classroom life. You reinforce your students' gestures of helpfulness and validate their contributions to the lives of others. You encourage them to build a better world, beginning with their own—the classroom. You realize the rewards of teaching lie mainly in seeing your students grow. As a result of your student teacher experience, your understanding of teaching has reached a new level: you realize the impact you can effect on your students' lives, and this realization sharply focuses the teacher characteristics you value.

Do you find yourself asking your supervising teacher or college coordinator "What do you do when ...?" You raised the question because you are searching for help in finding a specific, practical, and real answer for a situation or problems you encounter. You are eager to know the "answer," to know what

Focus One

Expected Performance

- Identify beliefs and expectations of yourself as teacher that you prize.
- Design model that communicates the professional teacher.
- Discuss questions you have about teaching and how they relate to your future goals.

you *should* be doing to alleviate a particular crisis, perhaps one that affects the climate of your classroom. While knowledgeable outsiders can be resources, answers to problems and situations in the classroom and school must come from individuals in touch with the multiple inside variables (Wasserman, 1993). You are an "inside variable" and grasp the importance of resolving the problem yourself in conjunction with your students. Like other beginning teachers, you are concerned about maintaining a learning climate, and you recognize that your thinking and decision-making practices about daily classroom life are keys to realizing this goal.

As the teacher, you recognize that goals you have for your students are the major factors that influence your academic decisions and classroom policies designed to maintain the learning climate. Most likely you find yourself deciding between two approaches—a teacher-directed, information-dissemination model of teaching or a more constructive, student-centered approach (Jones & Jones, 1998). Considering what you want your students to know and do, you may choose to integrate both approaches during an extended class period. Your decisions and the goals pushing these decisions are guided by such considerations as the engagement and maturity levels of the students and the overall behavior patterns of the group. Rather than spotting and punishing misbehavior, you work hard to plan and establish systematically classroom groups that maintain quality work standards (Doyle, 1986). Your reflective approach to planning enables you to better match activities to student interests, while allowing your expectations for individual students to remain high.

The goals and expectations you hold for yourself as teacher are guided by your beliefs about your students' needs and their responses when challenged to meet academic standards and goals. Your student teaching experience encourages you to recognize the connection between your curricular and instructional decisions and your beliefs about the academic ability of the class and of individual students.

Good and Brophy (1994) maintain that "high expectations and commitment to bringing about student achievement are part of a pattern of attitudes, beliefs, and behavior that characterize schools that are successful in maximizing their students' learning gains" (p. 106). Considering classroom instructional experiences and the school climate where you now work, do you recognize the powerful impact of teachers' beliefs and expectations for students? Your search for answers to the question "What do I do when . . .?" is an important one. You may find help from others who are closely connected with the internal variables of the classroom setting you so diligently strive to manage. Be aware that your own beliefs, expectations, and goals impact the routine responses you make.

You are engaged with the school on a personal level. These are your students and their activities occupy your thoughts and interests. You are aware of practices that promote ethical standards for you and your students. Daily, you make choices keeping in mind what is in your students' best interest. Your awareness of teachers' ethical practices grows day by day as you learn about school and state policies, and such routine tasks as grading, confidentiality of records, responsibilities toward student journals, and writing portfolios. Professional ethics carries new meaning for you as you struggle with these issues.

You find the social organization of schools to be an inviting atmosphere. Observing and interacting with other teachers help you gauge your own level of dedication to teaching. You enjoy working with peers, especially those who are caring and open and seem happy in their profession. You find yourself drawn to those willing to assume new perspectives and accept challenges. In working with a team of dedicated professionals you now identify numerous teacher behaviors worth emulating. Teachers engaged in study and professional development or actively involved in creating rich learning experiences for their students have all influenced your understanding of *teacher*. You want to be like those teachers. You think you have made progress in developing a solid relationship with your supervising teacher and with other members of the team or department. You feel like a professional, and a career as a professional teacher has multidimensional meaning for you.

As a result of your experiences do you have different expectations for yourself as teacher? Your satisfaction with the job you are doing as a teacher depends on the success you realize from meeting these expectations, while allowing yourself to learn by making mistakes. Ask yourself this critical question: Do you feel enriched by working with and for youth? If the answer is a resounding "Yes!", you understand more clearly now than ever before the importance of the expectations you hold for yourself as teacher. Your student/intern teaching experiences allow you to describe specifically and work toward the professional teacher you aspire to become. Upon careful reflection, what teacher characteristics do you truly value? How do these contribute to the sense of satisfaction you experience as a result of your work as a teacher? What would your list of prized teacher characteristics contain? How might you symbolize these?

We suggest that you design a monument that captures you, the teacher. The monument may include words, phrases, symbols, and any other design elements you choose. You want persons viewing your monument to recognize the professional characteristics you value and the personality traits you cherish in a teacher. Viewers will immediately grasp and recognize the essence of your creation. You are the designer with an eye on the future!

Seminar Leader Tasks

- Provide 4-by-6 pieces of high quality paper for designing a monument.
- Make available or remind participants to bring pens or other drawing instruments.

Discussion Questions

1. In designing your monument, did you concentrate more on the present or on the future? How is the future represented?
2. Looking at your monument, are there certain characteristics or repeated themes? If so, what are they? Do you see words such as dedicated, decision maker, student advocate, risk taker, searcher, and student centered? How do these correspond to the beliefs and expectations you hold for yourself as teacher?
3. As students remember you as one of their teachers, what would you most like them to recall about you?

Focus Two

In **Focus One** you identified and discussed your experiences of student success with activities you planned and taught. Recognizing that your talents and abilities positively affect students' interest and engagement in activities boosts your self-confidence as a teacher. This can motivate you to take other risks in using a variety of teaching techniques. Varying teaching techniques and thus increasing the amount of time your students are engaged with instructional activities is at the very heart of creating and maintaining a learning climate.

APPLICATION: MAINTAINING THE LEARNING CLIMATE

In the last chapter you focused on the teacher attitudes and actions that contribute to a learning environment. Teachers deliberately choose preventive discipline approaches that are intended to promote student self-control and

Expected Performance

- Show consistent sensitivity to individual academic, physical, social, and cultural differences and respond to all students in a caring manner.
- Use classroom management techniques that foster self-control and self-discipline. Encourage responsibility to self and others.
- Promote student willingness and desire to receive and accept feedback.
- Use instructional strategies that interest and challenge students in a positive and supportive manner.
- Motivate, encourage, and support individual and group inquiry.

responsibility. Also fitting into the preventive stage of classroom management are rules and procedures that your supervising teacher, and perhaps you, introduced at the beginning of the school year. Monitoring rules and procedures and implementing consequences span the entire year and play an integral part in maintaining the classroom learning climate.

What does it mean to maintain a learning climate? You may hear teachers say, "I really like this school. I am able to teach every day." Teachers may be referring to their desire to spend most of each day engaged in instructional activities. Their greatest challenges are planning creative lessons, obtaining resources, teaching students, and assessing student work. Carefully planned instructional activities and meeting student needs take priority and help prevent misbehaviors from occurring. Does the above description fit your current teaching placement? People living and working together over a period of time can expect to encounter problems. Even in ideal school settings discipline problems occur.

Maintaining a learning climate depends on decisions you make when discipline problems interrupt classroom instruction. What is your initial reaction to the student who falls out of the desk? When students are poking, wrestling, and/or teasing one another? When they break into gales of laughter over a double entendre you unconsciously make in class? How does your supervising teacher respond to these types of problems? Have students disrupted instruction while you are teaching? How do you respond?

As the person in charge of classroom instruction, you are expected to resolve any disruption quickly and effectively and refocus students' attention on instruction. Your classroom observations provide examples of how experienced teachers respond to discipline problems. When a student acts out, you may act spontaneously and then observe the effects of your response on the individual. Later, you reflect on the incident and the results of your actions. After assessing your response, how satisfied are you with the action you took? Did you rely on a specific management theory or model you learned from an earlier course or classroom management class? What might you do differently the next time a student chooses to disrupt the class?

MODELS OF DISCIPLINE STRATEGIES

Summaries of selected models and theories are included below to help you connect theories with observations and practice in your classes. These models can assist you in clarifying your beliefs and applying your knowledge about classroom management strategies to the less-than-perfect situations you encounter in your classroom.

Instructional Management Strategies

The instructional management approach consists of appropriate instruction so carefully planned and implemented that it prevents most discipline problems and solves those not prevented (Weber, 1994). In addition to planning appropriate activities that address student needs, the instructional management approach also incorporates Kounin's research (1970). His studies found that teachers maintain quality instruction within the classroom through (1) preventing misbehavior, (2) managing movement, and (3) maintaining group focus.

- Preventing misbehavior refers to the teacher's ability to demonstrate:
  withitness—communicating general awareness of the classroom to students
  overlapping—attending to two or more simultaneous events
- Managing movement includes the two instructional skills:
  momentum—keeping lessons moving and avoiding slowdowns
  smoothness—staying on track

- Maintaining group focus is accomplished through:
  group alert—sustaining whole class attention to ongoing activity
  accountability—communicating that participation will be observed and evaluated
  high participation formats—engaging all students, those directly and not directly responding to tasks

Kounin's concepts for managing group instruction enable teachers to analyze and identify areas needing improvement (Evertson, Emmer, Clements, & Worsham, 1997). Practicing and using these methods in your classroom will allow you to move closer to the vision you hold for yourself as teacher.

Behavior Modification Strategies

Teaching students with special behavioral needs requires skillful use of behavior management skills. A number of strategies based on behavior modification are available to teachers in the regular classroom and those teaching in self-contained classrooms for special learners. We use the term *behavior modification* here in referring to any stimulus that maintains or increases the behavior exhibited immediately prior to the presentation of the stimulus. For example, in praising a student for raising a hand before responding, you increase the chances that every student in your class will raise their hands and wait to be called on before speaking.

Other strategies grounded in behavior modification theory include chaining, modeling, contingency contracting, and extinction.

- **Chaining** is a series of tasks you want students to perform independently and in a sequence. Its advantage is that you can teach and assess each task independently. Morning routine tasks are one example.
- **Modeling** means you demonstrate or publicly acknowledge actions and attitudes you want individuals or the entire class to display. You will want to be sensitive in using modeling with older students and not embarrass them before their peers.
- **Contingency contracting** is a written behavioral agreement between you and a student and can be applied to a variety of settings. Involving students in planning their own behavior improvement can lead to other positive results. Using positive reinforcement creates an inviting atmosphere, and you are likely to prefer these strategies.

If, however, your goal is to decrease an inappropriate behavior, you may need to apply some form of **extinction**, withholding from the student a reinforcing event or object. For example, if a student is acting inappropriately, withholding attention or assigning time-out from a reinforcing activity or situation may effectively reduce or eliminate an undesirable behavior.

Most student and intern teachers find using punishment a difficult choice to make. You may even squirm when reading the word. **Punishment** refers to using a strategy that decreases an undesirable behavior such as incompletion of work (Zirpoli & Melloy, 1997). What may appear to students as "punishment" (having the student complete an assignment before participating in a class activity) is simply providing them an opportunity to meet your expectations.

Socioemotional Climate Strategies

Appearing throughout the text are examples emphasizing the importance of strategies that contribute to the social and psychological (socioemotional) climate of the classroom. These strategies are appropriate for maintaining a learning climate and preventing discipline problems. Socioemotional strategies include skills such as listening attentively to others and teaching students to listen to each other (Weber, 1994). Think about the times when students come to your class with problems and you have the opportunity to help them. Most days you can relate to students in a positive and interpersonal manner and show empathy and understanding to students' expressing sadness, pain, and negative feelings about themselves. Modeling attentive listening and being present to students are powerful means toward establishing a positive learning climate.

Other strategies associated with creating a socioemotional climate call for honing interpersonal skills through one-to-one interactions, the use of conflict resolution, and other group processes. Teachers can model and teach students about Gordon's (1974) "I Messages" (clearly and without blame stating one's needs) and adopt suggestions from Glasser's **reality** and **control theories** (Glasser, 1969, 1986, 1990). You may want to research Glasser's suggestions for becoming personally involved, accepting the student but not the student's misbehavior, and confronting students with unacceptable behavior. Glasser also proposes a classroom meeting process that you can use to teach a whole class how to deal with the groups' behavior problems.

Assertive Discipline Strategies

Strategies from the assertive discipline model are authoritarian and directly address misbehavior. In using these strategies you convey to individuals and to the total group that you are in charge. When you observe that a rule is not being kept and you implement the consequence for breaking rules, you are using assertive discipline. Other strategies prevalent in the assertive model include proximity control (standing close to a misbehaving student or one not engaged in the assigned activity) and mild desist (a brief statement of disapproval quietly, gently spoken). These actions convey the message that you see your role as being responsible for students behaving according to classroom rules and administering consequences (Canter & Canter, 1992; Weber, 1994).

Teacher implementation of classroom rules and procedures plays a pivotal role in maintaining a learning climate. Student/intern teaching offers you an opportunity to experience the effect class rules have in meeting students' personal and nonacademic needs. Have you been "tested" by students to see if you and your supervising teacher are in agreement with the class rules and procedures? When you see a student breaking class rules, what do you say and do? You are aware that teachers need to know and follow up students' responses to school and district rules. The student teaching/intern experience provides you opportunities to formulate, implement, and monitor rules both in the classroom and the entire school setting.

We encourage you to consult with other teachers and to read and review theories and suggestions by other educators as you continue to learn about classroom management. The Reference and Suggested Readings section at the end of this chapter offers sources on models and theories and other discipline-related topics.

SAFE SCHOOLS

The concern about school safety includes and extends beyond the routine care you take in storing and using materials and in physically arranging furnishings as precautionary safeguards against classroom accidents. Schools reflect society, and the escalating incidences of violence in schools corresponds with what is happening in society. Along with considerations of strategies used when behavior problems occur, we ask you to consider issues related to current emphasis on safe schools. Rather than focus on the word *violence*, many educators prefer the positive term *safe schools*. The emphasis is on dissipating situations and problems before they result in violence, a preventive approach to creating a safe school.

Violence is defined as physical and nonphysical harm that causes damage, pain, injury, or fear (Dear, 1995). In presenting school violence we want to help you learn your school's plans for maintaining safety. Even though you may have thought about your role as teacher in providing safety for your students and you, we encourage you to use your current experience for present and future planning. Part of planning is to gather information about school board policy and determine how the information involves you. What do you do when name calling and verbal put-downs occur in your classroom? What is expected of teachers when fights break out between students in the classroom or hallways? What are you expected to do if you suspect a student is carrying a weapon or using drugs? Providing a safe environment for you and your students can be accomplished generally with foresight and planning.

Most boards of education are addressing issues pertaining to safe schools. Policies are adopted for possession of drugs, bringing guns, knives, and other weapons to school, and eliminating gang activity. Schools collaborate with community resources, especially law enforcement officers, on safety issues affecting children and adolescents. You might inquire about programs that exist for teachers in your school district and how you can become better informed about existing threats to safety in the community where you teach.

Learning about and obtaining available community resources, working with parents, and taking advantage of programs for preventing outbreaks of violence are some suggestions for promoting safe schools. You may locate sources within your school and seek assistance from community groups. With students in your classes, you can contribute to the safe school environment by sharing your expertise and teaching them to deal nonphysically with everyday conflicts.

The Reference and Suggested Readings section at the end of this chapter provides you with information about school violence, safe schools, and suggested approaches for schools and teachers. Due to a number of extreme cases currently threatening school safety, new programs and information continuously emerge. You are encouraged to take advantage of opportunities that prepare and protect you and your students.

As a student/intern teacher you are adjusting to being in charge. In accepting your role as leader, you are responsible for choosing strategies for managing student behavior. As teacher, you decide which strategies you think will sustain student involvement in learning tasks. When students are disruptive, you select another set of strategies aimed at eliminating the disruption and refocusing attention to the task at hand. Adjusting to the authority role and deciding on intervention and prevention strategies for specific situations takes time and continued practice. We intend that these Assigned Activities offer you the opportunity to reflect on decisions you make for maintaining a safe and positive learning climate in your classes.

ASSIGNED ACTIVITIES

The following activities are intended to help you consider strategies for maintaining a learning climate. You are asked to respond to them as part of your reflections on what you are observing and implementing in the classroom and on the effects of your actions.

1. For which rules and procedures do you most frequently need to apply consequences? Which rules do you periodically review? How has your student/intern teaching experience changed your understanding about class rules and procedures?

2. From what sources can you learn the school and district policies for promoting a safe school? Are there written expectations of teachers in promoting a safe learning environment? Are student/teacher policy handbooks readily available and implemented?

3. Table 9.1 lists discipline techniques described in this chapter. While reflecting on your teaching each day refer to the Discipline Techniques Table and mark those you used.

4. Describe three incidents that challenged you to resolve a discipline problem this week. What techniques did you use in resolving the problem? Under which model are the techniques listed? How effective are the techniques you choose in maintaining a learning climate in your classroom?

    Problem:

    Technique used:

    Under which model is the technique listed?

    How effective was the technique you used in maintaining the learning climate in your classroom?

5. In assessing your growth as a teacher, discuss an important insight you now have about maintaining a learning climate? Name an area of classroom management that you want to strengthen.

SUMMARY

Over the past weeks you have reflected on the different components contributing to a learning climate. Your journal entries address the management of instruction and explain your reasons for decisions you made to meet student needs. Every day you monitor and apply rules and procedures established for the class. When looking back to your first days in the classroom and comparing that time with now, you perhaps can sense an increase in student self-control and personal responsibility. Are you feeling a sense of ownership toward this shift? Sharing the responsibility for helping create and maintain a positive atmosphere? You want your students to experience success in your class. You want students to be happy and behave! In this seminar you are encouraged to recognize what you know about discipline strategies and to consider *when* and *why* you apply them in the school setting. After sharing your concerns and questions with peers, you may discover that yours are quite normal. You may feel more confident about managing student behavior and find yourself better able to de-escalate situations before they flare out of control.

FOLLOW-UP QUESTIONS AND SHARED INSIGHTS

As you converse with your peers about the discipline techniques you observed and used last week, refer to your journal. The following questions offer you an opportunity to share your experiences with preventing and/or eliminating misbehavior.

1. Explain what connections you see between instructional planning and management and managing student behavior. You might consider specific topics: teacher enthusiasm, questioning techniques, group work, use of technology, etc.

2. Which class rules do you most often remind students to observe? What seems to renew students' motivation to follow procedures? How successful are the stated consequences in preventing repeated rule breaking?

TABLE 9.1 *Discipline Techniques*

	Discipline Techniques	Times Used	Individual	Group	Effect on Individual Learner/Class Discipline
1	Ignores inappropriate behavior				
2	Rewards appropriate behavior				
3	Refers to another learner model ("I like the way . . .")				
4	Assigns time-out				
5	Assigns cleanup area				
6	Student compensates for damages				
7	Withholds privileges				
8	Assigns extra work				
9	Sends student to the office				
10	Calls parents, solicits support				
11	Demonstrates withitness/ overlapping				
12	Maintains group focus: alert-accountable-participative				
13	Manages movement				
14	Moves close to student				
15	Places hand on shoulder— behavior noticed while class continues				
16	Listens and encourages learner to express problems				
17	Encourages cooperation				
18	Student describes own behavior; states improved course of action				
19	Describes situation, expresses feelings, clarifies expectations				

3. Using the Discipline Techniques in Table 9.1, share with others what you consider to be effective techniques in maintaining a learning climate. Explain why you think they are effective.

4. Name a technique that you were not successful in applying and explain why you think the technique did not work. How might others help you to successfully apply this technique?

5. What discipline techniques do you want to acquire? You might describe specific events in your classroom and ask others' suggestions for dealing with them.

6. With which aspects of discipline are you now feeling more comfortable?

Journal Excerpts

High School

"Sixth period was the only class that gave me trouble today. The problem was not students talking too much but it was talking too little! That class does not like to participate! We were discussing a short story they had read in their books. I was using the discussion questions as my starting point. Then I moved away from prepared questions and lost the focus. Unfortunately, they would not respond to me! They would give me an answer from the book, but if I asked for any type of opinion-based answer they clammed up. I think one of the factors is that they are a quiet group, and I have not taught them a lot. We just need to 'get used' to each other."

"I have been working hard at using myself to model behavior. I'm aware of my body position, location, eye contact, hand on shoulder, etc. This has been working well. Today in the 4th period I had a group of students who were easily distracted. I decided to pull up a desk and sit between them for part of the period. This really worked. They spent the remainder of the period working and utilizing every moment and were surprised at how much they had accomplished. I did this again in 5th period. Although I'm still not where I want to be with this class, I feel like I am well on my way. I think that I have come a long way in a week, and that mainly is because of my desire and determination to teach this class, and for my students to be successful."

"There are times that I need to ignore the students who are only 'acting up' to get attention from me. By always acknowledging them, they are receiving a message that reinforces their behavior. On the other hand, I also must pay attention to students who may need me but are too quiet or self-conscious to call their needs to my attention in any way. I have to make sure to always include them in my interactions . . ."

"As I watched the students in small groups, I noticed one girl was talking with another about her boyfriend, while the others were trying to complete the group assignment. I slowly walked up to the group and pretended to intently study the group's guiding question. After a couple of seconds, the two not working looked at me. I said, 'Oh! I was just trying to figure out where (boyfriend's name) was in the question I gave you!' They both turned red and smiled nervously at me—they knew what I meant!"

Middle School

"As I watched the students come into the classroom, I mentioned to my supervising teacher that one student in our 6th period class had gotten in trouble every period today. In holding true to form, the boy shoved another boy and threatened him, and a serious shoving match ensued. Luckily, Mrs. A. was right behind them and she broke it up quickly (which she normally doesn't do—she's pretty small compared to these boys). She conferenced with the boys, calmed them down, and set up a peer mediation meeting between them for tomorrow."

"I was taken aback today when our notoriously loud and unfocused 4th period class performed so well. Normally they get one or two lectures about behavior and respect everyday. However, today for some reason, they focused beautifully, read well and acted out the words in an interesting manner. It was a pleasant way to end the day because it reaffirmed my belief that all students are capable of focusing on learning and succeeding!"

"I did a lot of one-on-one work with students today. We have a hyper student who never does his work, sits still, or stops talking. Today, I sat down with him for awhile and encouraged his ideas. I kept telling him he wasn't stupid (as he said), he could do it, and I praised him when he did. After awhile, I left him on his own. When the class went on to the next activity, he came to show me that he had finished. I was stunned . . . so proud . . . of him and myself, too."

"What a day! I had the class by myself and looking back, I can tell I was tense about teaching. I gave one warning and then I threatened detentions if they weren't quiet. One student said I wasn't a teacher and couldn't give a detention. I said I could and felt badly for being so harsh. Sometimes I worry they will take advantage of me, looking so young and being so small."

Elementary School

"I found that Mrs. J. uses a great many techniques. I have been watching and learning a great deal. I am very impressed by the way she handled a student that lied. Mrs. J. made it very clear to that student and the entire class that she would not tolerate lying in her class. She asked the other students what they thought about lying. She turned this situation into a true learning experience for everyone."

"I do not feel good about how I managed behavior today . . . . I think I need to prepare myself better. I should look at the pages before I introduce them to the learners even though the book is on tape. I had serious problems with one student. For some reason I have the hardest time getting him to mind me. When I try to talk to him, he covers his ears or runs from me. I wonder if it's because he doesn't think there will be any solid consequences for disobeying me. I must decide how I want to discipline him and then follow through with my plan. It just gets to me because he intentionally misbehaves. I have a hard time dealing with this."

"After today, I feel much more confident. During my learning center time, I set rules and established consequences. I stuck to them and also used a lot of sticker reinforcement."

"I'm still struggling to gain the respect of the children. While many of the children see me as their teacher, there are still those few who test me every single day. I give warnings, and I talk with each child, but they could care less about what I am saying. When I am with these students, I feel as though I am losing control quickly. I need to find ways to keep the ball in my court. I know I need to be in charge and maintain control. I just feel as though these few students are throwing me for a loop and holding me back. This is something I will work on during this placement."

Special Education

"C. had a rough day for the first time this year. I am not really sure what targeted his outburst today but he had to be placed in time-out twice. He ran around the room pulling books off the shelves and turning over chairs. I was in the room with the assistant when this first occurred. I began taking points from him and could see his behavior was escalating. It was very uncomfortable for me to feel I could place a child in time-out. I know Mrs. B. would support my action but it still was very scary. Mrs. B. returned to the room just as C. would have to be put in the time-out room. She came in and placed him in the time-out room without hesitation or question."

"I was talking to L. about appropriate behavior since he had run to the chalkboard and charged me with his head. When I told him he could answer again if he were sitting in his seat, he said, 'like the way I am sitting?' He squats down like he is sitting, however, there is no chair. This is when it becomes difficult to correct his behavior because his actions are so sporadic and funny. I continued to go on with the lesson and bragged about R. for sitting properly. L. jumped in his seat and said, 'I want to be good.' He is so funny, yet needs so much help."

"The fifth grade student who comes from the Behavior Disorders room wore me down today in reading class. Finally, after many cues and direct corrections, I deemed it necessary to explicitly conference with T. about appropriate and inappropriate behaviors. I think it is very difficult to instruct when you continuously have to stop and correct behavior. I have to learn to ignore a lot more of T's behaviors than I have been."

REFERENCES AND SUGGESTED READINGS

Bauer, A. M., & Sapona, R. H. (1991). *Managing classrooms to facilitate learning.* Englewood Cliffs, NJ: Prentice Hall.

Bey, T. M., & Turner, G. Y. (1996). *Making school a place of peace.* Thousand Oaks, CA: Corwin Press.

Burden, P. R. (1995). *Classroom management and discipline: Methods to facilitate cooperation and instruction.* White Plains, NY: Longman.

Canter, L., & Canter, M. (1992). *Assertive discipline: Positive behavior management for today's classroom.* Santa Monica, CA: Lee Canter & Associates.

Charles, C. M. (1996). *Building classroom discipline* (5th ed.). White Plains, NY: Longman.

Cipani, E. (1998). *Classroom management for all teachers: 11 effective plans.* Upper Saddle River, NJ: Merrill/Prentice Hall.

Dear, J. D. (1995). *Creating caring relationships to foster academic excellence: Recommendations for reducing violence in California schools.* Sacramento: California Commission on Teacher Credentialing.

Doyle, W. (1986). Classroom organization and management. In M. C. Wittrock (Ed.), *Handbook of research on teaching* (pp. 392–425). New York: Macmillan.

Edwards, C. H. (1997). *Classroom discipline & management* (2nd ed.). Upper Saddle River, NJ: Merrill/Prentice Hall.

Emmer, E. T., Evertson, C. M., Clements, B. S., & Worsham, M. E. (1997). *Classroom management for secondary teachers* (4th ed.). Boston: Allyn and Bacon.

Evertson, C. M., Emmer, E. T., Clements, B. S., & Wortham, M. E. (1997). *Classroom management for elementary teachers* (4th ed.). Boston: Allyn and Bacon.

Glasser, W. (1990). *Quality school: Managing students without coercion.* New York: Harper & Row.

Glasser, W. (1986). *Control theory in the classroom.* New York: Harper & Row.

Glasser, W. (1969). *Schools without failure.* New York: Harper & Row.

Good, T. L., & Brophy, J. E. (1994). *Looking in classrooms.* New York: Harper Collins College Publishers, pp. 83–127.

Gordon, T. (1974). *T.E.T. Teacher effectiveness training.* New York: David McKay.

Guskey, T. R. (Ed.). (1996). *Communicating student learning 1996 ASCD yearbook.* Alexandria, VA: Association for Supervision and Curriculum Development.

Hamby, J. V. (1995). *Straight talk about discipline.* Clemson, SC: National Dropout Prevention Center.

Jones, V. F., & Jones, L. S. (1998). *Comprehensive classroom management: Creating communities of support and solving problems* (5th ed.). Boston: Allyn and Bacon.

Koenig, L. (1995). *Smart discipline for the classroom: Respect and cooperation restored* (Rev. ed.). Thousand Oaks, CA: Corwin Press.

Kounin, J. S. (1970). *Discipline and group management in classrooms.* New York: Holt, Rinehart and Winston.

Savage, T. V. (1991). *Discipline for self-control.* Englewood Cliffs, NJ: Prentice Hall.

Wallach, L. B. (1994). Violence and young children's development. Urbana, IL: ERIC Clearinghouse on Elementary and Early Childhood Education EDO-PS-94-7.

Wasserman, S. (1993). *Getting down to cases: Learning to teach with case studies.* New York: Teachers College, Columbia University.

Weber, W. A. (1994). Classroom management. In J. M. Cooper (Gen. Ed.), *Classroom teaching skills.* Lexington, MA: D.C. Heath.

Weinstein, C. S. (1996). *Secondary classroom management: Lessons from research and practice.* New York: McGraw-Hill.

Weinstein, C. S., & Mignano, Jr., A. J. (1997). *Elementary classroom management: Lessons from research and practice* (2nd ed.). New York: McGraw-Hill.

Zabel, R. H., & Zabel, M. K. (1996). *Classroom management in context: Orchestrating positive learning environment.* Boston: Houghton Mifflin.

Zirpoli, T. J., & Melloy, K. J. (1997). *Behavior management: Applications for teachers and parents* (2nd ed.). Upper Saddle River, NJ: Merrill/Prentice Hall.

Assessing Student Learning

Focus One

I'm Feeling Proud of . . .

When was the last time a student asked you, "How am I doing?" Have you asked the same of your supervising teacher or university coordinator? A one-word verbal or written response does not satisfy your need to know, nor does it satisfy your students' desire for feedback. Reflecting on your day-by-day teaching can be a tool for authentic learning, a means for analyzing your performance in the classroom. You are actively connecting your knowledge of teaching with your understanding of the learning community, the instruction, and the mission of your school. Higher-level thinking, creativity, basic and cultural literacy, disciplinary mastery, and responsible membership in society are expected of you in this professional setting (Newmann, Secada, & Wehlage, 1995). Feedback and other authentic assessment measures indicate how you are doing in this learning-to-teach situation and enable you to set goals and work toward meeting or exceeding them. Likewise, you want to facilitate your students' academic growth and develop further competencies in assessing their progress.

Your professional need to learn and apply an assortment of authentic assessment tools leads you to content standards and standards established by states and national goals. Using standards aligns your teaching with that of the National Commission of Teaching and America's Future: ". . . new curriculum and assessments need to support challenging academic coursework from elementary school to high school and higher standards for graduation that better reflect the demands of today's society. Assessments of performance should provide richer information about learning throughout the grades and evaluations at the end of high school that are relevant to the decisions of colleges and employers." You want students to be happy, productive, and well-educated citizens. Clearly stating performance standards helps students know the expectations they have to meet and recognize where they need to improve. You grasp the connection between a student's sense of accomplishment and growth as a learner. You understand the importance of students' meeting goals and

Expected Performance

• Examine what is involved in the assessment process.

• Explore the implications of assessment for teachers and students.

• Share feelings connecting your students' successes with your accomplishments as teacher.

standards and work hard to assess their progress in myriad ways (Urban, 1999; Zmuda & Tomaino, 1999).

The contemporary emphasis on changing student assessment practices mirrors the trend in teacher education's evaluative practices. For example, the constructivist approach to learning (the model you are observing and practicing) influences such instructional methods as integrated language arts, "hands-on, minds-on" approaches in science, writing to learn across the curriculum, problem solving and reasoning in mathematics, and cooperative learning. Likewise, these complex teaching methods/philosophies require authentic and multiple assessment measures. As a practicing professional, you write journals, create lessons and teaching units that address standards, demonstrate teaching practices, develop a professional portfolio, and initiate dialogue with your supervisors. Each of these measures provide information about the question, "How am I doing?" These sources communicate a more complete road map of what you have accomplished and highlight directions for where you are heading next in learning to teach. These authentic assessment processes tell the unfolding story of your learning and growth as an educator.

Do you remember the story of Peter Pan? Peter Pan repeatedly begged Wendy to tell him stories. Like Peter Pan most of us like to hear stories, especially animated stories embellished with details that capture our imagination and emotions. We identify with the characters and we learn from them by vicariously living the story. Do you enjoy hearing stories? Do you delight in sharing or hearing stories about yourself? Through stories we come to know ourselves on a different level and learn to evaluate our actions in light of the events that shape the story.

Your story includes the events, decisions, and learning that make up your personal experience of becoming a teacher. Your evolving understanding of the teacher's role validates your beliefs and knowledge about teaching. Your deeper involvement in the teacher's role helps you analyze your prior experiences in a new light. Your talents and special abilities have helped you refine your dreams about teaching as a career. Unlike Peter Pan, you have grown, ever moving toward becoming a "grown-up" teacher—a new, unique creation, willing to take on the responsibilities of educating young people. Taking time to assess your personal story and the events, actions, and choices you make along the way encourages your growth as a professional.

Like Peter Pan, teachers can also delight in stories. The nature of teachers' work makes for good storytelling because they come to this experience wanting to make a difference in the lives of children and adolescents. Whether this is your first career choice or you come to teaching from another background, you are becoming a teacher! Your prior experiences contribute to the many wonderful and unique characteristics you bring to the art of teaching. Through interactions with your seminar group, you are likely to discover that you and your peers share similar motivation for wanting to teach. In the following activity you are invited to share your stories and the gifts you bring to the profession.

Through your classroom stories you are brought to the realization that your success is a result of your students' success stories. Your stories are intertwined, overlapped. They are created together. In assessing your students' progress, you assess your own and often find reasons to celebrate and acknowledge growth—theirs and your own! When your students engage in creative activities you planned, it validates your ability to plan effectively. When your students can't believe it is time for class to end, their enthusiasm motivates you to make the next lesson more creative! When peers ask you to share a teaching technique and later thank you for the success they experienced, it affirms your belief in yourself as an effective teacher.

How do you evaluate yourself as a professional? Is it linked to others' successes, your own initiative, positive responses, and engagement with others?

How does it feel to work with students who are engaged in a learning activity you planned, one based on professional standards? How does it feel when others listen to your innovative teaching suggestions and include them in their lesson plans? How does experiencing a sense of pride in what you do and knowing how you affect others deepen your understanding of teaching?

Discussion Questions

1. Name an ability or talent that others have recognized in you and tell how you used this ability or talent in teaching.
2. When your students are happy with their accomplishments, you very likely "feel proud" of them and of yourself. Give examples of students' "proudest moments," times when they met an instructional goal or performance standard you designed. Think about your response to your students' success. How might seeing your students succeed help you become a better teacher?
3. Telling others about your abilities and talents may sound like bragging or boasting, and you may feel uncomfortable doing so. What connections are there between describing your abilities and talents and documenting ways you meet certain professional teaching standards?

Focus Two

Expected Performance

- Demonstrate multiple assessment and sources of data.
- Use formal and informal assessment strategies to evaluate and ensure the continuous intellectual, social, and physical development of the learner.
- Accurately assess student performance using established criteria and scoring guides consistent with the school system assessment program.
- Make appropriate provisions for assessment processes that address social, cultural, and physical diversity.

Focus One addresses the teacher you aspire to become. You identified the teacher characteristics you value and the different expectations you hold for yourself as teacher. During this time of tremendous personal learning about the different teacher roles, you are better able to clarify and prioritize your goals. One of the most demanding roles you experience as teacher is that of assessor. Understanding the assessment process is critical to your development as a professional educator. **Focus Two** addresses the importance of assessing what students know and have learned because of your instructional goals. Communicating these results to students and parents or guardians involves a thorough understanding of the assessment process.

The key to effective assessment connects the assessment with intended learner outcomes. All students learn differently and their needs vary. As educators, we want to take students beyond rote learning into discovery and higher levels of thinking. Teachers use a variety of teaching strategies to help students learn, assess the degree of learning, and determine how successfully learners have translated the strategy into personal learning.

APPLICATION: ASSESSING STUDENT LEARNING

As a 21st century teacher you will use multiple means for assessing student thinking, problem solving, and verbal and written responses to learning tasks. No process is more central to teaching than evaluation, a process that involves collecting information, forming judgments, and making decisions. Properly designed assessment instruments and procedures can improve decision making regarding learner performance. Assessment, therefore, is essential for improvement of the curriculum, of instruction, and of student learning.

You want to reflect with your students on the learning process, and their progress in achieving the stated expectations. The assessment methods (such as scoring guides or rubrics) you select will inform and challenge the learners to reach higher levels of thinking, self-learning, and self-assessment.

> "When students and teachers make use of reflection as a tool for learning and assessment, they are creating an opening that allows them to enter into students' work, making sense of their endeavors and accomplishments, and learning how they judge their success."
>
> Zessoules & Gardner (1991) p. 58

A number of methods of assessment can measure student performance and progress. Testing is the most conventional source of data, and probably the most familiar to you. Alternative assessments are becoming more common in classrooms today, and many educators design their own criteria and standards for student work.

Alternative, Authentic, and Performance Assessment

The terms, *alternative assessment*, *authentic assessment*, and *performance assessment* are often used synonymously, yet have different meanings. Reviewing the terms at this point gives you a broader picture of assessment.

- **Alternative assessment** usually applies to all assessments different from the multiple-choice, timed approaches that characterize most standardized and many teacher-made tests. Alternative assessment affects teachers and students in a number of ways. Teachers continually reflect on student needs and assessment results and begin to view every activity in light of assessment. Students become more reflective and self-assessing; they begin to take responsibility for their own learning.
- **Authentic assessment** conveys the idea that students are engaged in applying knowledge and skills to real-life situations and problems. The purpose of authentic assessment is intended to help students understand their own work in relation to that of others, to see new possibilities and challenges in their verbal and written assignments, and to refine and redesign their responses. Reflection and self-assessment are vital to this process. Planning for authentic assessment has a significant influence on the instruction provided the student.
- **Performance assessment** indicates students' progress through demonstrating their understanding and application of knowledge, skills, and attitudes. As instructional strategies become more diverse so must the form of assessment change. These assessments over time result in a tangible product or observable performance assisting the students to improve their learning.

Information gained from student performance assists the teacher with instructional decisions. Learner performance is evaluated not only to determine the extent to which your students meet your expectations; it also provides you with information to make sound instructional decisions. Once your assessment is designed to be educative, you no longer separate it from instruction. It is a major, essential, and integrated part of teaching and learning (Wiggins, 1998).

Standards for Authentic Pedagogy and Student Academic Performance

Newmann, Marks, and Gamoran (1995) have developed standards for authentic pedagogy and student academic performance. Their model is designed to determine the extent to which teachers use authentic assessment tasks and teach authentic lessons. These authors are clear that not every instructional or assessment activity need fulfill all three standards. But they encourage you to keep

authentic achievement as your ultimate goal. Reflect on their criteria that serve as guides for student achievement:

Construction of knowledge—students interpret, synthesize, and evaluate complex information producing new meaning for them.
Disciplined inquiry—students demonstrate an in-depth understanding of a particular problem or issue.
Value beyond school—students make connections between school activities and their own experiences and the world beyond the classroom.

At this point, your development of assessment activities may be at the novice or apprentice stage. Nevertheless, having a grasp of the relationship between the instructional objectives and the assessment activities is an important step toward authentic achievement, your ultimate goal!

Keep in mind several attributes related to assessments as you develop your assessment system. Effective assessment is:

- **continuous or ongoing.** Daily and weekly assessment of identified teaching goals and assessing the progress of each learner are the first steps toward authentic assessment. Redesigning the curriculum to suit the learner's individual needs leads to success for the teacher and the learner.
- **flexible.** Assessment needs to concentrate on the identified areas of weakness or goals for each learner. Effective teachers are always adjusting their instructional activity to meet the needs of the individual learner.
- **cumulative.** A longitudinal approach to assessment puts the results of any one assessment into perspective. A sampling of student work (portfolio) over time is one example of implementing a cumulative approach to assessment.
- **diverse.** Multiple instruments should be used to assess learner progress. Combining a variety of views of performance paints a clearer picture of learner achievement. There simply is no one right way to assess students.

Your selection and use of the various assessment instruments involve much reflection and research. The choice of an assessment instrument depends on the evaluative decisions you want to make about student learning. When you assess what you value and value what you assess, you remain true to your mission of educating those in your care, challenging them to meet or exceed your expectations for them as learners. Educational integrity begins with you, the classroom teacher, before you can encourage integrity in the schools that are vital within a community.

Table 10.1 provides a variety of assessment instruments and their use in making evaluative decisions.

TABLE 10.1 *Assessment Instruments: Type and Use*

Prior to (Diagnostic)	Ongoing (Formative)	Final (Summative)
Pretests	Quizzes	Teacher-made tests
Observations	Discussion	Portfolios
Journals/logs	Assignments	Projects
Discussions	Projects	Standardized tests
Placement tests	Teacher-made tests	Discussion
Standardized tests	Checklists	
Questionnaires	Observations	
Interviews	Portfolios Journals/logs Standardized tests	

The learner's response to any one of the assessment tasks can be influenced by a variety of environmental factors. Preparing learners by discussing the assessment strategies with them may give you new insights about the individuals and allay some learner anxiety. Your sensitivity and encouragement may increase their ability to stay on task, think for themselves, and complete the assessment with a positive attitude.

ASSIGNED ACTIVITIES

1. Select one assessment instrument you are currently using or have recently used. The questions below are intended to help you examine the assessment process. Referring to the instrument you selected, respond to the questions about the assessment process you are conducting.
   a. What outcome(s) are to be measured?
   b. Is it group or individual work? If group work, what roles are expected to be fulfilled?
   c. What options or choices are allowed? Describe the choices, i.e., written, verbal, action, etc. Who makes the choice? Teacher, student, or both?
   d. What materials or equipment will be available to students? Are there any specifications?
   e. Are the activities given a time limit? How does the time affect student performance? Is peer assistance permitted?
2. Which of the assessment strategies in Table 10.2 have you examined and/or used with learners?

TABLE 10.2 *Assessment Instruments*

Assessment Instruments	Examined	Used
Observations		
Student interviews		
Written tests		
Performance events/exhibitions		
Journals		
Autobiographies		
Criterion-referenced tests		
Group work		
Checklists		
Standardized achievement tests		
Homework		
Videotapes		
Case studies		
Anecdotal records		
Portfolio entries		
Rubrics		
Conferences		
Rating scales		

SUMMARY

Focusing on assessment, you are more conscious of the connection between learning strategies and student performance. Perhaps your reflections include questions about the academic levels of the learning strategies you use. Did you ask yourself: Were my students engaged in activities of value that produced new meaning? Do my students' activities reflect an understanding of a specific concept, problem, or skill? Did I meet the ability levels of all my students? Can my students relate or apply this task, this activity to the world beyond the classroom?

If authentic assessment is to influence the learning process, then the various assessment instruments need to reflect the academic expectations of the teachers. You as the teacher, or with other team members, select the assessment instrument that matches the stated expectations. Through your choice of the appropriate assessment, you communicate to the learners what is important, what they are expected to know and be able to do, and what deserves their attention and focus.

FOLLOW-UP QUESTIONS AND SHARED INSIGHTS

Using the following questions, share the results you found from examining, planning, and using assessment instruments.

1. Using Table 10.2, which assessment instruments have you used this week? How does this information help you make decisions concerning learner progress?
2. In what ways did you use assessment in making changes to improve instruction? Give specific examples.
3. Using the information written in your journal, explain how assessment strategies influenced the instructional techniques you planned.
4. To what extent do your test items correspond with the learner outcomes stated in your lesson plans?
5. How was student progress determined? Were any provisions made for exceptional learners?

Portfolio Tasks

Assessing and Communicating Learning Results
New Teacher Standards
- The teacher proposes both formal and informal assessment experiences that are developmentally appropriate for learners, allow different modes for student response, and reflect the specific content being taught.
- The teacher makes appropriate provision for assessment processes that address social, cultural, and physical diversity.
- The teacher provides students with information about a systematic way of assessing student work that is consistent with the school system's performance assessment program.
- The teacher focuses student attention on what needs to be done to move to the next performance level.

Performance Guidelines
1. Briefly address the social, cultural, and physical diversity of your class and school community. Specify the content areas you are teaching.

2. Describe how you help students understand the performance level you expect of them and what is needed to progress to the next level.
3. Draft a letter to the parents helping them understand the assessment process used with your classes.
   a. Name and briefly describe the different assessment instruments you plan to use with your students.
   b. Explain how grades for assessment activities will be decided.

Performance Criteria

The quality of your entry will be assessed to the extent that evidence provided:

- Proposes both formal and informal assessment experiences that are developmentally appropriate for learners, allow different accommodations for student response, and reflect the specific content being taught.
- Makes appropriate provision for assessment processes that address social, cultural, and physical diversity.
- Provides students with information about a systematic way of assessing student work that is consistent with the school system's performance assessment program.
- Focuses student attention on what needs to be accomplished to progress to the next performance level.

Journal Excerpts

High School

"The assessment strategy for my freshman English class was a scoring guide that I made to help me grade their independent novel projects. I made up this rubric before I ever introduced the independent novel project to the students. I wanted to make sure that they knew exactly what was expected of them. When I introduced the project, I gave each student a handout which stated the specific criteria on which I would be grading the project."

"Projects assigned to students are evaluated briefly at the formative level to keep students 'on track.' For example, various stages of writing are collected to check progress. Then, students receive a summative evaluation on the final result. Portfolio entries are often items which students are allowed to revise at least one time before receiving the summative evaluation. All of these entries are placed on file with all of their other pieces of work."

"I have to really try to stay focused and fair when I am reading and grading several papers in a row. This is difficult, because the mind can wander off, or become tired and miss things in a paper. I always try to keep my responses positive in at least one aspect, while also offering constructive criticism. I actually enjoy responding to papers, and the more I do, the more confident I feel."

Middle School

"In first period, I am grading notebooks. Ms. L. is conferencing with writers from another class and I listened in on some of those! The class is writing 'memoirs.' I'd never even heard of those and they are required for state portfolios, so I am learning along with the students."

"I was pleased to read the limericks from those students who handed in their homework. I found that most of the limericks the students turned in did fit the qualifications for being a limerick. However, the most common mistakes were: (1) there were too many or too few syllables in a particular line, (2) the words at the end of the lines didn't rhyme. To address this, I commented on each student's paper accordingly and deducted points for limericks with errors in rhyme, form, syllabication, and humor qualifications."

"Today's test offered a new challenge. I caught one of my favorite students cheating on the exam. He had made a cheat sheet with all of the formulas in small, block print. I took his exam from him and told him to see me after class. I knew if I tried to handle it right then I would have lost my temper and would not have thought rationally. As I walked to the back of the room, I began thinking to myself, 'I wonder how many of my other students have cheated on my exams? Have I paid close enough attention?' After class, I called him over to talk about the situation. I talked to him for at least fifteen minutes. I asked him, 'What do you think I should do?' He would only respond with 'Give me a zero.' I wasn't going to give him a zero because I did not want to destroy him, but I wanted to teach a lesson. So I told him to be at study skills the next day to take a new test that would be much harder than the previous. He then had to take the grade he received on the test. I hope it works."

Elementary Education

"An oral performance type of test/project was performed by the students each day last week. The students were required to give oral book reports (3–5 minutes) about a person's life. These were videotaped. They also had to turn in a written report."

"One method of formative evaluation that I use often is journaling. I give them a topic to journal at the end of every class period. The topic usually flows directly from the lesson/discussion and is in addition to homework (as they are given the last few minutes of class time to complete it). I take these up every day and make comments on every one before I return them. This allows me to gauge their progress in grasping crucial elements and also to direct their thinking in the direction of deeper meanings."

"I taught Reading formally today for the first time. It went okay, but I'm trying to think of ways to spice up the discussion. I think I might allow them to act out scenes tomorrow. I think that would also be a neat assessment activity instead of the formal test that would normally follow the completion of a unit."

Special Education

"I was asked to give another Brigance. So first thing this morning, I gave the test. I almost cried. This little boy should already be in a self contained unit. He is in the second grade and he does not have accurate letter recognition. On the test, he could only recognize four to five letters. I cannot believe a child has gotten this far in his education without services. I was told that last year he was not tested in because his attendance was so poor. He is a sweet child that tries hard, but I can see that if we do not get him some help soon he is going to acquire behavior problems due to the frustration level."

"I got pretty involved today in the collaborative classroom. During math, the students had a test. At first we walked around and answered questions, helped the students understand the questions, and made sure they were writing the answers correctly. It was multiple choice, and the math teacher wanted the students to write both the letter and the answer. After this, we graded tests as the other students were finishing up their tests."

"I was working independently with one student in particular because they were making pictionaries. This required writing, and he needed a lot of help.

After this, they took a spelling test. The test was on homophones; a word was used in a sentence and the students had to decide whether or not it was correct. I read the test to him. I realize it is hard to read a test, without hinting at the answer. After he would answer, he would look at me to see if it was correct. Of course, I would not tell him, but he would watch my face and try and figure it out. I just looked away. He knew most of the answers, but I do not think he trusted himself."

REFERENCES AND SUGGESTED READINGS

Airasian, P. (1996). *Assessment in the classroom* (2nd ed.). New York: McGraw-Hill.

Allman, J., & Brophy, J. (1998). Assessment in a social constructivist classroom. *Social Education, 62*(1), 32–34.

Alverno College Faculty. (1994). *Students assessment-as-learning at Alverno College.* Milwaukee, WI: Alverno College.

Caine, R. N., & Caine, G. (1997). *Education on the edge of possibility.* Alexandria, VA: Association for Supervision and Curriculum Development.

Carpenter, S. L., & King-Sears, M. E. (1998). Classroom assessment practices for instruction. In M. S. Rosenberg, L. O'Shea, & D. J. O'Shea, *Student teacher to master teacher: A practical guide for educating students with special needs* (2nd ed.). Upper Saddle River, NJ: Merrill/Prentice Hall.

Checkley, K. (1997). *Assessment that serves instruction in education.* Update 39(4). Alexandria, VA: Association for Supervision and Curriculum Development.

Diez, M. E. (Ed.). (1998). *Changing the practice of teacher education: Standards and assessment as a lever for change.* Washington, D.C.: AACTE Publications.

Diez, M. E., & Moon, C. J.(1992). What do we want students to know? . . . and other important questions. *Educational Leadership, 49*(8), 38–41.

Hart, D. (1994). *Authentic assessment: A handbook for educators.* Menlo Park, CA: Addison-Wesley.

Herman, J. L., Auschbacher, P. R., & Tinters, L. (1992). *Alternative assessment.* Alexandria, VA: Association for Supervision and Curriculum Development.

Jamentz, K. (1994). Making sure that assessment improves performance. *Educational Leadership, 51*(6), 55–57.

Kuhs, T. M. (1994). Portfolio assessment: Making it work for the first time. *The Mathematics Teacher, 87*(5), 332–335.

Linn, R. L., & Gronlund, N. E. (2000). *Measurement and evaluation in teaching* (8th ed.). Upper Saddle River, NJ: Merrill/Prentice Hall.

Marzano, R., Pickering, D., & McTighe, J. (1993). *Assessing student outcomes: Performance assessment using the dimensions of learning model.* Alexandria, VA: Association for Supervision and Curriculum Development.

McMillan, J. (1997). *Classroom assessment: Principles and practice for effective instruction.* Needham Heights, MA: Allyn and Bacon.

Murphy, J. (1995). Changing role of the teacher. In M. J. O'Hair & S. J. Odell (Eds.), *Educating teachers for leadership and change: Teacher education yearbook III.* Thousand Oaks, CA: Corwin Press.

Newmann, F. M., Marks, H. M., & Gamoran, A. (1995). Authentic pedagogy: Standards that boost student performance. *Issue Report No. 8.* Madison, WI: Wisconsin Center for Education Research.

Newmann, F. M., Secada, W. G., & Wehlage, G. G. (1995). A conception of authentic human achievement. In *A guide to authentic instruction and assessment: Vision, standards and scoring.* Madison, WI: Wisconsin Center for Education Research. pp. 7–13.

Perrone, V. (Ed.). (1991). *Expanding student assessment.* Alexandria, VA: Association for Supervision and Curriculum Development.

Rothman, R. (1995). *Measuring up: Standards, assessment and school reform.* San Francisco: Jossey-Bass.

Simmons, R. (1994). The horse before the cart: Assessing for understanding. *Educational Leadership, 51*(5), 22–23.

Stenmark, J. K. (Ed.). (1991). *Mathematics assessment: Myths, models, good questions, and practical suggestions.* Reston, VA: The National Council of Teacher of Mathematics.

Stiggins, R. J. (1998). *Student-centered classroom assessment* (2nd ed.). Upper Saddle River, NJ: Merrill/Prentice Hall.

Urban, V. D. (1999). Eugene's story: A case for caring. *Educational Leadership, 56*(6), 69–70.

Wiggins, G. (1998). *Educative assessment: Designing assessments to inform and improve student performance.* San Francisco: Jossey-Bass.

Zessoules, R., & Gardner, H. (1991). Authentic assessment beyond the buzzword. In V. Perrone (Ed.), *Expanding student assessment.* Alexandria, VA: Association for Supervision and Curriculum Development.

Zmuda, A., and Tomaino, M. (1999). A contract for the high school classroom. *Educational Leadership, 56*(6), 59–61.

11 Communicating Learning Results

> *"To gain in knowledge of self, one must have the courage to seek it and the humility to accept what one may find."*

A. T. Jersild (p. 83)

Focus One

Expected Performance

- Trace your journey through the student teaching experience.
- Describe your affective and cognitive responses to the different phases of learning to teach.
- Examine and discuss the different types of communication about your progress in becoming a teacher.

Look Where I Am!

Standing near the top of a hill and looking back at the path leading up, you clearly see where you've been. As you approach the end of your student/intern teaching journey, this may be an ideal time to look back at the past months and examine your personal experiences during your transition to TEACHER. These experiences include your reflections and discussions about the teaching/learning process and your concerns while moving through these experiences. Having the courage to engage in self-analysis and accept what you find has the power to motivate you to become a more effective teacher. Likewise, others' offers of professional expertise and interactions give you deeper insights into the effectiveness of your teaching. You are better prepared to communicate the value of what you learn about yourself as teacher to others. Giving voice to your increasing levels of understanding of a practicing professional and your involvement in the process validates and affirms your learning experience.

What concerns about teaching have you had during this period of transition to teacher? Looking forward to student/intern teaching you may have felt anxious. You had butterflies in your stomach. There were so many concerns and questions racing through your mind! You eagerly awaited the announcement of your assigned school and your supervising teacher, along with your university supervisor. Upon arriving at the school, you found yourself involved in various activities, and your concern about your evaluation escalated. "How do I find out when I succeed and when I fail? How will I ever be able to put it all together and really be a teacher?" Do you recall having these questions? Later, other questions about your teaching arose and you asked, "How effective am I?" You wondered if your voice was loud enough and if students would follow your directives and behave during class. Do you remember worrying about knowing the content well enough to respond to students' questions?

In the early weeks of student/intern teaching you may have been concerned about how your students felt about you and if you were becoming too personally involved with them. You may have been concerned about your lack of experience. There may have been times when your own status was unclear to you or you felt conflicting expectations were thrust upon you. By now you have discovered that individuals taking on new roles usually have these or similar initial reactions.

After several more weeks you began designing, planning, and teaching for extended periods of time. Along with additional instructional responsibilities came new questions: "Are students learning what I'm teaching?" "Are students learning what they need?" At this time you may have asked yourself, "How can I improve myself as a teacher?" You examined your instructional strategies, experimented with different methods, and assessed your teaching effectiveness against student success and productivity. This is exactly what you should have been doing! Questioning yourself as teacher is part of the process of your transition to teacher. According to Fuller (1970), these are the kinds of persistent questions of student teachers. These questions develop sequentially and accompany the growth of student teachers as they assume more of the teacher role. Seeing your questions in this light, do you feel more like a professional teacher?

Take a look at where you are. Are the above questions the same ones that have nagged you from time to time during this experience? We pose these questions for two reasons. First, we want you to realize that to ask questions like these is normal for student/intern teachers. Secondly, we want you to recognize the importance of such questions as you adapt to your new role. As you develop professionally, expect to encounter and respond repeatedly to changes in education that challenge you. Be prepared to have similar concerns and questions as you make transitions to other new roles within your school. Your response to these concerns is critical to your growth as teacher. When moving through change, you are encouraged to pay attention to your feelings and seek support (Fuller, 1969; Sprinthall, Reiman, & Theis-Sprinthall, 1996). Your journals, reflections, and conversations with peers and supervisors are intended to help you address your questions and personal concerns to understand yourself as a learner. Engaging in this process helps you adopt more complex behaviors as a result of your questions and expanding insights.

You have been invited to explore and analyze your affective and cognitive responses to student/intern teaching. Throughout the student teaching seminars, conversations with peers, and conferences with supervisors, you have assessed your professional progress on many levels. Further explorations lie ahead as you enter the teaching profession and your understanding of teacher continues to expand. New and creative approaches to professional growth are developing. Rust (1999) reports that teachers (beginning, experienced, and teacher educators) coming together to research and learn actively and promote change in their professional lives. Within these supportive learning opportunities teachers from diverse groups reflect on their own experience and knowledge, explore their attitudes and beliefs about teaching and learning, and share a host of skills and strategies—those that form the underpinnings of their work. Through professional conversations about classroom life and as stories unfold, new insights about the teaching and learning processes are deepened. As you look forward to your own professional growth, you will want to keep in mind that cognitive development is not automatic. Rather than growth happening as a result of accumulating years and experience, your growth as a professional depends largely on your interactions with other professionals and your ability to give voice to all you have learned. Self-reflection and interpersonal communication are catalysts for professional growth.

The **Focus One** activity presents the different phases of transition to the teacher role and invites you to examine your own experiences using these questions. Which ones match your experiences as a student/intern teacher moving toward becoming teacher? How is your experience similar to that of your peers? So much is happening each day and one fast-paced day follows another! You may not even be aware of the progress you have made in this transition to teacher. You may not have taken time to compare your initial steps into student/intern teaching with your present performance. Noting events and identifying feelings associated with each turning point in your experience is valuable in sorting out all that you've learned so far. Perhaps you are now able to be more objective, to have different insights, and to take a broader perspective of prior events. Perhaps you've come to understand and value the processes necessary to learning. Perhaps you recognize the need to pause, to take stock of your professional journey thus far.

To help you connect your experiences with the sequence of development phases associated with professional growth, a list and brief description of each one follows. Read the description and make notes that help you recall specific situations from your experience. These notes can help you make connections and give voice to your growth as you interact with your group members.

Phase I *Concern about Self*

- I'm anxious. What do I need to be concerned about?

_____

_____

Phase II *Concern about Self as Teacher*

- What am I supposed to do?
- Will I know enough to teach? What if students ask questions I can't answer?
- What happens if I lose control?
- Where do I stand in this new situation as a teacher?
- How do my students see what I'm doing? Do they like me?

_____

_____

Phase III *Concern about Students*

- How can I explain this idea to students?
- Is what I'm teaching what students really need to know?
- How can I be a better teacher?

_____

_____

Discussion Questions

1. Which of the questions listed under the different phases match those you ask during your student/intern teaching experience? Which questions caused you the most anxiety?
2. As you grappled with the questions, what other feelings about your new role resurfaced?
3. When you had questions similar to those listed under the various phases, what sources of support have you sought? What might have caused you to be hesitant about seeking support?
4. Looking back over this experience, what new insights have you gained about your progress toward the role of teacher?
5. Summarize your growth and communicate the results of your learning with the members of your group.

Focus Two

Expected Performance

- Communicate results to students and parents or guardians.
- Use multiple assessments and sources of data.
- Use formal and informal assessment strategies to evaluate and ensure the continuous intellectual, social, and physical development of the learner.
- Promote student self-assessment using established criteria and focus student attention on what needs to be done to move to the next performance level.
- Systematically collect and analyze assessment data and maintain up-to-date records of student progress.

Throughout your preservice education you have heard repeatedly that communication is essential to becoming an effective teacher. You are learning during this student teaching or intern experience that communication involves not only interacting with students and your supervising teacher, but with many teachers, administrators, and parents or guardians. Communicating learning results means encouraging, challenging, listening, and providing the learners with information about their achievement and continuing progress. (Think for a moment of the valuable insights you had regarding your professional growth as a result of reflective communication!) Written or verbal comments on papers, projects, journals, portfolios, progress reports, and or report cards communicate to the students what they have achieved. Much like conferences scheduled with your supervising teacher, individual conferences with the students gives you opportunities to discuss questions, academic progress, and class behavior and to listen to their perspectives. This communicates to the students that you care. You are interested in their learning, you want them to succeed, and you are encouraging them to take charge of their learning. What a professional approach to establishing a trusting relationship and rapport with students!

APPLICATION: COMMUNICATING LEARNING RESULTS

One of the primary uses of assessment is to determine what students know or have learned with regard to specific instructional objectives. Multiple examples of assessment communicate clearly to students, to other teachers, and often to parents the range of the student's performance. Students receive feedback from teachers in a variety of ways. In considering how students are performing and assigning summary scores, Marzano, Pickering, and McTighe (1993) make the following suggestions:

- Use as much information as possible even information not recorded in the grade book.
- Weigh the various scores using sound criteria.
- Assign summary scores if adequate information is available.
- Consider the nature of the standards issued by the state or learned societies (diversity of knowledge or skill and the consistency of knowledge or skill).

Grading

Nothing seems to be more controversial in education than grading and communicating student learning results. Grades provide limited information about how the student is performing and are oftentimes misunderstood by the student and parent. In addition, teachers find the grading process very difficult and time consuming.

The meaning of the grade must be clearly defined and easily understood by the learner so that it clearly communicates the level of student achievement. Feedback regarding your students' performance should be continuous and allow your students to know where they stand. Although the teacher's subjective perceptions and insights inevitably influence the grading process to some extent, they should not be allowed to greatly distort the subject matter grade. (Arasian, 1996).

Multiple measures provide a more complete picture of student performance. Skills and attitudes that a student is developing become part of your reporting system. Most subject matter assessment is done with teacher-made tests, papers, quizzes, projects, activity sheets, and homework. Some aspects of student achievement can be better assessed by performance than by a multiple choice or essay test. Using scoring guides for performance assessment tasks will assist you in making decisions and reporting the results of your learners' achievement. In addition, it will encourage student self-assessment and cooperative group reporting for accountability purposes. Finally, when conferencing with students and parents or guardians about results of performance assessment, scoring guides will provide a more sophisticated analysis of student achievement.

Forms of Assessment

Watts (1996) encourages the use of alternative forms of assessment for communicating student learning. To get a clearer and more comprehensive picture of student achievement, she outlines a formula for successfully and fairly assessing student learning:

1. presenting visible evidence of student growth and achievement
2. ranking or rating of student achievement against clearly stated, predetermined standards
3. involving students in grading through self-assessment and/or peer evaluation
4. conferencing with students, parents, or guardians to open the lines of communication

Incorporating these assessment strategies may at first seem daunting to you. As you practice and use them with your students you may experience a new sense of purpose and direction in your lessons. You are empowering your students by having them experience assessment as a process rather than "giving" them a grade at the end of the quarter! These strategies enable you to work with individual students to help them set goals and engage them in learning. The learner is validated through this model, and learning is seen as real, tangible, and valuable.

Visible evidence of student growth and achievement is accomplished through a variety of exciting classroom performance tasks. Employing portfolios in the classroom and creating opportunities for exhibitions of student knowledge are sound assessment practices. Other highly visible alternative methods include displays of student work, student presentations, and anecdotal records. Videotaping your students' work, and at work, is a remarkable record of their achievement and potential.

Portfolios are purposeful collections of student work and may include:
- student-selected works in progress illustrating their learning, application of knowledge, and risk-taking
- student rationale statement supporting selection of work
- student samples of their best work
- student reflection about their work
- criteria developed by teacher and student used for assessment
- teacher evaluative comments and student self-assessment

Presentations may include students conducting experiments, teaching a skill or concept to others, performing a play, or working as a cooperative group in solving a problem.

Exhibitions may include a visual display, chart, graph, concept map, written report, or science fair project.

Anecdotal records include teacher-recorded observations of individual student behaviors. Only behaviors are recorded that are significant and cannot be obtained from other classroom assessment methods. Specific points to keep in mind in recording effective anecdotal records adapted from Orlich et al. (1998):

- Be brief and record only the unusual behaviors.
- Be consistent.
- Be factual.
- Record positive and negative indicators.
- Be careful not to draw inferences from a single incident.

Ranking or rating student achievement is difficult unless you prepare ahead of time clearly stated standards for student performance. Using report card checklists, rubrics or scoring guides, and standards found in work samplings helps to provide a road map for your students as they move toward achievement.

Scoring Guides or Rubrics

Different ways to label criteria for evaluating student performance include: rubrics, scoring rubrics, scoring criteria, and scoring guides. Each describes the guidelines for evaluating learner performance and usually includes a scale of values for rating the quality of the task or performance and the learner expectation for a specified performance. The criteria that you develop or select for the task or performance depends on the purpose for the assessment. When criteria is clearly communicated to the learner and the parents or guardian, it helps them understand what you, as teacher, intend the learner to accomplish. In designing your own rubrics or scoring guides, Martinello and Cook (1994) suggest guidelines that may be helpful to you as you determine how well students perform according to an appropriate model:

- The behaviors described in the rubric are the behaviors described in the learning objectives or in the description of the task.
- There are no required number of points on the scale for a rubric. Most include four to six depending on the activity.
- The descriptors for each point on the scale should be as clear and unambiguous as possible.
- Students may participate in the construction of rubrics by specifying the expected behaviors for each point on the scale.

Involving students through self-assessment and/or peer evaluation gives them opportunities to become active learners. They become more articulate about their progress and what they need to work on to improve their performance. Early in the school year you will want to communicate to students your grading system and encourage them to take responsibility for tracking their personal progress and setting academic goals. Giving your students the opportunity to journal, reflect on their learning, and record their grades enables them to see progress in various areas over time.

Peer and Self-Assessment

Students can assess themselves and their peers in cooperative group settings with rating checklists and performance criteria. Johnson, Johnson, and Holubec (1993) describe a step in the writing process where students are actively involved in learning. Each group member drafts a composition that will be read and responded to by peers. After responding to the piece and making suggestion for revisions, each composition is revisited for editing purposes. Students proofread each others' work, helping with necessary corrections, by using the criteria set by the teacher for this particular writing piece. Before the individual student writes the final copy, each student signs a statement that the criteria has been met by each group member. This process allows each student in the group to read, review, and rate another student's work against an established performance criteria. By using a peer's work as a model students not only gain a better understanding of the performance criteria, they engage more deeply in the multifaceted processes of learning, oftentimes resulting in improvement in productivity, creativity, and accountability.

Peer assessment activities used for writing purposes are highlighted here as one example. Teachers use other self- and/or peer assessment activities in reading, math, learning logs, journals, and goal setting for behavior management. The bottom line is getting your students involved in self-assessment and peer evaluation across the curriculum. This involvement motivates students to take a more active role in their own learning.

Conferencing with students, parents, or guardians to open the lines of communication will frequently save you time and trouble later. While it is time consuming, careful planning is necessary to ensure productivity. Parent, guardian, and student response is usually positive. Conferencing is proactive! Your students see the connection between their performance and the need to talk about it and communicate the results of their hard work (or lack of it!) to their parents or guardians. Two-way communication ensures that the message received is the message sent. All parties feel secure and informed about academic expectations, goals, problems, and academic standing.

Reporting Guidelines

Guskey (1996) recommends the following guidelines to help ensure that grading and reporting practices are fair, equitable, and useful to students, parents, and teachers:

- Begin with a clear statement of purpose. A statement of purpose would address why grading or reporting is done, for whom the information is intended, and what are the desired results.
- Provide accurate and understandable descriptions of student learning.
- Use grading and reporting methods to enhance, not hinder, teaching and learning.

Reporting to Parents

The report card is the most common form of communicating to parents or guardians a student's progress. Each school system usually has a set format. You may discuss with your supervising teacher the reporting form your school uses and the procedures used for grading and commenting to parents or guardians.

The written progress report is another method of communicating learner progress. Written in clear, easy-to-read, everyday language, the report communicates to parents or guardians specific areas indicating learner progress. Many teachers write student progress notes to parents or guardians periodically throughout the school year. In the near future, with electronic capabilities, you may be communicating with parents even more frequently.

Conferences

Conferencing is the most effective way of communicating with parents or guardians and the student. When you invite parents or guardians for a conference, you are actually saying, "We would like to communicate what your son or daughter is learning in school. What would you like to know? There are many different ways to give you a picture of your son's work. We can show, discuss, send, or invite you to see examples, attend a performance, read student writing, or examine your daughter's portfolio."

In a conference you, as teacher, can clearly discuss demonstrated achievement and any learning difficulties. As you plan for the conference, begin saving samples of students' work, perhaps their portfolio, and any other pieces of information that will enhance the discussion. Using an individual self-assessment form (designed by you) invites students to participate in the conference and take an active role in their development as learners. Time is always a factor; therefore, it is highly recommended that you prepare an agenda of the items you wish to discuss.

During the conference you will want to listen to the parents' concerns. This helps you learn about the student from the parents' perspective. Working together as partners, as teacher with the parent or guardian, you provide opportunities for sharing valuable information about the learner from each other. Planning jointly for the student's benefit is the overall goal of the conference. At the conclusion of the conference you will want to review what was discussed and summarize the actions planned and agreed upon by all.

Responsibility for completing report cards or preparing conference reports for parents or guardians may not be entirely your task at this time. Assisting other teachers with developing a reporting process greatly increases your competence and contributes to your confidence in this important area of teaching.

ASSIGNED ACTIVITIES

The activities this week draw attention to the variety of ways you communicate with the parents or guardians concerning the learner's progress.

1. Discuss with your supervising teacher the plans used by the school and teachers for communicating with parents or guardians. Journal a summary of the key points you will implement as teacher.
2. Describe your involvement in the following assessment reporting methods.
    - Open house
    - Parent/teacher/student conferences
    - Report cards/progress reports
    - Individual educational plan (IEP)
    - Performance events
    - Parent/teacher organization meetings
3. Comment on the formative and summative evaluative reports given students this week. How were the results recorded, used and/or analyzed? What was the follow-up for students who were not reaching their potential?

    Reports

    - Tests (written, oral, performance)
    - Daily assignments (class presentations)
    - Projects (problem solving, thematic)
    - Group work
    - Journals, notebook, lab books
    - Home assignments
    - Portfolio entries
    - Student interviews
    - Conferencing with student

SUMMARY

To communicate learning results effectively it is imperative that you fully appreciate the processes involved and the opportunities for individual growth that stem from reflective communication. Effective communication of learning results calls for the use of a number of assessment strategies and tools. As a professional, you engage in reflection, self-analysis, and other assorted ways to mark your progress. You recognize the need to communicate your growth and receive feedback from others. You better understand students' need to engage in communication about their progress as learners.

Current research suggests that a partnership between parents and teacher results in better planning and decision making affecting students (Guskey, 1996). Conferencing with parents or guardians can be an effective means for creating and continuing cooperative relationships between home and school. You may have been present for the Open House or Parent Night when your supervising teacher communicated with the parents for the first time this school year. Perhaps you have been present or even participated in scheduled conferences with parents or guardians. You observed as your experienced supervising teacher enabled parents to share mutual concerns, ideas, and opinions in a comfortable, secure setting. In a special education meeting you witnessed all committee members contributing to the individual educational plan and reaching a consensus on reasonable expectations for the individual student.

Actively listening to your students, parents, or committee members encourages communication rather than confrontation. Your understanding of effective communication skills can result in a more productive dialogue between you and parents or guardians. You have also discovered how essential it is to be well prepared and organized if parent conferences and meetings are to be successful. Positive, well-conducted conferences can serve as encouragement and direction for the learner if appropriate information is shared.

FOLLOW-UP QUESTIONS AND SHARED INSIGHTS

From your journal, experiences with learning assessment, and the assigned activities, share responses to the following:

1. What kind of information do parents/guardians want to know about their son or daughter's achievement?
2. What information is helpful for teachers to request from parents or guardians regarding the learner?
3. In what ways does the teacher communicate learner progress or achievement to the student?
4. Which reporting plans used by the school and teachers were valuable in building and strengthening the partnership among the parents, teachers, and students?
5. What suggestions do you have for getting parents more actively involved in the student's educational achievement?

Technology Tips

Electronic Portfolios

Throughout this chapter considerations are given to alternative and authentic strategies for assessing student learning. You have reflected on your choice, your reasons, results of the assessment, and strategies selected for your students. One of the many strategies you have been considering is using the portfolio.

Earlier chapters of the text encourage you to develop a portfolio and suggest specific items to include. In compiling a portfolio you could use a word processing application on a computer and illustrate its contents with photographs, tapes, and copies of students' work. You might choose more sophisticated technology requiring a great amount of memory and pressed onto a CD-ROM. This high-tech medium, known as the *electronic* or *digital portfolio,* holds burgeoning interest as a valued assessment of teaching.

What is an Electronic Portfolio?

The electronic portfolio is a purposeful collection of work you assemble by electronic means and use as an exhibit of your efforts, growth, and achievements in one or more areas. It allows you to use scanned images of projects, other examples of student work, diagrams, and drawings (Wiedmer, 1998). The electric portfolio, like other types of portfolios, requires that you plan and choose its contents giving careful consideration to its purpose and goal. You would want to go beyond collecting and displaying evidence of teaching/learning tasks to provide as complete as possible a representation of your teaching competencies and a holistic view of yourself as a teacher (Hurst, Wilson, & Cramer, 1998).

What Are the Benefits of the Electronic Portfolio?

Benefits of electronic portfolio are similar to those for developing the hard-copy portfolios. The multimedia capacity offers additional ways to display your unique talents and abilities. The prospective employer gains insight into your knowledge and use of technology along with your personal and professional abilities, knowledge, attitudes, and values as a teacher. Journal writing, seminar conversations, and follow-up are examples of ongoing reflection that adds depth and value to your portfolio. The electronic portfolio allows you to represent visually the reflection process and its effect on your development as a teacher.

Authentic assessment of your skills, knowledge, and attitudes as a teacher can be captured through the multidimensional capacity of the electronic portfolio. Including resource materials you have downloaded from the Internet demonstrates your knowledge of content and creativity in connecting the classroom with the outside world. Lesson plans can include these resources. You provide the viewer examples of your ideas along with rationale for choosing the instruction and your comments about ways you might change things the next time you teach. In addition to communicating what you think, the multidimensions available through the electronic portfolio provide evidence that you are a thoughtful teacher.

For Whom Is the Electronic Portfolio Intended?

Teacher portfolios serve a variety of purposes and can satisfy a number of goals. As a student/intern teacher you are looking for a job. Many educators eager to bring cutting-edge ideas into the school are looking for technology-literate teachers. Viewing your electronic portfolio and interacting with you about its contents, the interviewer gets an understanding about your level of expertise and attitude toward the use of technology with your students.

You are greatly benefited in the process of compiling an electronic portfolio. Just as you encourage self-assessment in your students, the electronic portfolio offers you an ongoing process of self-assessment. It allows you to see your progress over a period of time. A progression of teaching techniques can be assessed using video clips of your teaching.

Examples of electronic portfolios are increasingly available from education and technology journals. Backer (1997), Ryan et al. (1997), and Wilcox et al. (1997) provide examples you may find helpful in planning and compiling yours. You may view examples of electronic portfolios created by preservice teachers at this web site: <http://www.students.uiuc.edu/~ozee/miscellaneous/portlist.html>. Information about the hardware and software requirements, HTML, tutorials, links to other sources, and discussion of design models for delivering instruction on the World Wide Web (Hackbarth, 1997) is available at: http://dpwebl.dp.utexas.edu/edapp/placement-service.html. Go to "Education Career Services" for job assistance and sources. For an example of a commercial resume service, you may want to view Eagle's Resume Services:

http://www.richmond.infi.net/~leeann.electron.htm

Other suggestions of the necessary hardware and software for creating an electronic portfolio are available in the following list of publications.

Backer, P. R. (1997). The use of portfolios in professional education: A multimedia model of instructional methodology, ERIC Document: ED408356.

Holt, D., et al. (1997). Integrating preparation and practice through a technology-based approach to portfolios for professional development using IBM technology, ERIC Document: ED405325.

Hurst, B., Wilson, C., & Cramer, G. (1998). "Professional teaching portfolios: Tools for reflection, growth, and advancement," *Phi Delta Kappan 79*(8), 578–582.

Khan, B. H. (Ed.). (1997). *Web-based instruction.* Englewood Cliffs, NJ: Educational Technology Publications.

Niguidula, D. (1997). Picturing performance with digital portfolios, *Educational Leadership, 55*(3), 26–29.

Riggsby, D., et al. (1995). Electronic portfolio: Assessment, resume, or marketing tool, ERIC Document: ED387115.

Riggsby, D. (1997). Supporting student teachers with laptop computers: A project of the school of education at Columbus State University, ERIC Document: ED410934

Ryan, C. W., et al. (1997). Teacher education field experiences: Impact on self-esteem of professional year program interns via electronic portfolios, ERIC Document ED405329.

Ryder, R. J., and Hughes, T. (1997). *Internet for educators.* Upper Saddle River, NJ: Merrill/Prentice Hall.

Wiedmer, T. L. (1998). Digital portfolios: Capturing and demonstrating skills and levels of performance. *Phi Delta Kappan 79*(8), 586–589.

Wilcox, B. L., et al. (1997). Intelligent portfolios for professional development, ERIC Document: ED408250.

High School

"Today we had Parent-Teacher Conferences. It was quite fascinating to experience this aspect of teaching. I got to see how Mr. R prepared and dealt with specific situations. It was wonderful to meet the parents. No one was mad or frustrated with me so I felt really good. After these conferences, I feel much more comfortable and confident about my interactions and relationships with parents. In general, they are very supportive of their sons and daughters and also our efforts. Wonderful learning experience!"

"Formative and summative evaluative reports take the form of tests, home assignments, portfolio entries, and conferencing. We give vocabulary tests as a written form of evaluating the new words students study. After the tests are returned, students discuss their answers and reasoning behind the correct answers. For one home assignment students read two short stories and were asked to map a story element sheet for each of the stories. This was used to assess student reading comprehension and application of student knowledge of story elements. We explained the purpose of the assignment and the evaluation strategy that we would use in grading. In the next class students discussed their completed assignment and in this way the assessment gave students further help in understanding the story elements."

"Portfolio entries are the major form of evaluation that we gave this week. Students handed in their portfolio pieces to be given a revision grade. They will eventually be graded on their final portfolio—complete with four writing pieces. For now, though, students are only able to see revision process through this evaluative report. After the revision of the portfolio piece is evaluated, students have the option of coming to conference about their writing to gain a more complete understanding of the evaluation process."

Middle School

"We had Open House tonight. I was nervous, but I did not have to speak to the entire group of parents. In a way, I wish I would have had the practice. I'll be so nervous when I do have to face parents. I need to work on being assertive. Parents are scary! I felt so proud when Ms. P.J. would turn to me for specifics about an individual student. Since I grade so much of their work, I know them well and know how they're doing. Luckily, I only had to speak of good things and Ms. P.J. handled the tough cases. I learned a lot about approaching problems because my supervising teacher is great with parents. Tonight was very beneficial for me."

"Today Ms. H. handed out grades for the past grading period. She shared with the class her disappointment at the number of *D*s and *U*s. She confided to me, 'Just when I thought I was doing something good by getting all these students published and representing the school in numerous publications—BLAMMO, something like this brings me back down to earth and makes me think I'm doing a lousy job!' I am impressed with how humble she is! I hope I can keep a similar perspective when I teach—I want to feel confident in my ability while at the same time realizing I am *always* improving my techniques/methods!"

"Today we worked on revising the *Anne Frank* papers the students turned in last week. Ms. H. held a serious discussion of how poorly they had performed on the piece. She informed them that many pieces were rated at the Novice level.

She cited a lack of effort shown during the two days that students were given for working on the draft. She referred to the many good ideas that were poorly developed during this time. During each period I circulated and gave advice and questioned students on how they could more clearly state their ideas. I found it rewarding to spend quality time helping students who really want to be better writers and wanted my advice."

Elementary School

"We had Open House tonight. It was great to get to speak with some of the parents about their children's progress. We have some very dedicated, concerned parents. I felt empowered when I was asked to tell the parents what I hoped to be doing with their sons and daughters while I am in the classroom."

"The Parent-Teacher Organization sends a newsletter to parents informing them of dates and times of meetings, school programs, and other current happenings. Parents are also informed about their child being involved in a performance event, usually in the 4th grade. Before this day and other test-taking days, the counselor sends home a letter reminding parents to make sure that children get plenty of rest and eat a nutritious breakfast before coming to school."

"Ms. W. uses a weekly recording journal that is sent home with the students. I am very interested in this procedure and I think it works very well. I was involved in charting these reports today and recording their results in the grade book. I also gave and graded their spelling tests. The students work hard and I enjoy grading the tests so I can see the results."

Special Education

"This week was very eventful. Tuesday I attended an ARC (parent meeting) along with 10 other individuals. I never realized so many people could fit into Mr. O.'s office. It was really neat to be part of the large team which was formed for one of my students. I also had the opportunity to give a student a one-on-one social studies test. This student is so fearful of taking tests. We didn't discuss the modifications that Ms. M. and I began on Friday after Ms. M. met with the social studies teacher. I was very impressed with Ms. M. and the approach she used in explaining to the other teacher why and how she was teaching in order to help this student improve in the social studies class."

"I was able to sit in on G.'s IEP meeting. While in the meeting with his mom and step dad, Mrs. B asked me to explain the intervention I started with G. today. I started a stamp book. I explained to G. that each time he responded to a question with verbal cues from an adult or peer he would receive a stamp in his book. After five stamps he would receive a treat from the treat box. This was a great hit! Before the IEP meeting he had already earned two treats. So, I shared with Mom and Dad that the general idea was to start with G. receiving a treat after only five stamps, but that number would be increased over time."

"We had conferences, but did not have any parents come. One parent came yesterday and a few came last week. We went to the ECE resource center and to the audio visual center. Working with Mr. D. all day helped me feel more comfortable around him and his style of teaching. I think he is an excellent teacher. He is great with both instruction and behavior. He is very dedicated to his job and wants his students to succeed."

REFERENCES AND SUGGESTED READINGS

Airasian, P. W. (1996). *Assessment in the classroom.* New York: McGraw-Hill.

Arends, R. I. (1997). *Classroom instruction and management.* New York: McGraw-Hill.

Callahan, J. F., Clark, L. H., & Kellough, R. D. (1998). *Teaching in the middle and secondary schools* (6th ed.). Upper Saddle River, NJ: Merrill/Prentice Hall.

Fuller, F. F. (1969). Concerns of teachers: A developmental conceptualization. *American Educational Research Journal, 6*(2) 207–226.

Fuller, F. F. (1970). *Personalized teacher education for teachers: An introduction for teacher educators.* Austin: University of Texas, R & D Center for Teacher Education (ERIC Document ED 048–105).

Gersten, R., Vaughn, S., & Brengelman, S. U. (1996). Grading and academic feedback for special education students and students with learning difficulties. In T. R. Guskey (Ed.), *Communicating student learning 1996 ASCD yearbook.* Alexandria, VA: Association for Supervision and Curriculum Development.

Guskey, T. R. (1996). Reporting on student learning: Lessons from the past-prescriptions for the future. In T. R. Guskey (Ed.), *Communicating student learning 1996 ASCD yearbook.*

Herman, J. L., Aschbacher, P. R., & Winters, L. (1992). *A practical guide to alternative assessment.* Alexandria, VA: Association for Supervision and Curriculum Development.

Jersild, A. T. (1955). *When teachers face themselves.* New York: Teachers College, Columbia University.

Johnson, D. W., Johnson, R. T., and Holubec, E. (1993). *Cooperation in the classroom* (6th ed.). Edina, MN: Interaction Book Company.

Johnson, D. W., & Johnson, R. T. (1996). The role of cooperative learning in assessing and communicating student learning. In T. R. Guskey (Ed.), *Communicating student learning 1996 ASCD yearbook.* Alexandria, VA: Association for Supervision and Curriculum Development.

Martinello, M. L., & Cook, G. E. (1994). *Interdisciplinary inquiry in teaching and learning.* Upper Saddle River, NJ: Prentice Hall.

Marzano, R. J., Pickering, D., & McTighe, J. (1993). *Assessing student outcomes: Performance assessment using dimensions of learning model.* Alexandria, VA: Association for Supervision and Curriculum Development.

Orlich, D. C., Harder, R. J., Callahan, R. C., & Gibson, H. W. (1998). *Teaching strategies: A guide to better instruction.* (5th ed.) Boston: Houghton Mifflin.

Perrone, V. (Ed.) (1991). *Expanding student assessment.* Alexandria, VA: Association for Supervision and Curriculum Development.

Popham, W. J. (1997). What's wrong and what's right-with rubrics. *Educational Leadership, 55*(2) 72–75.

Rich, D. (1998). What parents want from teachers, *Educational Leadership, 55*(8), 37–39.

Rust, F. O. (1999). Professional conversations: New teachers explore teaching through conversations, story, and narrative. *Teaching and Teacher Education.* (In press).

Schmoker, M. (1996). *Results: The key to continuous school improvement.* Alexandria, VA: Association for Supervision and Curriculum Development.

Sprinthall, N. A., Reiman, A. J., & Thies-Sprinthall, L. (1996). Teacher professional development. In J. Sikula (Ed.), *Handbook of research on teacher education* (2nd ed.) New York: Simon & Schuster, Macmillan.

Stiggins, R. (1997). *Student-centered classroom assessment* (2nd ed.). Upper Saddle River, NJ: Merrill/Prentice Hall.

Tancock, S. M., & Ford, K. L. (1996). Facilitating reflective thinking: Technology-based portfolios in teacher education, *Journal of Technology and Teacher Education, 4*(3/4), 281–295.

Watts, K. H. (1996). Bridges freeze before roads. In T. R. Guskey (Ed.), *Communicating student learning 1996 ASCD yearbook.* Alexandria, VA: Association for Supervision and Curriculum Development.

Weinstein, C. S., & Mignano, A. J. Jr. (1997). *Elementary classroom management: Lessons from research and practice* (2nd ed.). New York: McGraw-Hill.

Wiggins, G. (1998). *Educative assessment: Designing assessments to inform and improve student performance.* San Francisco: Jossey-Bass.

Collaborating with Colleagues, Parents, and Other Agencies

> *" . . . understanding and teaching the complexities associated with collaboration will avert putting the proverbial bandwagon before the horse and ultimately keep us on the bandwagon known as collaboration."*

M. Welch (p. 26)

Focus One

Expected Performance

- Identify the ways you see yourself as a team player.
- Engage in a problem-solving activity with peers.
- Apply your understanding of cooperation and collaboration to your current teaching situation.
- Discuss the necessity for cooperation and collaboration within the changing role of teachers.

Am I a Collaborator, a Team Player?

New expectations are emerging for schools in the 21st century and for individuals working in schools. Many schools are changing from a hierarchical pattern of organization and structure to one more decentralized, thus changing the traditional roles of administrators and teachers. These changes in structure are made for promoting a sense of community in schools and are focused on meeting human needs. The roles and responsibilities of the administrators, teachers, and others in these schools are more general and flexible than in the past.

Today, teachers are considered more as professionals and are given opportunities to demonstrate their expertise within the school and provide input for the larger school community. You may have heard teachers' roles referred to as guides, leaders, decision makers, learners, student advocates, and colleagues (Murphy, 1995). In your student teaching placement you may be working with administrators, the curriculum coordinator, and a social worker; in addition, you may be a member of an instructional team. Each of these teacher roles supports the idea of teacher as collaborator—part of a collective group contributing to the school's overall climate.

Creating the school community and establishing a healthy climate (one in which teachers, students, and staff come together to learn and to teach) requires cooperation and collaboration. In the text you have extensive descriptions and suggestions for structuring and maintaining cooperative group activities. You may be using these techniques and observing group members working and showing mutual respect toward each other. Likewise, new teacher roles such as leader and colleague require that teachers collaborate. Henderson (1996) explains that "when teachers collaborate, they support one another's professional autonomy and celebrate their diversity in the context of shared pragmatic reconsiderations and critical examination. Collaborating professionals treat one another as fellow inquirers" (p. 187). You may already be engaged in collaborative activities in providing services to special education and English as a second language students in your school. You join the efforts of others in addressing students' needs and school-related problems (Zabel and Zabel, 1996). Teacher assistants may direct the instructional activities you design. Does this resemble the school where you are now teaching? How do you interact with these professionals and paraprofessionals?

The working relationship among the school-based professional and paraprofessional is often labeled as collaboration and teamwork. Are you a team player? Do you collaborate with others? Individuals engaged in this collaborative relationship share and promote a common goal. In the school the common goal is generating and maintaining a teaching/learning climate for all members of the school community. Consider your own student/intern teaching situation and the collaboration and teamwork that exists within your classroom, the team, and the school. What elements are present that create the interdependent relationships you experience? Are you and others willing to participate actively in the formation of a dynamic community? Is there recognition and respect for each other's competence? Is diversity celebrated among the community members, individually and collectively? Do members interact with each other to communicate pragmatic concerns and identify common problems? Are conflicts resolved through a critical examination process that promotes a wise and decisive course of action? Whether you are a regular classroom teacher, a special educator, a bilingual or ESL teacher, these components necessarily supply the impetus and motivation inherent in working collaboratively toward a common goal.

Being fully cognizant of expectations you hold for yourself (and others working with you) is an important starting point for reflecting on collaboration and teamwork. **Focus One** offers a hands-on activity that demonstrates the elements critical to effective collaboration and teamwork. It invites you to participate with your group in working toward a common goal and analyze the process involved, the underlying framework that encourages success. During the activity you will want to recognize and respect the competence of others and to interact with all group members. This activity provides you and your group with a problem, asks you to identify the problem, and then determine a course of action for solving the problem. Specific directions serve as parameters in which the task is performed. By adhering to the confines of this activity, you can better understand the challenges associated with real-life problem-solving events in the school or in your classroom.

Directions for the Rectangular Puzzle Activity

Each member assembles a rectangular puzzle that has the same dimensions when completed. No two puzzles have pieces with the same shape. Using the pieces given by the seminar leader and those received from others, group members work independently solving the problem and are aware of what other members need for completing their puzzles. When the seminar leader confirms that yours and other members' puzzles are accurately assembled, your group has completed the activity (Goethals & Howard, 1985).

Puzzle Pieces

All correctly completed puzzles have the same size.
Pieces to each puzzle have different shapes.
Edges of all correctly placed puzzle pieces fit smoothly together.

Directions

Remove puzzle pieces from the envelope.
Examine puzzle pieces to see if the pieces fit together to form a rectangle.
Pass puzzle pieces you do not want to the person on your right.
Receive puzzle pieces *only* from the person to your left.

Seminar Leader Tasks

- Prepare puzzles using diagram found in Appendix A. Puzzle pieces can be made of tagboard.
- Provide each student with an envelope. Each envelope contains one or more geometric pieces. The pieces may or may not fit the same rectangle.
- Form groups of five students each.
- Monitor and check the accuracy of puzzles assembled by each group.

Be aware of puzzle pieces held by other group members.

Mentally picture the completed rectangle, yours and others'.

Engage in the activity without gesturing or verbally communicating with other group members.

Be aware of how you feel toward yourself and toward others while performing the task.

Helping Other Group Members

Pass puzzle pieces you are not using.

Allow others to work assembling their own puzzle.

Be mindful that other group members are capable of completing their task.

Be willing to restructure your rectangle to help other members try out other solutions.

When your group completes its task, reflect on the process and your participation.

Discussion Questions

1. Describe the myriad feelings you experienced while you and your group assembled the puzzles. How did you feel toward yourself? Toward others in the group?
2. When you observed that others in the group needed help, what did you do? How did your interactions with others during the activity mirror your attitude toward them as capable and competent professionals?
3. To what extent did you remember the group's common goal? What caused you to lose focus of the goal?
4. Consider your experience of this activity and analyze which collaboration and teamwork elements are most important to individual and group success.
5. Apply what you have learned to a current situation in your school and analyze the effectiveness of collaborative effort.

Focus Two

In your **Focus One** activity, you worked together as a team to build a puzzle, which demonstrated a way to collaborate. There were tense moments, humorous times, frustrating moves; you may have wanted to just take charge! In your discussions that followed, you began to relate this experience to real life situations with you as the teacher. Working with your supervising teacher has its ups and downs. Teaming with other teachers can be frustrating and time consuming. When conferencing with the learners' parents or guardians, you may want to take charge and dismiss their concerns, setting a course with yourself in charge! It's easier to do it yourself rather than involve everyone else in decisions about a student's academic concerns.

APPLICATION: COLLABORATING WITH COLLEAGUES, PARENTS, AND OTHER AGENCIES

Collaboration is the shared responsibility of teachers, parents, administrators, and community members. As a participant in conferences and meetings with colleagues, parents, and other agencies, your desire to become an effective collaborator is confirmed. You realize the ability to work collaboratively within diverse groups takes great sensitivity. Likewise, making joint decisions, resolving conflicts, setting goals and following through on assigned tasks is a real commitment of time and energy. Collaboration with colleagues, parents, and others working together for the benefit of the learner is a great feeling!

Collaboration Skills

Sometimes the collaboration process seems overwhelming. Your supervising and team teachers may have collaborated for years but are still working on overcoming specific roadblocks to effective communication. Good collaborators, according to Pugach and Johnson (1995), are willing to invest the time and energy necessary to improve their own professional practice. Improving collaborative skills leads to a sense of collegiality, creating a climate for successful student achievement.

Throughout your beginning teacher experience you realize the importance of interpersonal skills, communication skills, joint problem solving, decision-making strategies, and conflict resolution strategies in working with others. These skills are necessary to collaborate and work with others to more effectively provide the most productive learning climate for all your students.

Howard, Williams, Port, and Lepper (1997) describe factors discussed in the literature necessary for successful collaboration:

- trust
- face-to-face interaction
- interpersonal skills on the part of all team members
- voluntary collaboration
- equity among participants

Collaboration Forms

Friend and Cook (1996) define collaboration as interaction between parties sharing resources to reach a common goal. Collaboration may take many forms within the school. Gable and Manning (1997) list the more popular teacher collaboration arrangements to include:

- grade-level collaboration, where first grade teachers are paired with a reading specialist or resource teacher
- subject-area collaboration where teachers teach specific subjects
- "cluster" collaboration where teachers are located in the same wing

General and special education teachers are participating in more collaborative teaching arrangements whereby two teachers share equal responsibility for planning, teaching, and assessing students. This provides the teachers involved with numerous problem-solving and cooperative teaching opportunities. Research shows that both students with and without disabilities benefit (Gable & Manning, 1997). Teachers begin to develop flexibility and are more creative in strategies to meet the needs of all students. Wood (1998) found that in initial stages of an inclusion or collaborative environment, teachers maintained discrete role boundaries, but as the year progressed, role perceptions became less rigid and the teaming became more cooperative. Contradicting previous results suggesting that educators prefer pull-out programs, a comprehensive assessment of general and special education teachers and administrators indicated the respondents from 32 school sites favored full inclusion of all students (Villa, Thousand, Meyers, & Nevin, 1996).

Whether you are in a collaborative situation or general classroom, there are numbers of students within classrooms with special needs. It is essential that you learn to consult other colleagues and seek their assistance when needed.

Familiarize yourself with the various special resources and learn how to obtain the available services that will benefit all your students.

Collaborating with Parents

Collaboration extends beyond the environs of the school. Parents are a valuable asset to the school, and their involvement and support needs to be fostered. Encouraging parents to express their concerns and soliciting their ideas and support in making academic or behavior decisions regarding their child benefits the learner. The Metropolitan Life Survey of the American Teacher (Harris & Associates, 1998) found that students who do better academically are more likely than students who have academic difficulties to feel that their parents take an active interest in their school lives, provide them with the home support they need to succeed academically, and encourage them to pursue their dreams.

Parents and community representatives are important resources for meeting the mission and goals of schools. Site-based decision making engages parents and teachers working together in planning school improvement. How do we get more parents involved as active partners in the collaborative interrelationship between home and school? Adapted from Giannetti and Sagarese (1998) is a list of 10 approaches to turn parents into partners:

1. Welcome and invite the parents to the classroom.
2. Advertise your expertise through newsletters and other media.
3. Implement an early warning system with frequent progress reports.
4. Show parents a positive picture of their child.
5. Convey to parents your shared values—effort, discipline, responsibility, standards, and integrity.
6. Cast yourself as a child advocate.
7. Share your inside information about the learner's world.
8. Empathize with parents that parenting is a tough job.
9. Be an effective and fair disciplinarian.
10. Be a consistent role model.

Collaborating with Other Agencies

Other people and resources in the community may contribute to your students' learning and behavior. Family resource centers, foster or group homes, social service agencies, and residential treatment centers may be of assistance to one or more of your students. In addition, parents and/or physicians may confer with you about students on medication or under emotional or physical therapy, asking you to report the effectiveness of the medication dosage or therapy.

Developing appropriate relationships with colleagues, parents, and others is a significant segment of teaching. The quality of interactions between you and colleagues, parents, and others within agencies involved with learning programs affects your success as teacher. Your experience as beginning teacher provides extensive opportunities for interacting with a variety of professionals. Sharing insights, efforts, and abilities enhances the quality of instruction provided learners. As an effective collaborator, you contribute to—and benefit from—exchanging views, opinions, and experiences.

ASSIGNED ACTIVITIES

Recall the number of professionals and others with whom you relate as a teacher. The activities below are intended to guide your reflection on the quality of your interactions, how you have benefited and contributed to a collaborative effort.

1. Chart the length of time spent during a week as you interacted with the following:

	M	T	W	Th	F
Supervising teacher(s)					
University supervisor					
Team members					
Principal(s)					
Counselor					
Other school personnel					
Parents					
Community members					

2. Journal ways you used your interpersonal skills in your collaboration with two or three of the above.
3. In your interactions describe at least two ways in which you demonstrated productive leadership or active team membership skills.
4. What skills do you want to work on to become a more effective collaborator? Journal your plan for development or progress toward achievement.

SUMMARY

Focus One invited you to continue to interact with your students, your colleagues, your supervising teacher, parents, and others with a new awareness of the numerous personal benefits derived from refining your collaborative skills. As you gain confidence and a sense of belonging, you are more likely to contribute to the valuable insights you have received from observations and daily interaction with the students. Developing collaboration skills takes practice and is an ongoing process. **Focus One** provided ways to pool your resources, clarify your ideas, share and receive suggestions, and make decisions in the form of an action plan. This cooperative, collaborative interpersonal activity presented practice with collaborative skills and allowed you to analyze the underlying framework necessary for effective collaboration among members of a community.

Effective communication skills and positive interaction in collaborative settings lead to shared decision making, benefiting students, parents, and families. No one course or workshop can prepare you adequately to work effectively with families and agencies. Activities that may help you increase your confidence and competence may include the following:

- Attending guest lectures and discussions led by teachers, parents, or community experts provide opportunities to interact and learn different approaches to collaboration.
- Peer sharing of case studies and school and community experiences presents a type of action research where your responses can be analyzed and discussed against learning theories presented in your preservice courses.
- Serving on a school or community committee with a variety of teachers, parents, and/or community consultants is a great experience.
- Working cooperatively with other group members by actively listening, determining when to question for clarification, or initiating an action leads to joint decision making and productive problem solving.

FOLLOW-UP QUESTIONS AND SHARED INSIGHTS

As a beginning teacher you have been observing and participating in curriculum integration efforts in a variety of collaborative approaches to accommodate learner needs. Reflect on your own family background, your basic assumptions about social and cultural differences of your students' backgrounds, and your attitude toward working with all your students and their families as you share insights and discuss the following:

1. Describe collaborative efforts in which you are presently engaged (i.e., student portfolio development, thematic units, individual education plan (IEP), school-based decision making, conferencing).
2. When conflicting ideas and opinions are expressed, how do partners, team members, administrators, parents, and other group members respond?
3. Examine the chart under Assigned Activities that shows the number of your interactions during the past five days. With whom do you most frequently interact? Share an experience about when collaboration was necessary to your decision making.
4. Which skills do you most frequently use or would like to use in all collaborative activities? Describe the degree of success you experienced in applying these skills.
5. Role play one of the following situations. Alternately play the roles of parent and teacher. Discuss the collaborative behaviors demonstrated by each in the role.
   - Discuss a son or daughter's performance or behavior with a parent.
   - Talk with parents who are upset about their son or daughter's grades.

Collaborating with Colleagues, Parents, and Others
New Teacher Standards
- The teacher identifies the purpose and scope of the collaborative effort.
- The teacher demonstrates tolerance for alternative perspectives and options and encourages contributions from parents and community resources.
- The teacher demonstrates sensitivity to differences in abilities, modes of contribution, and social and cultural backgrounds.

Performance Guidelines
During your education program you have had various experiences that provided opportunities for collaboration. You have interacted with instructors and colleagues in university classes, and as a student or intern teacher you are working extensively with supervising teachers and other support personnel in the schools. In addition, you are increasingly involved with the school community and social service agencies. When addressing the collaboration section of your portfolio, you will want to describe these and similar experiences. The three tasks below are intended to guide your reflective experience with collaboration.

1. Identify three different types of collaborative experiences you have had in university classes, school settings, and in community or social service agencies.
2. Describe when and where the collaboration occurred, the purpose and scope of the collaboration, and your specific contributions to the effort.

3. Critique the effectiveness of each collaboration in terms of:
- How the collaborative effort met its stated goals.
- What was learned from your experience about negotiation, conflict, and compromise.
- How you use what you learned in working collaboratively with parents, colleagues, and others.

Performance Criteria

The quality of your entry will be assessed to the extent that evidence provided:

- Identifies the purpose and scope of the collaborative effort.
- Demonstrates tolerance for alternative perspectives and options, and encourages contributions from parents and community resources.
- Demonstrates sensitivity to differences in abilities, modes of contribution, and social and cultural backgrounds.

Journal Excerpts

High School

"I will be conferencing with all my students' parents this evening. Mr. T. and F. will assist me in preparation, provide input, and answer any questions I can't handle. T. and F. said we'll get about 30% of our parents, with more coming in the Spring to concentrate on scheduling. Most all the parents I have met are very supportive and enthusiastic. They said I'll get a few apologetic parents concerning their child and perhaps a few hostile ones. I'm excited to meet with the parents, but also very nervous."

"Today was a busy and long day. I met at 7:15 with my supervising teachers to discuss my upcoming schedule at school and my soccer schedule. They never seem to be impatient or uninterested in helping me. I am thankful for this. Mr. G. has helped me get acquainted with Resource Period which means I supervise students' study time. I now understand the sign out/in process and I think I'll be fine. We also began planning with Mr. S. for the new classes I am assuming responsibility for teaching. During first and second periods the guidance counselor came in to speak to the sophomores about the PSAT they will be taking later this month. I think several in Mr. G's class are beginning to trust me. This makes me feel more confident."

"Teacher education can prepare you for many things except for the tragic event that happened today at our high school. One of the school's outstanding students and a football player was killed while waiting for his bus. First, the players were called down and told; then, the vice principal came around and told each teacher before making an announcement over the P.A. After the announcement bursts of screams, yelps, and loud crying were heard throughout the building. Upset students were asked to go to the library where there were counselors to talk with and comfort students. Crises members from the school district office came, police officers, and some gang specialists were all available. Teachers and staff were there to counsel, comfort and love the hurting friends, team members, and classmates. Not only were the student's family and friends affected by his death, but the entire school and community. I can't begin to describe the hurt I felt these students were going through and the many unanswered questions of 'Why?' Although none of us has the answer, many teachers stopped class and dealt with the issue in different ways. Some students were asked to write journal entries, some just sat quietly, and some teachers just hugged and comforted those students who needed a shoulder to cry on. I was very impressed at the way the staff, faculty, and school district representatives handled this tragic event and the way they were there for each student. College classes can't prepare you for such tragedies and all week I've been asking God, 'why?' and I have learned a lot. It seems that what helps most is that teachers, schools, businesses and community members all pull together for the kids and changes happen. I can't imagine how incredibly well students would do if they always had this kind of love and support from all!"

Middle School

"I had a great day! Dr. S. observed me and had positive things to say about my teaching. Ms. N., the Principal, sent my recommendation letter to the school district office, another middle school called to set up an interview, and the newspaper called and said it was publishing the article I sent. I'm elated!"

"Another student teacher and I collaborate quite a bit. He gave me a really creative lesson plan on irony that I tried with this class today. Of course, they loved it. It involved listening to music. S. is so creative in so many ways. I thought I would miss talking with him when I move, but then I remembered we both have e-mail. Another thing we talked about was my eighth grade class. He sensed that I was frustrated with them. I can't help it; I try not to get irritated with them, but I always seem to anyway. Their behavior definitely needs work. It's getting to the point where I worry about doing hands-on lessons and cooperative learning with them. They're fine in small groups but when the entire class is there, for example language arts, I have to keep a very tight reign or they get out of control. S. gave some suggestions that I plan to try."

"Yesterday we met as a team to discuss upcoming field trips. We are going to the zoo and later we will take a three-day camping trip. I expect it to be a lot of work. Field trips require so many forms, especially the over-night camping trip. There are packing lists, permission slips, money to be paid, and plans for students staying at school during this time. The list seems endless and each one has a deadline. Fee waivers cover the zoo trip but not the camping trip. Most students sold candy to go to the camp for free. Parents are also involved. Our school holds 'Chit-Chat' sessions with parents and most of their questions this week were about the upcoming camping trip."

Elementary

"One problem with the lesson occurred when students who received special help returned after I began teaching the class. Everything is orderly and all students are working until these two students come into the room. I lose all control and everyone loses focus on what they are doing. As I see it, the rules and consequences are not followed for these students and this bothers me. If they get two or three marks, it doesn't matter because nothing happens to them. I know I need to stick to my guns and apply consequences."

"Today was my first day with Mrs. W. and the third grade class. It was very new and interesting. I came in and was greeted with a warm welcome. The day was spent getting familiar with routine procedures in the room. I charted students' names and drew seating charts to help me learn the names of the children. The class was reading their *Storybook* magazine. This is an extra that she uses for reading. The magazine is full of short stories and clever activities. I noticed that after reading the magazine, Mrs. W. asked them to identify the genre of the story. Later she filled me in and told me she is emphasizing the genre this year and including it in the assessment process. I learned the markings that she uses in her grading system; A+ means very good and a check mark means adequate. This is a bit different from what I have been using to grade homework."

"I arrived early today to share my plans with Mrs. R. I have completed the plans for my lessons for next week and I wanted to show her my ideas to make sure that she approved of the plan and the activities I had selected. She seemed pleased with the plan and the activities."

Special Education

"My day began with an ECE Meeting. This session was very informative. We talked about a number of issues, specifically the new IEP forms and how to complete them. Actually I shared some of the things I knew from the classes I've taken on campus."

"I was very happy to be with Ms. M. on Friday. We didn't have time to really discuss my role but I know it is a conversation we will soon have. With her I think I will really experience what team teaching is like."

"We had another parent volunteer again today. I've met this mother before and really like her. Apparently she paid a compliment about me to Ms. L. It felt good to hear something positive because very often I only think the worst. Although I don't feel as though I change my style when parents come in, I am very aware of their presence."

REFERENCES AND SUGGESTED READINGS

Berger, E. H. (2000). *Parents as partners in education: The school and home working together* (5th ed.). Upper Saddle River, NJ: Merrill/Prentice Hall.

Berres, M. S., Ferguson, D. L., Knoblock, P., & Woods, C. (Eds.). (1996). *Creating tomorrow's schools today: Stories of inclusion, change, & renewal.* New York: Teachers College, Columbia University.

Center for the Future of Children. (1996). *The future of children: Special education for students with disabilities.* Los Altos, CA: Center for the Future of Children.

Finn, J. D. (1998). Parental engagement that makes a difference. *Educational Leadership, 55*(8), 20–24.

Friend, M. & Cook, L. (1996). *Interactions: Collaboration skills for school professionals* (2nd ed.). New York: Longman.

Fuchs, D., & Fuchs, L. S. (1995). What's "special" about special education? *Phi Delta Kappan, 76*(7), 522–530.

Gable, R. A., & Manning, M. L. (1997). The role of teacher collaboration in school reform. *Childhood Education, Summer,* 219–223.

Giannetti, C. C., & Sagarese, M. M. (1998). Turning parents from critics to allies. *Educational Leadership, 55*(8), 40–42.

Goethals, M. S., & Howard, R. A. (1985). *Handbook of skills essential to beginning teachers.* Lanham, MD: University Press of America.

Guskey, T. R. (Ed.). (1996). *ASCD Yearbook 1996: Communicating student learning.* Alexandria, VA: Association for Supervision and Curriculum Development.

Harris, L., & Associates, Inc. (1997). *Building family-school partnerships: Views of teachers and students.* The Metropolitan Life Survey of the American Teacher (1998). New York: Metropolitan Life Insurance Company.

Henderson, J. G. (1996) *Reflective teaching: The study of your constructivist practices.* Upper Saddle River, NJ: Merrill/Prentice Hall. pp. 183–203

Howard, V. F., Williams, B. F., Port, P. D., & Lepper, C. (1997). *Very young children with special needs: A formative approach for the 21st century.* Upper Saddle River, NJ: Merrill/Prentice Hall.

Johnson, L. J., & Pugach, M. C. (1991). "Peer collaboration: Accommodating students with mild learning and behavior problems." *Exceptional Children, 57*(5), 454–461.

Long, C., and Stansbury, K. (1994). Performance assessment for beginning teachers: Options and lessons. *Phi Delta Kappan, 76*(4), 318–322.

Murphy, J. (1995). Changing roles of the teacher. In M. J. O'Hair & S. J. Odell (Eds.), *Educating teachers for leadership and change.* Thousand Oaks: Corwin Press, Inc. pp. 311–323.

Pugach, M. C., and Johnson, L. J. (1995). *Collaborative practitioners: Collaborative schools.* Denver: Love.

Rosenberg, M. S., O'Shea, L., and O'Shea, D. J. (1998). *Student teacher to master teacher: A practical guide for educating students with special needs.* (2nd ed.). Upper Saddle River, NJ: Merrill/Prentice Hall.

Villa, R. A., Thousand, J. S., Meyers, H., and Nevin, A. (1996). Teacher and administrator perceptions of heterogeneous education, *Exceptional Children 63*(1), 29–45.

Welch, M. (1998). Collaboration: Staying on the bandwagon, *Journal of Teacher Education, 49*(1), 26–37.

Wood, M. (1998). "Whose job is it anyway? Educational roles in inclusion," *Exceptional Children, 64*(2), 181–195.

Zabel, R. H., and Zabel, M. K. (1996). *Classroom management in context: Orchestrating positive learning environments.* Boston: Houghton Mifflin.

13 Reflecting and Evaluating Teaching

"To cultivate good teaching we must begin with ourselves."

C. M. Clark

Focus One

Expected Performance

- List gifts, talents, abilities, and sources of these gifts in your life.
- Examine ways these gifts allow you to fulfill some aspect of the teacher role.
- Share with others your insights about gifts and their effect on who you are and what you do as a teacher.

For Who I Am and What I Have, Thanks!

Welcome to the changing profession of teaching! You join the profession at a time when the teacher role is expanding its terrain, encompassing new expectations for you as collaborator, colleague, leader, and learner. Throughout the student/intern teacher experience you reflect on teaching practices, collect data, and share your understandings and insights with colleagues. Performing the teacher role requires you to have a deep knowledge base, effective methodologies and teaching strategies, and critical thinking skills. To be an effective teacher it is also necessary to have a focused understanding of yourself as an individual.

Focus One activities invite you to share with peers your perceptions and feelings about your development as a teacher. We intend that these activities allow you to highlight the positive feelings you have about your growth as a professional and your ever-widening perceptions of the teacher role. Your group and seminar discussions may even extend into the school and generate conversations with other teachers willing to share their insights about teaching! As you look to yourself and others, your understanding of the teacher role continually expands and changes. You clarify your beliefs about teaching and highlight those aspects you value and intend to acquire. You are changing, developing, advancing, and experiencing the joys and disappointments of life as a teacher.

Understanding yourself and valuing your beliefs influence your teaching, and this ongoing process is critical to your development. We teachers need help from others, urges Clark (1995), and we learn to respect our students by learning to respect and love the "child" within ourselves. To connect with students it is important to remember what it was like for you to be their age. "To cultivate good teaching we must begin with ourselves" (p. 16). This "beginning with ourselves" includes identifying what we believe, where these beliefs come from, and how they impact who we are as teachers. As members of the profession, we are also charged to consider these beliefs in light of principles associated with the teaching profession: honesty, fairness, protection of the weak, and respect for all people. The ongoing exploration of yourself as a teacher calls you to recognize and appreciate others, assist and encourage those in need, and appraise and direct others with integrity and courage.

One dimension of exploring self is to consider the gifts you bring to the teaching career. These gifts are the characteristics and abilities that make you unique and special. Do you think of yourself as a gift? Webster's definition of gift is "something given; talent." Implied in the definition is the existence of a receiver. In how many ways do you as a teacher give of yourself? Is your ability to give to others the result of someone giving to you? Robert Coles (1993) describes people who provided models of service for him: Dorothy Day, Simon Weil, Anna Freud, Erik Erikson, his mother and father. He describes his parents as gifts in their modeling of service:

> I have been given so much, and shown so much, by so many individuals. My parents still hover over, even haunt, this subject matter. . . . I have heard my mother's and my father's voices . . . I have a tape of a radio interview done with my father, discussing his extraordinary work with ailing and poor elderly people, and I have a tape of a talk my mother gave to a charitable group devoted to the needs of children. (p. xxvi)

Who are the people in your life you consider gifts? How did the values they embody and their principled living influence your development?

Your reflections, conversations, and journal writing act as a wetstone in sharpening your awareness of gifts you bring to others each day. As a student/ intern teacher, do you discover being and doing things you never expected of yourself? Are you moved to act, to help, to instruct and assist students and colleagues? These experiences are invitations to learn about the abilities and characteristics—gifts—that you may not have been aware of possessing! Have you thought or said, "I didn't know I could do it!" Can you name a gift you recently discovered? Teaching uses all of your gifts, and your awareness of these gifts better enables you to direct and expand their use.

From whence did these gifts come? Your talents and abilities are justifiably treasured and remembering them you feel enriched. Perhaps earlier generations passed these gifts to you and they became your heritage. Preservice teachers involved in service learning are reported to have gained in their social and personal responsibility, moral reasoning, and self-esteem. Opportunities to reflect on what they learned from service-centered activities and the total impact of these experiences contributed even more to their personal development (Root, 1997). Do your experiences within the school community bear out this type of learning for you? Acknowledging and using your talents and gifts enables you to develop an attitude of gratitude.

The media repeatedly reminds us that we are a nation of power and luxury compared with many other countries throughout the world. Once a year, particularly at Thanksgiving, we are reminded to count our blessings. Among these blessings are the founding fathers' and mothers' ideals of freedom, human rights, and justice for all. You can name heroes, heroines, and saints whose lives and words embody these ideals and continue to inspire. Taking time to reflect briefly and affirm ourselves reminds us that our gifts are indeed bountiful.

On a more personal basis, consider the support systems you have come to count on: your family, your education, your moral convictions. Contrast these with what you may see in the classroom. As a student/intern teacher you may be surprised at the level of isolation some children and adolescents live with daily. Some may know little of the "good life," and you marvel at their resilience. You may be surprised at the amount of neglect experienced by children and adolescents in your school. In this land of plenty you recognize that a sense of family is not necessarily present in the lives of some youth. Perhaps, you note that a sense of pride and approval is not part of every student's experience. Their eyes and their interactions tell you volumes about the need to communicate and a longing to be accepted.

This activity asks you to take a few minutes to consider your gifts, and name two or three that you prize. These could be people who have always been there

Seminar Leader Task

You may want to provide students with special materials for listing their gifts. The Appendix contains a wrapped-gift design that may be copied and distributed to students.

for you—your parents, extended family members, a teacher, a neighbor, or a member of your church, synagogue, or mosque. There may be events and memories you treasure, times when others recognized and praised your special abilities. From conversations and interactions with others you realize that you have a positive attitude toward yourself, toward others, and toward life's challenges. You take risks, possess a vision of what you want to become, and are determined to move ahead. What gifts have brought you to this time in your life? Who are the people who inspired, motivated, supported, and believed in you? Using the space below, list the persons, abilities, and events you consider the treasured gifts to which you credit much of who you are and what you have to give as a teacher.

_____

_____

_____

_____

Discussion Questions

1. Describe some gifts you deeply value and are most grateful to have. Which of your gifts do you want to share with students? With teachers and other members of the school community?
2. What student/intern teaching experiences have helped you recognize your gifts? Without your current experiences, which gifts might you ignore and take for granted?
3. Consider these principles of the teaching profession: honesty, fairness, protection of the weak, and respect for all people. Select the principles you see as especially important for you to practice and explain the reasons for your choice.
4. When considering the role of teachers in preparing citizens for a democratic society, what would you add to the list of professional teaching principles?

Focus Two

Reflection and self-assessment are essential to progress and achieve teaching tasks: planning, implementing instruction, assessing learning, creating and managing the learning environment, reflecting, and evaluating instruction. Assigning specific activities offers you the opportunity to review and reinforce the best teaching practices and processes most critical to student learning.

Quality performance and continuous growth require self-reflection, assessment, and analysis. Conferences with your classroom and university supervising teacher, in which you share reflections, successes, concerns, suggestions, and future plans, are intended to help you progress and become comfortable, competent, and confident. Supervisors' encouragement and constructive comments reinforce your efforts.

You want to try so many new strategies. Looking at the assessment results of your lesson or unit, you ask yourself a number of questions: Was this the best strategy for the content I taught? Perhaps if I used cooperative learning groups, students would be engaged in the discussion. Why was student writing not up to standard? Questions such as these demonstrate how you are internalizing reflective practices and becoming increasingly self-reflective.

APPLICATION: REFLECTING AND EVALUATING TEACHING

You are assuming a more active role as teacher and becoming responsible for the class instruction. How exciting! What an awesome feeling! You have worked so hard to develop the necessary characteristics and skills to become an effective teacher. We have defined reflection as a reasoned response through either pre-planned or spontaneous but conscious actions. In recalling learning from liberal arts and educational courses and previous work with students, you are developing your teacher behaviors within the classroom and integrating your knowledge and experience. Reflection on your classroom practices encourages growth. Learning to teach well is a result of reflective practice.

Reflective Teaching Techniques

You are in a setting with extensive opportunities to practice reflection. During this beginning teacher experience, trying out new ideas, instructional strategies, and assessment instruments and sharing your planning and self-assessment with your supervising teacher and university supervisor reveal your commitment to reflective practice. You have a desire to hone your reflective skills and wonder how to assess your own strategies.

Ross, Bondy, and Kyle (1993) describe characteristics and abilities essential to developing effective reflective techniques:

- Demonstrate introspection, responsibility, and open-mindedness.
- See things from multiple perspectives.
- Use adequate evidence to support or assess decisions.
- Use educational, ethical, and practical criteria.

You are asking reflective questions: What do my students need? How will I plan for these needs? Why am I selecting these activities? What approach will I use to communicate this concept? Which assessment instruments will I use to determine how well my students are learning? Why are some students still not engaged? What can I do differently to keep my students focused? On and on. All of these questions assist you in looking at ways to expand and deepen your knowledge of the learners, content, and instructional and management skills. Reflective questions result in answers or movement toward more student-centered teaching.

Journaling and conferencing with your classroom and university supervising teachers, administrators and other school personnel, colleagues, and parents have provided extensive opportunities for reflective practice. You have been asked to share specific responses to questions relating to best practice each week. By writing journal entries regarding specific assigned activities, you are analyzing classroom events, testing your beliefs, and building your educational philosophy. Participating in cooperative groups and testing and discussing educational issues with your colleagues bring you into contact with new ideas and different perspectives.

Beliefs about teaching and learning are built over a lifetime. Teachers who approach teaching reflectively often view themselves as problem solvers, even change agents. Meeting the challenges of diversity and change will require your talents and resourcefulness. There is a sense of movement to change and to innovation, and there is often a sense of excitement and/or apprehension in the way individuals greet it (Rust, 1993, p. 14). Continually collecting evidence about student learning, you will learn to make wise choices and ethical decisions, to identify strengths and weaknesses of your instructional decisions, and to analyze ways to improve your teaching. As a promising effective teacher, you will never be satisfied with the status quo.

Helping Learners Become Reflective

Influencing the development of your students' learning each day is a tremendous opportunity for you as teacher. When students see you excited and eager to learn new things, they become motivated to become active learners. Reflecting with students, probing to find out what they learn from assigned activities, who their favorite character is and why, how the experiment could have different results, and what approach the students used to solve the problem encourages the reflective process. Reflection is actually modeled for the students. Such thinking, openmindedness, discernment, rational judgment, and creativity is likely to transfer to other aspects of students' lives. Teaching students to become reflective thinkers enables them to take more responsibility for their learning and become active participants in the process.

What are some strategies to increase reflective practice among your students? Adapting Van de Walle's (1998, p. 34) suggestions to structure mathematical lessons promoting reflective thought, we generalized them for all areas of the curriculum. You may find them useful in assessing whether you are encouraging reflective thinking among your students.

- Create a rich and safe learning climate.
- Pose worthwhile, engaging instructional tasks.
- Use well-planned cooperative learning groups.
- Use models, multimedia, and physical materials as thinker tools.
- Encourage thoughtful discussion and writing.
- Require students to defend and explain their responses.
- Listen actively.

Careful analysis and reflection are necessary to guarantee learning. Journal writing, group work, higher-level questions, projects, presentations, discussions, and creative homework assignments are ways students may demonstrate reflective critical thinking. Students who are critical thinkers and independent learners are the hallmarks of quality education. Incorporating reflection into your objectives leads students toward deeper insights, whatever the topic of study. Helping young people become reflective learners gives them a sense of confidence and ownership about personal learning.

Reflective Practice

Throughout your beginning teaching experience, you are reviewing and monitoring your goals and expectations, assessing what progress is made, and deciding what reinforcement is needed. All strengthen your reflective practice because they increase your confidence and competence in the teaching role. As a perceptive observer and a full participant in the learning process, you gradually assume more responsibility for all aspects of instruction and assessment. You are planning, preparing all the materials and activities, and teaching learners with varied talents and needs. You are also realistic and realize the commitment and energy it takes to fulfill this demanding role of teacher.

Reflection requires looking back, reviewing goals and priorities, and continually asking questions: What have I learned? How has this learning helped me? What are the implications embedded in this teaching experience for my students? Bridging theory and practice is a gradual process requiring continuous and systematic focus.

As a reflective beginning teacher, you are aligning instructional practices with major outcomes designed to facilitate effective instruction outlined by state and national standards. Learning to teach using those outcomes and standards allows you to review and reflect (self-assess) your teaching. To what extent are you:

- designing and planning instruction and learning climates that develop student abilities?
- introducing, implementing, and managing instruction that develops student abilities?
- assessing and communicating learning results to students and parents or guardians?
- reflecting and assessing teaching/learning situations and/or programs?
- collaborating with colleagues, parents, and others?
- engaging in professional development?
- demonstrating knowledge of subject matter?

ASSIGNED ACTIVITIES

For this assignment, reflecting on your instructional behaviors, examine an entire class instruction from preparation through assessment.

Journal your self-assessment of your instruction during one setting each day this week. Include the following components:

- grouping for instruction
- content area and concept, skill, or process
- instructional resources and materials
- students' special needs
- objectives, outcomes, expectations
- introduction, anticipatory set, advance organizer
- strategies and procedures (direct instruction, group investigation, cooperative group discussion, learning centers, creative problem solving, multimedia presentation)
- management of learning environment and student behavior
- closure, transition
- learning assessment
- assignment

SUMMARY

Focus One provided you an opportunity to examine your individual talents and gifts as teacher. In addition to seeing your role as collaborator, colleague, leader, and learner, you can also identify the skills you have that guarantee your success in these roles. Naming and owning your gifts and talents is not an easy task for some, especially if you are gradually becoming aware of what you have to offer others. You may have surprised yourself by more freely sharing your ideas, asking for suggestions, and voicing your beliefs. You realize that to become the teacher to which you aspire, you cannot flourish in isolation. Reaching out to others validates your gifts and talents as you begin to establish a close network of colleagues. This network paves the way toward collaborative endeavors such as solving school problems and making long-term decisions that affect learners.

When you become self-reflective, self-evaluative, you think deeply about every aspect of your teaching. Your everyday teaching provides ample experiences to analyze and determine strengths and areas needing improvement. Keeping a journal of your thoughts and feelings about your teaching is an additional means of self-evaluation. Studying and analyzing your teaching moves you toward becoming, as Cruickshank (1987, p. 3) says, a thoughtful and wise teacher.

FOLLOW-UP QUESTIONS AND SHARED INSIGHTS

Throughout your beginning teacher experience the activities emphasized reflection and evaluation of your teaching behaviors. You journaled comments on specific components of your instructional performance and initiated change where necessary. The following questions will aid in sharing your reflective evaluation of the lesson using the components from your Assigned Activities.

1. To what extent did you consider the diversity among learners in preparation for this lesson? How are you providing for the individual learner?
2. Do the materials and procedures match your objectives or learning outcomes for the lesson taught? What is the learning value of the activities planned for this lesson?
3. To what extent do you assess student performance using the established criteria and scoring guides consistent with the school system performance assessment program?
4. In what ways do you promote student reflective self-assessment?
5. What are the strengths you exhibit in your teaching performance? What teaching strategies reinforce your creativity?
6. What areas of the curriculum present your greatest challenge?
7. Discuss your growth as a reflective self-evaluator in making decisions about curriculum content, classroom management, collaborative teaching, and performance assessment.

Reflecting and Evaluating Teaching and Learning
New Teacher Standards

- The teacher continually evaluates the effects of choices and actions made concerning students, parents, and other professionals in the learning community.
- The teacher accurately assesses, analyzes, and communicates the effectiveness of instruction and makes appropriate changes to improve student learning.
- The teacher analyzes and evaluates the effects of learning experiences on individuals and on the class as a whole, and makes appropriate changes to improve student learning.

Performance Guidelines

Teachers as reflective learners accurately assess, analyze, and make appropriate changes to instruction. Read the following guidelines and submit the evidence described in step 7.

1. Provide three lesson plans you have taught with learner academic expectations or objectives, course content, and core concepts identified.
2. Refer to your lesson plans as evidence of meeting performance criteria for your first portfolio task as you make your selection.
3. Reflect on different classes or content areas in your choice of plans.
4. Evaluate the effectiveness of the learning experiences for your students.
5. Reflect on your instructional strategies and your interaction with students throughout the lesson.

6. Describe how you would improve student learning.
7. Submit **evidence** to include the following:
   - a copy of three lesson plans (refer to lesson plans from Portfolio Task in chapter 3)
   - evaluation of student learning experiences in the lesson
   - self-evaluation as you reflect on the teaching experience
   - description of changes you would make

Performance Criteria

The quality of your entry will be assessed to the extent that evidence provided:

- Accurately assesses, analyzes, and communicates the effectiveness of instruction and makes appropriate changes to improve student learning.
- Analyzes and evaluates the effects of learning experiences on individuals and on the class as a whole, and makes appropriate changes to improve student learning.

Journal Excerpts

High School

"I am now responding to freshmen and sophomores concerning their writing portfolios. I really enjoy learning to do this and I feel it's one of my strengths. I do have a tendency to put too much information on student evaluations and this can overwhelm them. So, I'm really working on choosing the most important things the students need to work on. I try to stay positive and always find something good about each piece I see. It is hard, draining work to respond to everything; however, students have put a lot of time into their writing and it deserves my time as well. This is making me feel much more prepared to teach and evaluate."

"I think I showed productive leadership in an English Department meeting today. I shared with others a creative group activity for teaching my freshmen how to write a letter to the newspaper editor. All freshmen have to write this letter. I suggested topics such as sports, teen smoking, and others they were interested in. I made copies of some examples of student work and handed them out at the meeting. Sharing ideas is what being a good department member is all about."

"I went over the answers to the Diagnostic Tests for grammar using basic presentation skills. I discussed *why* we review grammar since I wanted them to know the *purpose* of this lesson and see its relevance. I had to review basic grammar rules before feeling comfortable answering the students' questions. I had written out reasons, page numbers for all answers so I could effectively explain it to the students. As a form of reinforcement I asked students to explain *why* they answered as they did. Teaching grammar at first glance seems a very simple task. I thought, 'I'm an English major. This should be easy.' Once again I was wrong. I had to go back and relearn basic grammar rules in order to be confident in teaching them to the sophomores. I had to write grammar rules and page numbers just to teach the basic rules I take for granted!"

"Wow! I think my emotions, fatigue, confidence, cluelessness, happiness, compassion, anxiety, detachment, etc . . . are all swirling around endlessly! My student teaching is rapidly drawing to a close and I think I have grown tremendously. It is going to be extremely sad to leave. I'll miss it."

Middle School

"The peer mediation activities were excellent. It was such a valuable educational experience for the students and for me! I was totally engaged in the discussions and I enjoyed participating every chance I got. Mrs. H. and I even participated as disputants in a mock mediation. The students got a big kick out it. I think it helped them grasp the idea. These skills will benefit me in the future. Conflict resolution is a skill we all need. I think it is encouraging that these middle schoolers care enough to be part of the solution to the problem of violence in schools."

"After I taught sixth period Ms. P.J. gave me a note about my teaching and I asked for more critiquing. She helped me out by saying that I had left out some minor details, and when I used the overhead I looked at students to my left, but needed to keep eye contact with others as well. She praised my getting a girl on task who was talking and couldn't answer the question I asked. I had stayed with the student until she responded to the question."

"I used to think closure came at the end of the lesson—boy was I wrong! I sometimes use closure as part of a transition at the end of each activity such as a review and before giving new material. I have also used closure after explaining projects and writing assignments and at the end of class or group discussions. This is something that I have gotten good at over the last few months. I often use the agenda that is written on the board to help students make the transition from one activity to another. Closure is important because it gives students a sense of accomplishment and if done well is a form of reflection."

Elementary School

"I taught the math lesson and it went well. I am continuing to focus on my strengths—planning well, providing an overview, and I even included closure. I have found that keeping students involved in the lesson by varying the responses keeps them on-task. I'm also working on some of my 'weaknesses,' such as circulating more."

"I taught a chapter review preparing students for tomorrow's test. I felt rushed and forgot to go over the directions for each problem. The students had many questions so we spent extra time. Mrs. D. was called out by the vice principal and couldn't help me deal with the problem at the time. This lesson went poorly but I think it was good for me to experience this. I think that I recovered and the important thing for me to remember is to take my time and not get rushed."

"I accomplished another goal that was that I pretended that I was the only teacher in the room, and many times I was! I directed the instruction and moved students to and from places such as the bathroom and P.E. I took initiative in beginning and ending tasks, and in following through with rules and consequences. I had a much better day because of this. The students listened to me because I asserted myself and believed that I was in charge. I feel much better about myself when I assume my role in this way."

Special Education

"Student behavior was not awful today but it was not as good as usual. We had three students go to the center, but they all walked themselves. Although I had been responding to student behavior pretty well before, I got more forceful today. For some reason they were wound up. I never had to be very forceful before, but they responded well to me when I was. I took more points than usual and gave two students tickets (a few problems on a worksheet). This calmed down the students and things went well."

"I am getting very attached to some of these kids. Every day it gets harder and harder to leave their problems at school. The environment some of these kids live in—it's a wonder they behave as well as they do. In order to reach these students I realize I have to relate to them personally while remaining professional. When I do this, it is very difficult to separate myself from their problems."

"Today was a good day although I have come to realize that I really need to set goals and a schedule for myself. I feel that by setting a schedule I can keep the students and myself in line. I really have a hard time moving the learners along, but I think setting time limits on activities contributes to their ability to attend to tasks."

References and Suggested Readings

Barth, R. S. (1990). *Improving schools from within.* San Francisco: Jossey-Bass.

Brubacher, J. W., Case, C. W., & Reagan, T. G. (1994). *Becoming a reflective educator: How to build a culture of inquiry in the schools.* Thousand Oaks, CA: Corwin Press.

Clark, C. M. (1995). *Thoughtful teaching.* New York: Teachers College Press.

Clark, C. M. (1990). The teacher and the taught: Moral transactions in the classroom. In J. I. Goodlad, R. Soder, & K. A. Sirotnik (Eds.) *The moral dimensions of teaching.* San Francisco: Jossey-Bass.

Clift, R. T., Houston, W. R., and Pugack, M. C. (1990). *Encouraging reflective practice in education: An analysis of issues and programs.* New York: Teachers College Press.

Coles, R. (1993). *The call of service.* Boston: Houghton Mifflin.

Cruickshank, D. R. (1987). *Reflective teaching: The preparation of students of teaching.* Reston, VA: Association of Teacher Educators.

Eby, J. W. (1996). *Reflective planning, teaching, and evaluation K–12.* (2nd ed.). Upper Saddle River, NJ: Merrill/Prentice Hall.

Harmin, M. (1994). *Inspiring active learning: A handbook for teachers.* Alexandria, VA: Association for Supervision and Curriculum Development.

Henderson, J. G. (1996). *Reflective teaching: The study of your constructivist practices* (2nd ed.). Upper Saddle River, NJ: Merrill/Prentice Hall.

Jersild, A. T. (1955). *When teachers face themselves.* New York: Teacher College Press.

Osterman, K. F., & Kottkamp, R. B. (1993). *Reflective practice for educators.* Newbury Park, CA: Corwin Press.

Posner, G. J. (1996). *Field experience: A guide to reflective teaching* (4th ed.). White Plains, NY: Longman.

Root, S. C. (1997). School-based service: A review of research for teacher education. In J. A. Erickson and J. B. Anderson (Eds.), *Learning with the community.* Washington, DC: American Association of Colleges for Teacher Education.

Ross, D. D., Bondy, E., & Kyle, D. W. (1993). *Reflective teaching for student empowerment: Elementary curriculum and methods.* New York: Macmillan.

Rust, F. O. (1993). *Changing teaching, changing schools.* New York: Teachers College Press.

Shartrand, A. M., Weiss, H. B., Kreider, H. M., & Lopez, M. E. (1997). *New skills for new schools: Preparing teachers in family involvement.* Cambridge, MA: Harvard Family Research Project.

Schön, D. A. (1987). *Educating the reflective practitioner: Toward a new design for teaching and learning in the professions.* San Francisco: Jossey-Bass.

Stern, B. S. (1997, March). Relations among college supervisors, cooperating teachers, and student teachers in a reflective teacher education program. Paper presented at the Annual Meeting of the American Educational Research Association, Chicago.

Van de Walle, J. A. (1998). *Elementary and middle school mathematics: Teaching developmentally.* New York: Longman.

Wilson, J., & Jan, L. W. (1993). *Thinking for themselves: Developing strategies for reflective learning.* Portsmouth, NH: Heineman.

14 Continuing the Professional Journey

> *Being a good teacher is not an end point; it is a continuous process—a process of action, a process of reflection and planning, and a process of collaboration.*

L. A. Baloche

Expected Performance

- Examine short and long-term goals of a professional teacher.
- Identify professional goals attempted and/or met.
- Share insights gained from engaging in the *Process of Reflective Practice.*
- Provide evidence of performance levels achieved as student/intern teacher.
- Develop a professional development plan to improve performance.

You are becoming a professional teacher! What does the descriptor *professional* mean? Your journey thus far has provided you many new and challenging experiences. Throughout this student/intern teaching experience you have participated in a variety of activities reinforcing your professional and personal growth. You are expected to develop new instructional techniques, refine your practice, and continually grow as a teacher and individual. These expectations may be imposed internally and externally. You may be quite familiar with state or local school system standards. Professional organizations offer curriculum frameworks and formats for designing and implementing instructional practices. Decisions and actions by these external groups influence your short- and long-term goals. As a partner with your supervising teacher and others, you have set professional goals for yourself prior to each lesson, and following each lesson you used these goals to assess your teaching. Critically reflective teaching and learning encourages and scaffolds lifelong learning (Rodriguez & Sjostrom, 1998). Reflective teaching promotes your dream of becoming truly professional.

PROFESSIONAL GROWTH: LOOKING INWARD

In previous chapters you examined your stages of growth beginning with the concerns you have about yourself as teacher and moving on to the concerns you hold about students' learning. This chapter engages you in the total reflective process. Asking reflective questions like "How can I change the approach to engage more of my students?" and "In what way did I improve my questioning strategies?" gets to the very heart of reflective teaching. "A teacher's understanding of others can be only as deep as the wisdom possessed when looking inward" (Jersild, 1955). Becoming increasingly critical and reflective of your teaching enhances professional growth and an understanding and acceptance of yourself and others. Likewise, your reflective modeling enables your students to become more critical and reflective in their learning tasks.

PROFESSIONAL GROWTH: PARTNERS IN THE PROCESS

Your supervising teacher and university supervisor are instrumental in guiding you on your professional journey. The feedback addressed in your conferencing with them provides specific insights into the progress you are making. These professionals, observing your instruction and interaction with students, help you consider the impact of your teaching on student learning. You have no doubt relied on their advice and suggestions in designing, planning, and implementing instructional improvements. These kinds of opportunities enhance your ability to reflect and analyze your teaching. Making curriculum and instruction adjustments necessary to ensure maximum student learning is essential for professional growth.

Administrators also help you clarify and establish your professional growth goals and assess progress toward reaching them. Communicating with these individuals as often as opportunities arise demonstrates your strengths in interpersonal skills. Requesting and preparing for classroom observations by the principal, team leader, and/or department chair provide you a variety of evaluation experiences. Observation reports and recommendations from these individuals can become part of your university credential file and gives a prospective administrator a broad picture of your instructional performance. In selecting good teachers, administrators consider teaching performance during an applicant's student/intern teaching the most important indicator of their future success as teacher (Ralph, et al 1998).

PROFESSIONAL GROWTH: A CULMINATING REFLECTION

Throughout this student/intern teaching experience you have been actively engaged in sequentially examining the process of transitioning from student/intern to teacher. Each week you considered one or more parts of this whole process. The group activities and the application sections encouraged your growth through active involvement. You continue to build a repertoire of best practice and learn to cope with many challenging situations. As you come closer to completing this student/intern teaching experience, we provide you a reflection for connecting the teaching/learning process with your next big step—becoming a professional **teacher.** This reflective activity is designed to help you holistically view your process and progress toward becoming a professional teacher.

You may feel pride in your past accomplishments and be energized with new perspectives for the journey ahead. The journey toward professionalism has begun! Your student/intern position has provided you numerous opportunities to document your growth toward the title *professional.* Your reflective processes have enabled you to recall with ease your experiences with planning, students, collaboration, and more. We have provided competencies to help you document your activities as an educator and showcase your work by creating a professional portfolio. The professional teacher competencies representing your student/intern teacher experience are presented in the following sections. You might want to jot down your thoughts as you move through each criteria. Onward with the journey!

Designs, Plans, and Implements Instruction

Compiling your portfolio during the past months is one means to connect professional development with teaching practice. Through conversations, seminar discussions, and journals you have reflected on the teaching strategies that you design, plan, and implement. You communicate evidence of your performance in all of these areas through the portfolio.

- What do you want others to know about your teaching?
- Do you see yourself as a professional teacher able to identify, plan, and implement teaching practices that are recognized as "best"?
- Which lesson plans demonstrate your best instruction?
- In what ways were you able to introduce computers across the curriculum?
- How does your portfolio present this aspect of you, the professional?

_____

_____

_____

_____

Accommodates Diversity

Believing that all students can learn is the first step in developing instructional strategies adapted to diverse learners. Treating all students with sensitivity and promoting racial unity and gender equity requires establishing a positive learning environment. Creating plans to include literature, art, music, multimedia, cooperative learning groups, community speakers, and other resources and activities contributes to cultural knowledge. Designing multiple learning experiences prepares students for working and living within a multicultural, pluralistic society.

- In what ways have you provided for classroom diversity in adapting your instruction to the cultural background, learning styles, and multiple intelligences of your students?
- How has your own ethnic, racial, gender, and cultural experiential background prepared you for teaching in a multicultural classroom?
- Would persons viewing your portfolio gain insight into your understanding and sensitivity toward other cultures and ethnic groups?

_____

_____

_____

_____

Assesses One's Performance

Reflection implies that as a professional teacher you continually assess your performance. Your student/intern teaching experience provides numerous opportunities to assess your performance class by class and to examine your teaching over a learning sequence and instructional units. Perhaps your supervising teacher and college supervisor provided suggestions and models for assessing best practice. As professionals, they observed your teaching and later in conferences guided you in looking at individual strategies and the overall instructional objectives as criteria for making assessment.

- How does your portfolio present you as a reflective professional?
- Which criteria included in your portfolio documents the breadth and depth of your self assessments?
- Have you solicited comments from administrators and others who observed your teaching?

- What written comments did you receive?
- How did these comments affect your subsequent planning and teaching?

_____

_____

_____

_____

Identifies Personal and Psychological Needs

The Focus One group activities and action plans encouraged you to identify your personal feelings, perceptions, and insights you experienced as you adjusted to different aspects of the teacher role. Role taking implies learning a set of new skills and adjusting to accompanying emotions.

- How might you communicate coping skills learned and growth in self-knowledge acquired through activities, conversations, and sharing with a variety of other professionals?
- How does your portfolio represent the growth and stretching that has occurred as the result of this student/intern teaching experience?
- How are you a different person as a result of this experience?

_____

_____

_____

_____

Seeks and Receives Support

Professional growth occurs when persons seek and receive support. On a daily basis you engage with peers, colleagues, and other professionals within and outside the school. Perhaps you share your perceptions and learn from others through their experiences from earlier teaching years. You observe their ongoing efforts to grow as directors, guides, and advocates of students, learners, and leaders.

- How have your interactions with these individuals encouraged you to pursue self-growth and consistent improvement?
- In what way have you grown more interdependent as a result of this experience?
- Toward what growth areas do you aspire?

_____

_____

_____

_____

Collaborates with Parents, Colleagues, and Others

Collaborating with parents, assisting a colleague in presenting a school program, sponsoring a student group, and participating on a school committee would be additional evidence that you are growing professionally. Parents and guardians look to you as expert in knowing how to direct and help their son or daughter. You experienced opportunities to communicate with them about their child and to work with them toward meeting a goal you shared. Perhaps you collaborated with other teachers on your team or in your department. Your portfolio allows you to demonstrate these and other collaborating activities you engage in now and throughout this experience.

- How do you see yourself as a collaborator?
- What portfolio entries present you as a partner and team or department member?

_____

_____

_____

Engages in Professional Growth Opportunities

Perhaps you attended workshops and inservice activities during student/intern teaching. You may belong to professional groups and have even shared ideas and strategies you used successfully with your students.

- How proficient are you with integrating technology into your classes?
- What evidence is there that you continue learning a variety of teaching techniques?
- How can your portfolio communicate to those viewing it that you are a learner?

_____

_____

_____

PROFESSIONAL GROWTH: THE PORTFOLIO

Your reflection using these eight performance outcomes as guides helps you to see just where this whole process has brought you. Your portfolio is the visual demonstration of your reflections and accomplishments. We have suggested a structured format to assist you with organizing your experiences. You are free to make choices that portray your "best" practice, your rationale for the choices you make in managing your classroom, your selection of assessment instruments, your reflective response to your collaborative experiences, your problem-solving and creative approaches in working with diverse learners, and your own philosophy—what you believe about your role as teacher at this time.

CONTINUING THE JOURNEY: A PROFESSIONAL DEVELOPMENT PLAN

The reflective process used in building your portfolio is actually professional development, an ongoing process. What an outlay of effort and energy is spent in this accomplishment! You have a well-prepared document demonstrating your growth in professional knowledge and expertise.

Setting goals for your students is an experience you practice daily. Setting goals for yourself, following up your instruction with self-assessment, and determining strengths and areas needing further improvement are part of the ongoing process for professional development. As an example, the following may be a framework for your plan:

- List one professional development goal for increasing the level of learner expectations that you set for yourself.
  Ex. Provide more activities that involve problem solving.

- Name the evidence you will use to determine the level of growth made toward reaching the goal.

  Ex. Introduce problem-solving activities each day as a regular part of my lessons. I will make an effort to assess one group of students each week.

- Determine a time line you will use for performing these activities.

  Ex. I will research math and science ideas for a variety of examples. I plan to begin on Monday with total group and assess Group #5 on Thursday. After one month I will assess the class with a written test. The results will determine the intervals for the next month.

- Name the external monitors that will provide feedback on progress made toward the professional goals.

  Ex. In this case my plan depends on continued practice and research by retrieving information from more experienced teachers. I will ask my supervising teacher to assess my progress in this area. I am comfortable in developing a lesson for my university supervisor and conferencing about my problem-solving strategies.

ONWARD AND UPWARD! JOURNEY ON!

Developing a plan of action now demonstrates commitment to professional growth. Some of the documentation will change as you meet future challenges in your first teaching position. Many states have a well-designed induction or internship program, which includes a professional development plan created by the beginning teacher. Having completed a professional development plan at this stage of your journey places you at an advantage. You are well on your way! Table 14.1 recaps criteria demonstrating professional growth as a teacher and identifies chapters in this text that address those criteria.

PROFESSIONAL ORGANIZATIONS AND YOU

Teachers are members of numerous professional organizations and engage in a wide range of development initiatives with peers. Organization members formulate standards for teaching and learning for specific content areas, generate and share teaching techniques, and address issues affecting the different age

TABLE 14.1 *Performance Criteria Demonstrating Professional Growth*

• Identify and seek to meet personal and psychological needs (**Focus One** activities).	Chapters 1–13
• Design, plan, and implement recognized best practice.	Chapters 1–13
• Accommodate for diversity.	Chapter 5
• Portray the professional teacher role through collaboration with parents, colleagues, and other school support personnel.	Chapter 12
• Assess one's performance based on best practice criteria.	Chapter 13
• Seek support from colleagues within and outside the school community, friends, family, and mentors.	Chapter 13
• Welcome assessment and recommendation of others.	Chapter 14
• Engage in professional growth opportunities: conferences, workshops, service organizations, advocacy groups, curriculum planning, and professional organizations.	Chapter 14

level of learners. You may already hold membership in one or more of the local, state, or national groups. Your involvement with any of these groups is a rich and ongoing source for learning and developing teaching strategies and exploring evolving issues in education.

Are you considering joining a professional organization? Will the next phase of your journey as a professional teacher involve you as a participant? Professional organizations provide multiple resources. As a member you receive journals and other publications by the organization and attend workshops and conferences sponsored by the organization. Members are invited to present research, ideas, and strategies at local and national sites throughout the year. Exchanges with other teachers are available through the World Wide Web. Using the Internet you can access the web site for each group and then join chat lines to dialogue current issues and teaching techniques with other members across the nation. The list below suggests several groups, journals, mailing, and Web site addresses.

American Alliance for Health, Physical Education, Recreation and Dance (AAHPERD) consists of six national and district associations with the research consortium:

American Association for Active Lifestyles and Fitness (AAALF)
American Association for Health Education (AAHE)
American Association for Leisure and Recreation (AALR)
National Association for Girls and Women in Sport (NAGWS)
National Association for Sport and Physical Education (NASPE)
National Dance Association (NDA)

AAHPERD address:

1900 Association Drive
Reston, VA 22091
<http://www.aahperd.org>

American Association for the Advancement of Science (AAAS)
AAAS address:

1200 New York Ave., NW
Washington, DC 20005
<http://www.aaas.org>

American Council on Teaching of Foreign Languages (ACTFL)
ACTFL address:

6 Executive Plaza
Yonkers, NY 10701-6801
<http://www.actfl.org>

Association for Supervision and Curriculum Development (ASCD)
ASCD address:

1250 N. Pitt St.
Alexandria, VA 22314-1453
Journal: *Educational Leadership* *<http://www.ascd.org>*

Association of Childhood Education International (ACEI)
Address:

11141 Georgia Avenue, Suite 200
Wheaton, MD 20902
Journal: *Childhood Education* *<http://www.asaenet.org>*

Council for Exceptional Children (CEC)
CEC address:

1920 Association Drive
Reston, VA 22091
Journal: *Exceptional Children* and *Teaching Exceptional Children*
    <*http://www.cec.sped.org/*>

International Reading Association (IRA)
IRA address:

800 Barksdale Road
P.O. Box 8139
Newark, DE 199714-8139
Journal: *Reading Teacher;* others are available at <journals@reading.org>
    <*http://www.reading.org*>

International Technology Education Association (ITEA)

ITEA Headquarters:
1914 Association Drive, Suite 201
Reston, VA 22091-1539
<*http://www.iris.org/~iteawww/index.html*>

Music Teachers National Association
MTNA address:

441 Vine St., Ste. 505
Cincinnati, OH 45202-2814
<*http://www.teachermagazine.org/context/orgs/mtna.htm*>

National Association for Gifted Children
Address:

1707 L St. N.W.
Suite 550
Washington, DC 10036
<*http://www.teachermagazine.org*>

National Association for the Education of Young Children (NAEYC)
NAEYC address:

1509 16th St., N.W.
Washington, DC 20036
Journal: *Young Children*
http://www./naeyc.org. or <*http://www.naeyc.org/text/*>

National Council for the Social Studies (NCSS)
NCSS address:

NCSS Headquarters Office
3501 Newark Street NW
Washington, DC 20016
Journal: *Social Education* <*http://www.ncss.org*>

National Council of Teachers of English (NCTE)
Address:

1111 Kenyon Road
Urbana, IL 61801
Journal: *English Journal, Primary Voices, Voices From the Middle*
    <*http://www.ncte.org*>

National Council of Teachers of Mathematics (NCTM)
NCTM address:

1906 Association Drive
Reston, VA 22091-1593
Journals: *Arithmetic Teacher* and *Mathematics Teacher* <*http://www.nctm.org*>

National Council on Economic Education (NCEE)
NCEE address:

1140 Avenue of the Americas
New York, NY 10036
<*http://www.nationalcouncil.org*>

National Middle School Association (NMSA)
NMSA address:

2600 Corporate Exchange Dr., #370
Columbus, OH 43231
Journal: *National Middle School Journal* <*http://www.nmsa.org*>

National Science Teachers Association (NSTA)
NSTA address:

1840 Wilson Boulevard
Arlington, VA 22201-3000
Journal: *The Science Teacher* and *Science and Children* <*http://www.nsta.org*>

School Science and Mathematics Association
Address:

Bloomsburg University
400 East Second Street
Bloomsburg, PA 17815-1301
<*http://www.teachermagazine.org/context/orgs/ssma.htm*>

Teacher Organizations:
American Federation of Teachers (AFT)
AFT address:

555 New Jersey Ave., N.W.
Washington, DC 20001
Journals: *American Educator* and *American Teacher*
<*http://www.aft.org*>

National Education Association (NEA)
NEA address:

1201 16th Street, N.W.
Washington, DC 20036
Journals: *Today's Education* and *NEA Reporter*
<*http://www.nea.org*>

Journal Excerpts

High School

"My student teaching experience has really proven how much I do know and also how much more I have to learn and develop. I realize I have certain strengths and weaknesses. As far as professional development, I think this is an ongoing (never-ending) process in becoming an effective educator. Some areas I should focus on include: classroom management and discipline, planning, less reliance on the textbook, more original and unique approaches, integration of content, the balance of quantity with quality in the English classroom. I must make future decisions such as where I want to teach and live. I guess my priorities will center around preparing my files for future employment. I've never even designed a resume. I need to decide where I want to be, and when, and how, and. . . ."

"I must admit that I was nervous about being observed this week by so many different people but everything went really well. The principal could only come to observe me during the time I was teaching freshmen. Two university supervisors from English and Education Departments came and I had already scheduled a class for the department chair to observe me. I am very used to people coming in and observing me, so when the principal came, I was not really that nervous. I did worry about his visit because I would really love to teach here and I wanted to impress him by teaching a fine lesson. My class was very well organized and I kept students engaged the entire class period. The principal later told me he was really impressed and made other positive comments on the report that he gave me. I was on "cloud nine" the entire day! I'm even thinking of asking the president of the school to observe me since his teaching area is English. The more people who see me teach and give me feedback the better!"

"Today was a fun and unusual day! It's the end of the quarter and we had a faculty retreat. The first talk was on mission effectiveness as it applies to our school, and then in small group discussions we tried to generate practical ways for applying the ideas. We took time to reflect and journal for ourselves. For me the day was relaxing and a great experience!"

Middle School

"Overall, I was happy with the results of the lesson. They seemed to really retain what I want them to know. A few students even offered examples of ironic things that have happened to them. Speaking of ironic, the inservice we attended was on reading in the content areas. The speaker mentioned that a good way to help students develop a schemata was to relate the reading to a story or song, which I have been doing all semester. Even if I didn't learn anything I didn't already know, the in-service was fun. I saw people there whom I knew. . . . That is always good!"

"I think I feel better now about how things went when I was observed today. It's hard for me to separate my personal and professional feelings. I had prepared well, I was having a *blast,* and the kids were so excited. These same students who constantly say they don't like to write or can't write were writing beautiful poetry. It makes me want to cry. I know I'm too much a perfectionist and I wanted everything to be perfect. I should know better. There's always something that can be improved. I agree with all of the comments that were made—positive and areas needing improvement. This is the purpose of 'reflective teaching'! The lesson wasn't perfect, but I will continue to learn and refine my skills."

Elementary School

"Our inservice today was given by a teacher from another college who gave a workshop on Claris Works. We created spreadsheets, made graphs, and inserted spreadsheets into a word processing document. Some teachers became frustrated and gave up. Since this was somewhat a review for me from our education classes, I did not get much new information from the meeting. In fact, I was helping others around me who were not as familiar with this program as I am. I felt good being able to do so. Computers are a difficult tool to master and quite frustrating when one doesn't catch on quickly and the instructor moves ahead."

"This past week I had the opportunity to attend the Regional Conference. We spent the evening talking in our hotel rooms. It was so interesting for me to see how different these teachers were outside of the classroom. My supervising teacher and I walked to the conference center and I visited the exhibits before the general session began. Seeing so much free stuff was exciting! I wanted to attend a session on Portfolios but there wasn't room. I went to a session on integrating Science and Literature and another on Mathematics and Literature. I received copies of several lesson plans which may be useful in the future. A session on phonics was terrific and the presenter provided a packet of wonderful ideas for creatively teaching it. I never knew there were so many interesting ways to teach phonics. Throughout the conference people commented on how young I looked and some took a personal interest in talking with me. Teachers from the school told me they were impressed that I was willing to attend the conference. I responded that I was impressed that they provided me the opportunity to attend."

"An area in which I am a bit cautious is Science, and more specifically knowing how to help students' understand scientific methods to solve real-life problems. There is no doubt that becoming more comfortable and confident with the subject of science is vital to my becoming a successful teacher. I find throughout my student teaching experience that when there is an area where I am uncomfortable, the best thing to do is get help and assistance from those who are comfortable and successful in that area. In this case my plan involves requesting information from more experienced teachers. It would also be helpful when planning a lesson to consult more than one source for ideas. In this way I will have 'more than one trick in my bag' . . ."

Special Education

"After school we had departmental meetings. It was neat to meet the other ECE teachers. I felt overwhelmed hearing them talk about the paper work they had to do for some students. The new IEP forms will take some getting used to, but will be worth our effort for our students. They did find out that they fill out a different form for the three-year review than they complete for the original form. There are so many forms for different things and it's easy to be confused. I plan to watch Ms. K. as she completes a few forms and I will better understand how to do it."

"I was privileged to attend the Council of Exceptional Children national conference these past two years with a group of Education students. This year I went to a presentation by a specialist in behavior disorders. He had researched strategies to help retain student attention. His research was current and reality based giving us the best intervention techniques to use with students. I always learn so much at these sessions."

"I can see that I have grown professionally by implementing a variety of teaching strategies. This enhances the learning process because every child has his or her own unique learning style. I believe that good teachers use different methods and also integrate technology to make learning more interesting. Special education students need more visuals and hands-on experiences and I try to have them in cooperative groups each day. As a result, I have noticed the students are gaining confidence as well as feelings of success. I want to set high expectations for my students and challenge them to go beyond the requirements of each lesson."

REFERENCES AND SUGGESTED READINGS

Baloche, L. A. (1998). *The cooperative classroom: Empowering learning.* Upper Saddle River, NJ: Prentice Hall.

Beattie, M. (1997). Fostering reflective practice in teacher education: Inquiry as a framework for the construction of a professional knowledge in teaching. *Asia-Pacific Journal of Teacher Education, 25*(2), 111–128.

Borko, H., Michalec, P., Timmons, M., & Siddle, J. (1997). Student teaching portfolios: A tool for promoting reflective practice. *Journal of Teacher Education, 48*(5), 345–357.

Brennan, S., Roberts, R., Thames, W., & Miller, K. H. (1998). *Guiding and assessing teacher effectiveness: A handbook for Kentucky teacher internship program participants* (5th ed.). Frankfort, KY: Office of Teacher Education and Certification Education Professional Standards Board.

Bullough, R. V., & Gitlin, A. (1995). *Becoming a student of teaching: Methodologies for exploring self and school context.* New York: Garland.

Darling-Hammond, L. (1997). *Doing what matters most: Investing in quality teaching.* New York: National Commission on Teaching & America's Future.

Davies, R., & Ferguson, J. (1997). Teachers' views of the role of initial teacher education in developing their profession, *Journal of Education for Teaching, 23*(1), 39–56.

Danielson, C. (1996). *Enhancing professional practice: A framework for teaching.* Alexandria, VA: Association for Supervision and Curriculum Development.

Fuller, F. F. (1970). *Personalized education for teachers: An introduction for teacher educators.* Austin, TX: University of Texas, R&D Center for Teacher Education (ERIC No. ED048105).

Huling-Austin, L. (1992). Research on learning to teach: Implications for teacher induction and mentoring programs. *Journal of Teacher Education, 43*(3), 173–180.

Jersild, A. T. (1955). *When teachers face themselves.* New York: Teachers College Press.

Louis, D. S., Marks, H. M., & Kruse, S. (1996). Teachers' professional community in restructuring schools. *American Educational Research Journal, 33,* 757–798.

Ralph, E. G., Kesten, C., Lang, H., & Smith, D. (1998). Hiring new teachers: What do school districts look for? *Journal of Teacher Education 49*(1), 47–56.

Rodriguez, Y. E. G., & Sjostrom, B. R. (1998). Critical reflection for professional development: A comparative study of nontraditional adult and traditional student teachers, *Journal of Teacher Education, 49*(3), 177–186.

Wolf, K., Whinery, B., & Hagerty, P. (1995). Teaching portfolios and portfolio conversations for teacher educators and teachers, *Action in Teacher Education, 17*(1), 30–39.

Zeichner, K. (1987). Preparing reflective teachers: An overview of instructional strategies which have been employed in preservice teacher education. *International Journal of Educational Research, 11*(5), 565–575.

Zeichner, K., & Tabachnick, B. R. (Eds.). (1991). *Issues and practices in inquiry-oriented teacher education.* London: Falmer Press.

Zubizarreta, J. (1994). Teaching portfolios and the beginning teacher, *Phi Delta Kappan, 76*(5), 323–326.

15

Acquiring Certification and a Teaching Position

"The search for a professional teaching position begins with you!"

Your journey now takes you beyond your student/intern teaching experience. Equipped with your professional portfolio you are anxious to continue moving into your first teaching position. The search for a professional teaching position begins with you! We intend that this chapter guide you in efficiently and effectively designing and creating materials you will use in pursuing a teaching position. The chapter format changes to accommodate the different activities that engage you as you step into a different whirlwind, that of entering the profession of teaching. You will want to consider tasks such as: contacting the career services center, inquiring about teaching positions, developing a resume, preparing for an interview, and completing the certification process. In addition, the chapter provides printed and electronic sources to assist you in researching, planning, and developing materials. These will enable you to seek that position you have dreamed about for years!

What's Ahead?

- Career Services Center
- Resume, Cover Letters, and Interview Techniques
- Inquiry about Teaching Positions
- Interviewing for a Position
- Suggested Interview Questions
- Questions for the Interviewee
- Professional Portfolios
- Obtaining Certification
- Career Advancement

CAREER SERVICES CENTER

Perhaps you have visited your campus career services center. One of the first tasks you undertake prior to seeking a position is to begin assembling your credential file. Establishing a credential file allows you to organize the observations and evaluations by supervising teachers, the college/university supervisor, team leaders, and department chair, and letters of recommendation. A single packet of these materials can be sent to the personnel specialists in the school district.

Many colleges and universities have special counselors to assist you in assembling your file and in completing other tasks in the job-seeking process. In addition to assistance with compiling your credential file, you will find resources for resume writing. Using an expert career counselor to review your resume and make suggestions will allow your resume to take on a more professional appearance.

Career service centers provide a number of other services. Listings are available of teaching positions in area school districts, the state, the nation, and international schools. You may also take advantage of practice-interview sessions as a means of strengthening your communication skills. Through using the Internet you can also benefit from career services departments in other colleges and universities. Assistance in posting your resume on the Internet is yet another service available to you in career services centers. You will want to research these World Wide Web sites to further expand your ideas for completing your resume and your credential file. You can examine World Wide Web sites and printed materials suggested below prior to writing your resume.

Resume, Cover Letters, and Interview Techniques

<http://www.jobcenter.org>

Maintains a database of resumes from prospective employees and matches them. Free resume posting.

Archeus Online: <http://www.golden.net/~archeus/worksrch.htm>
Resume, cover letter, and interviewing resources.

Student Center: <http://www.studentcenter.com>
Information on resumes, letters, and interviewing.

Career Lab: <http://www.careerlab.com>
Two hundred free cover letters, samples, and examples.

Anthony, R., & Roe, G. (1998). *101 grade A resumes for teachers* (2nd ed). New York: Barron's Educational Services.

Kennedy, J. L., & Morrow, T. J. (1994). *Electronic resume revolution: Create a winning resume for the new world of job seeking.* New York: Wiley & Sons.

INQUIRY ABOUT TEACHING POSITIONS

Let's start with your making inquiry about possible teaching positions within the school systems of your choice. Most school districts require an application form, which may be requested by mail or phone or directly retrieved from the personnel office of the school system. Otherwise, a letter of application is written to get your enclosed resume read and generate an interview. Communication skills are most important in your letter; it is the first introduction to your writing competency. Banis (1997) provides timely tips for writing and producing job-search correspondence and samples of several types of letters. Editing your own responses and giving careful attention to style, punctuation, and spelling may give the reader a strong first impression of you, the applicant. Suggested web sites and printed materials are listed:

<http://www.nationjob.com/education>

Lists education jobs by category: education/teaching/child care. Submit job preferences and e-mail address and receive weekly list of jobs matching choices.

<http://www.fowt.com>

Lists job openings in 1,000 American community schools, international schools, private schools, church-related schools, and multinational, industry-supported English-speaking schools and colleges in more than 100 foreign countries.

Online Career Center: <http://www.occ.com>
Search jobs using education category and location.

<http://www.ccsd.net/HRD/liOpp.htm>

Example of individual school district, Clark County in Las Vegas, listing employment opportunities for certified personnel.

Banis, W. J. (1997). The art of writing job-search letters, *Planning job choices: 1998* (41st ed.), E49-E55.

Bureau of Labor Statistics, US Dept. of Labor. (1998–1999). *Occupational outlook handbook.* Bulletin 2500. Washington, DC: US Government Printing Office. Highlights of job outlook 1996–2006. Provides job search methods, tips on applying for jobs, and evaluating job offers.

National Center for Education Statistics. (1998). *Condition of education.* Office of Educational Research and Improvement, National Center for Education Statistics. Washington, DC: US Department of Education Statistics.

Interviewing for a Position

Personal contact with the prospective personnel specialist or director is likely to culminate in an interview session. Make sure you provide the personnel office a phone number where you can be reached when you are out of town. When you are contacted and given an interview, make sure you are prompt for your appointment. Your interviewer/s may be an administrator, a group of administrators, a group of teachers and principal from the school, or a group of teachers from the district. Their goal is to find the best possible candidate to fill a position for their school or district. How do you prepare for a successful interview? You will want to research the suggested Web sites and print materials prior to the interview session. The following questions may be helpful to use either as a role-playing activity or for your own preparation.

Suggested Interview Questions

- What specific talents do you bring to the teaching profession that will benefit students?
- How do you think students learn? How do you stimulate their thinking?
- How would you go about maintaining discipline and creating an environment conducive to learning?
- Give an example of a time when you had to deal with a difficult student.
- If I were to encounter you three, six, and nine years from now, what would you be doing?
- To what extent are you willing to explore and share new ideas with others?
- In what ways have you integrated technology in your teaching?
- Describe any opportunities you have experienced to develop unit and/or interdisciplinary teaching?
- What can be learned from observations by supervisors and principals?
- Tell me about your student teaching experience.
- How prepared are you to work with diversity among learners?
- What resources have you used effectively in the classroom?
- What types of student assessment have you used? What were the results?
- How would you get parents involved in their child's learning?
- What is your philosophy of education?
- What do you consider are your greatest strengths? Any areas for improvement?
- Describe your collaborative relationships with your supervising teacher and university supervisor.

Questions for the Interviewee

In addition to preparing for the response to interviewing questions, you may want to generate a list to ask the interviewer or use the following:

- What types of professional development and supervisory programs does the school or district provide?
- What is the beginning teacher's salary? Are salary increments based on merit pay or automatic yearly increases?
- What is the school district policy for teacher evaluation?
- What opportunities will I have to demonstrate my leadership ability?

Keep in mind that an interview is significant in the hiring of new personnel. It is important that you arrive promptly for your appointment, dress professionally, and speak distinctly when responding to the questions.

Some schools and school districts use the Teacher Perceiver Interview Instrument in hiring teachers. The instrument administered during an interview is taped and later scored by the interviewer. The SRI Teacher Perceiver Instrument includes questions asked of the interviewee over 12 categories: mission, empathy, rapport drive, individualized perception, listening, investment, input drive, activation, innovation, gestalt, objectivity, and focus. In preparing for an interview of this type you would want to reflect on your convictions, beliefs, and experiences of teaching.

PROFESSIONAL PORTFOLIO

Opportunities for developing a portfolio based on state and national standards were provided you in chapters 3, 6, 8, 12, and 13 during your student/intern teaching experience. In addition, portfolio entries may include a transcript, resume, brief autobiography, your philosophy of education, descriptive picture of what would be expected in your classroom before students arrived the first day, your discipline plan, and your professional development plan. Many school districts require a portfolio in addition to the initial candidate interviews for employment. As you exhibit your thoughtfully selected entries, you can be proud of all the effort you extended in demonstrating your progress throughout the student/intern teaching experience.

OBTAINING CERTIFICATION

Certification is required in all 50 states and the District of Columbia and is confirmation that you have met the necessary requirements of that particular state department of education. Recent reforms have brought about many changes in teacher certification and it is advisable that you contact the state department of education in the state you are seeking employment. The teacher certification official on your campus can provide a listing of certification requirements and the address of the teacher certification officer in each state. Many states accept the requirements of another state granting what is called *reciprocity.* You can find the states with reciprocal agreements and a listing of individual state requirements for certified personnel in the following publication.

Tryneski, J. (1997). *Requirements of certification of teachers, counselors, librarians, administrators for elementary and secondary schools: Sixty-second edition, 1997–1998.* Chicago: The University of Chicago Press.

Each state has an certification office that handles teacher certification and licensing. The following is a current listing of addresses for each state.

Addresses for State Offices of Certification

Alabama
Teacher Education and Certification
State Department of Education
P.O. Box 302101
Montgomery, AL 36130-2101
334-242-9977

Alaska
Certification Analyst
Department of Education
801 West 10th Street, Suite 200
Juneau, AK 99801-1894
907-2831 or 2026

Arizona
Teacher Certification Unit-70016
P.O. Box 6490
Phoenix, AZ 85005-6490
602-542-4367

Arkansas
Teacher Education & Licensure
State Dept. of Education
4 State Capitol Mall
Little Rock, AR 72201-1071
501-682-4342

California
Commission on Teacher
Credentialing
Box 944270
Sacramento, CA 94244-7000
916-445-7254

Colorado
Educator Licensing
State Dept. of Education
201 E. Colfax Avenue
Denver, CO 80203
303-866-6628

Connecticut
Bureau of Certification and
Professional Development
State Dept. of Education
Box 2219
Hartford, CT 06145-2219
860-566-5201

Delaware
Teacher Certification
Dept. of Public Instruction
P.O. Box 1402
Dover, DE 19903
302-739-4686

District of Columbia
Teacher Education and Certification
Branch
Logan Administration Building
215 "G" Street, N.E.
Room 101A
Washington, DC 20002
202-724-4246

Florida
Bureau of Teacher Certification
Florida Education Center
325 W. Gaines, Rm. 201
Tallahassee, FL 32399-0400
904-488-2317

Georgia
Professional Standards Commission
Certification Section
1454 Twin Towers East
Atlanta, GA 30334
404-657-9000

Hawaii
State of Hawaii
Dept. of Education
Office of Personnel Services
P.O. Box 2360
Honolulu, HI 96804
808-586-3420

Idaho
Certification Division
State Dept. of Education
P.O. Box 83720
Boise, ID 83720-0027
208-332-6680

Illinois
Illinois State Board of Education
Certification & Placement Section
100 N. First Street
Springfield, IL 62777-0001
217-782-4321

Indiana
Indiana Professional Standards Board
Teacher Licensing
251 East Ohio Street, Suite 201
Indianapolis, IN 46204-2133
317-232-9010

Iowa
Board of Educational Examiners
Grimes State Office Building
Des Moines, IA 50319-0147
515-281-3245

Kansas
Certification Specialist
Kansas State Dept. of Education
Kansas State Education Building
120 SE 10th Ave.
Topeka, KS 66612-1182
913-296-2288

Kentucky
Kentucky Dept. of Education
Division of Certification
1024 Capital Center Drive
Frankfort, KY 40601
502-573-4606

Louisiana
Louisiana Dept. of Education
Teacher Certification, Room 700
P.O. Box 94064
Baton Rouge, LA 70804-9064
504-342-3490

Maine
Division of Certification and
Placement
Dept. of Education
State House Station 23
Augusta, ME 04333
207-287-5944

Maryland
Division of Certification 18100
State Dept. of Education
200 West Baltimore St.
Baltimore, MD 21201
410-767-0412

Massachusetts
Massachusetts Dept. of Education
Office of Teacher Certification and
Credentialling
350 Main Street
Malden, MA 02148
617-388-3300

Michigan
Office of Professional Services &
Certification Services
Michigan Dept. of Education
P.O. Box 3008
Lansing, MI 48909
517-373-3310

Minnesota
Teacher Licensing
State Dept. of Children, Families and
Learning
616 Capitol Square Building
St. Paul, MN 55101
601-359-3483

Mississippi
Teacher Certification
State Dept. of Education
Box 771
Jackson, MS 39205-0771
601-359-3483

Missouri
Teacher Certification
Dept. of Elementary and Secondary
Education
P.O. Box 480
Jefferson City, MO 65102
573-751-3486

Montana
Teacher Certification
Office of Public Instruction
P.O. Box 202501
Helena, MT 59620-2501
406-444-3150

Nebraska
Teacher Certification
State Dept. of Education
301 Centennial Mall South
Box 94987
Lincoln, NE 68509-4987
800-371-4642

Nevada
Licensure and Certification
Nevada Dept. of Education
700 East 5th St.
Carson City, NV 89701
702-687-3115

New Hampshire
Bureau of Credentialing
State Dept. of Education
101 Pleasant St.
Concord, NH 03301
603-271-2407

New Jersey
Office of Licensing and Academic
Credentials
CN 503
Trenton, NJ 08625-0503
609-292-2070

New Mexico
Director
Professional Licensure Unit
Education Building
300 Don Gaspar
Santa Fe, NM 87501-2786
505-827-6587

New York
Office of Teaching
University of the State of New York
State Education Department
Albany, NY 12230
518-4740-3901/2/3/4

Buffalo Board of Education
City Hall
65 Niagara Square
Buffalo, NY 14202
716-842-4646

North Carolina
North Carolina Dept. of Public
Instruction
Licensure Section
301 N. Wilmington Street
Raleigh, NC 27601-2825
919-733-4125

North Dakota
Education Standards and Practice
Board
Teacher Certification
600 E. Boulevard Ave.
Bismarck, ND 58505-0440
701-328-2264

Ohio
Teacher Education & Certification
State Dept. of Education
65 South Front St., Rm. 1009
Columbus, OH 43215-4183
614-466-3593

Oklahoma
Professional Standards
State Dept. of Education
2500 N. Lincoln Blvd.
Rm. 211
Oklahoma City, OK 73105-4599
405-521-3337

Oregon
Teacher Standards and Practices
Commission
Public Service Bldg.
255 Capitol Street, N.E.
Suite 105
Salem, OR 97310-1332
503-378-3586

Pennsylvania
Bureau of Certification
Dept. of Education
333 Market Street
Harrisburg, PA 17126-0333
717-787-2967

Rhode Island
Office of Teacher Certification
State Dept. of Education
Shepard Building
255 Westminster St.
Providence, RI 02903-3400
401-277-4600

South Carolina
Teacher Licensure
State Dept. of Education
1015 Rutledge Building
1429 Senate St.
Columbia, SC 29201
803-774-8466

South Dakota
Teacher Education & Certification
Division of Education
700 Governors Drive
Pierre, SD 57501-2291
605-773-3553

Tennessee
Office of Teacher Licensing
State Dept. of Education
5th Floor, Andrew Johnson Tower
710 James Robertson Parkway
Nashville, TN 37243-0377
615-741-1644

Texas
State Board for Educator Certification
1001 Trinity
Austin, TX 78701
512-469-3001

Utah
Certification and Personnel
Development Section
State Board of Education
250 East 500 South Street
Salt Lake City, UT 84111
801-538-7740

Vermont
Licensing Office
Dept. of Education
120 State Street
Montpelier, VT 05620-2501
802-828-2501

Virginia
Office of Professional Licensure
Dept. of Education
P.O. Box 2120
Richmond, VA 23216-2120
804-225-2022

Washington
Office of Professional Education
Teacher Education, Licensing and
State Board of Education
Old Capitol Building
P.O. Box 47206
Olympia, WA 98504-7206
206-753-6773

West Virginia
State Dept. of Education
Building 6, Room 337
1900 Kanawha Blvd., East
Charleston, WV 25305-0330
800-982-2378

Wisconsin
Teacher Education, Licensing and
Placement
Box 7841
Madison, WI 53707-7841
608-266-1027

Wyoming
2300 Capitol Avenue
Hathaway Building, 2nd Floor
Cheyenne, WY 82002
307-777-6248

CAREER ADVANCEMENT

Your journey onward takes you beyond your initial teaching experience, advancing to higher levels of instructional, interpersonal, and collaborative skills and knowledge of content. Advanced degrees or developing specialization areas for certification are in your future. As you gain at least three years of experience you may want to consider being certified by the National Board for Professional Teaching Standards (NBPTS). NBPTS has established standards for teaching practice and developed board certification assessments based on these standards. Many educators believe that NBPTS certification will mean higher salaries and contribute to creating a profession of superior teachers. Though NBPTS is for experienced teachers, it is wise to continue your journey forward, reaching for higher standards as a professional.

TABLE 15.1 *Timeline for Completing Teaching Position Search*

Activities	Beginning Date	Completion Date
Professional Portfolio		
Credential File		
Resume		
School District Inquiry Letters		
School District Application Forms		
Certification Application Forms		
Praxis/State Teacher Examinations		
Interview 1		
Interview 2		
Thank You Letter		
Acceptance Letter		
Letter to Inform Other Interviewing Schools of Your Decision		

Cooperative Group Approach to Focus One Activities

CHAPTER 1 FOCUS ONE: COOPERATIVE GROUP APPROACH

First Observations

Focus One activities promote greater self-understanding. These cooperative learning group activities ask you to share your classroom experiences with your peers. You are letting others get to know who you are, what you are learning, and how you feel about it. Likewise, sharing and attending to others promote a sense of trust within your small group. Having an open mind toward participation contributes to your personal enrichment through these group activities. Allow yourself time to feel comfortable with those in your group. At the same time, let others know that you respect their sharing. Assure them that what is shared will remain within the group and will not be repeated to anyone outside your circle.

Are You Actively Listening?

As you actively listen to your peers,

- give each person speaking your full attention.
- look at them, observe facial expressions, tone of voice, and body posture.
- listen to the total message being sent, verbally and nonverbally.
- allow the other person to finish talking before you speak.
- respond, giving back some feeling words along with rephrasing the content of what you heard the person saying. This validates each person's contribution and serves as a model of listening for others.

Review of the Group Process

Since the cooperative learning group process in **Focus One** is still new to you, review the roles and expectations of the group members. Keep in mind what you want to contribute as an individual group member and as a total group.

Tasks for the Group Process

- Decide on roles for each group member.
- Obtain materials for group—encourager (observer in a four-member group).
- Refer to the individual accountability form; review specific tasks assigned your role.
- Reflect on your responses in the group.

Writing the Action Plan

The action plan is a summary of the discussion points with the greatest significance for group members. As you consider the meaningful insights shared during this session, name one idea that motivates and inspires you and that would be a realistic and helpful goal for you to attain this week. Choose a practical action incorporating this idea—one that you can practice during the coming week. For example, your group members may decide to identify specific strengths each of you brings to the classroom and school. Even though the group's action plan is specific, it promotes an attitude and/or an action appropriate for the practicing professional you expect yourself to be. Acknowledging your talents and contributions daily enables you to see the progress you are making as a student teacher. Include the means you will use for remembering the plan. For example, in journal writing during the coming week, return to your action plan to record your experience with the particular goal.

Scribble Space for Action Plan Ideas

_____

_____

_____

The summarizer writes the group's action plan, and group members sign indicating that everyone agrees to practice the plan. The action plan, group accountability report, individual accountability report, and other materials are returned by the observer or encourager to a designated location. The facilitator will read and return the plan to you at the following session.

Group Discussion

The initiator-reader checks with other group members to see if all are ready to begin the discussion portion of the session.

- Initiator-reader directs group members to the Discussion Questions.
- All other group members assume their role for this session.

Individual Accountability Report

The quality of your participation as a group member is the focus of the individual accountability report. It serves as a guide helping you to mark progress in the different roles you assume during each session. Stating a specific and desired interpersonal skill assists you in practicing this skill during subsequent sessions. You likewise read and sign the individual accountability report of other group members. This gives you the opportunity to encourage your peers in their group process efforts. You and your peers gain confidence for facing greater challenges from the exchange of encouraging and supportive comments.

Materials Needed by Each Group:

- Group accountability report (action plan) from prior session
- Role markers
- Group accountability report
- Individual Accountability Report

Follow-Up to Action Plan

At the beginning of each session the facilitator returns the action plans to the groups. You will want to discuss how you used the plan since your meeting. Tell what you found helpful about the plan and how it might give you a clearer understanding and greater motivation for your day-to-day learning to teach.

CHAPTER 2 FOCUS ONE: COOPERATIVE GROUP APPROACH

Am I Initiating?

You again meet to share and reflect on your meaningful learning experiences and insights about becoming a professional teacher. This week you are asked to assume a new role within your group, paying close attention to the requirements of your role description. The facilitator opens the session and distributes to each group the individual and group accountability reports collected during the last session. You are given an opportunity to read the facilitator's comments to you and your group. With your group, discuss your experience with using the action plan in your day-by-day life in the school. Were you able to meet your goal? Go beyond it?

The initiator-reader assumes leadership in the group and all other group members likewise are expected to get into their new roles. Listed below are some points to help you recall this portion of the group process.

- Read the facilitator's comments.
- Think about how you carried out the action plan adopted during the last group session.
- Consider questions such as:
  Did you remember the Plan? If so, how useful was it in naming specific strengths you bring to the classroom and school?
  What aspect of the teacher role did you reflect on most often?
- The summarizer records your group's experience with using the action plan and its contribution to your learning as a professional teacher. You are now ready to reflect on another aspect of becoming a teacher, taking initiative.

Group Discussion

The initiator-reader checks with the group members to see that they have sufficient silent time to reflect and are ready to discuss. The three Discussion Questions in **Focus One** guide your analysis of your performance at this time. They can help you share with the group your insights about taking charge in the classroom. Be willing to risk being open and honest as far as you are comfortable. Share your insights and assess the extent to which you are initiating. Your sensitivity to others as they share examples of their taking charge in the classroom helps them in their openness with you.

Action Plan

What actions does your group plan to take as a result of your discussion about taking charge? Use the scribble space on the next page for jotting down actions that will remind you of the motivation and spirit of today's discussion while you work this week in the school. Include ways you will be accountable for the action plan. Share these with your group and listen to other's ideas.

Remember, a well-written action plan includes:

- common experiences shared by groups members
- specific self-assessment measures suitable to all group members
- practical actions for school use

Scribble Space for Action Plan Ideas

_____

_____

_____

The summarizer writes the group's action plan, and group members sign, indicating that all agree to practice the plan. The action plan (group accountability report) along with the individual accountability report and other materials are returned by the observer or encourager to a designated location. The facilitator will read and return the plan to you at the following session.

CHAPTER 3 FOCUS ONE: COOPERATIVE GROUP APPROACH
Analyzing Your Emotional Response to Beginning Teaching

Focus One offers another group activity designed to help you examine and learn more about your growth as a beginning professional. As you gather within the group, review and discuss the prior week's action plan. Below are guiding questions for review and discussion.

- Did you remember the plan?
- Did you find the means the group chose for remembering the plan workable?
- How are your experiences and the facilitator's comments about the plan connected?
- What comment does your group write after discussing its use of the action plan?

For the next part of this session you are assigned a new group. After group assignments are read, move to the new group. Introduce yourself and tell other members about the school, students, faculty, and staff with whom you work. Choose the role that you will perform and begin to carry out the responsibilities of that role. Joining different groups offers an opportunity to learn more about yourself and other people. You get to practice the different roles and to interact with others who respond in different ways to their roles in the group.

Action Plan

How do you plan to practice the insights gained from the discussion about becoming a professional teacher? Use the scribble space below for jotting down actions that will remind you of the motivation and spirit of today's discussion while you work this week in the school. Include ways you will be accountable for the action plan. Share these with your group and listen to other's ideas. If you need additional help with writing your action plan, refer to action plan examples in this appendix.

Scribble Space for Action Plan Ideas

_____

_____

_____

The summarizer writes the group's action plan, and group members sign, indicating that all agree to practice the plan. The action plan (group accountability report) along with the individual accountability report and other materials are returned by the observer or encourager to a designated location. The Facilitator will read and return the plan to you at the following session. Below is an example showing an action plan, the facilitator's response, and the follow-up to the action plan written by the group members.

EXAMPLES: ACTION PLAN, FACILITATOR'S RESPONSE, FOLLOW-UP TO ACTION PLAN

Action Plan

This week we will try to be more positive with what we do and to write about this in our journals. We need to focus more on positive things to help boost our confidence in ourselves. We all seem to focus on the negative more than the positive.

Facilitator's Response

Your group appeared to openly share your stories and your plan gives you a specific, practical goal. Best to you in following it!

Group Response to Action Plan

We all focused on our strengths and progress as student teachers. This forced us to think about positives while still thinking about improvements to be made.

CHAPTER 4 FOCUS ONE: COOPERATIVE GROUP APPROACH
Analyzing the Affective Dimensions of Inclusion

You are now ready to share with peers in your cooperative group your response to the Discussion Questions. Your feelings and reasoned considerations about your experiences of being included and excluded are the beginning points of the discussion.

Action Plan

Along with the action to be taken, include the means you will use for remembering the plan. For example, in your journal writing during the coming week, you may comment on some new insights you gain about the background of at least one student you teach.

Chapter 5 Focus One:
Cooperative Group Approach
What Am I Saying? What Am I Hearing?

After completing the drawing portion of the activity (see Figures A.1 and A.2), you are invited to join members of your cooperative learning group and share your experiences with each style of communication. The initiator-reader checks to see that you each take a different role and then leads the group into discussing. The Discussion Questions are intended to guide your conversation and help you to apply what you are learning toward improving the quality of your verbal communication in the classroom.

You are now ready to move into groups and begin the cooperative group process. The initiator-reader checks to see that you take your different roles and directs your choice of questions to discuss. Consider which of the Discussion Questions are the most helpful for sharing insights and experiences about the communication styles you experience.

FIGURE A.1

Communication Diagram #1

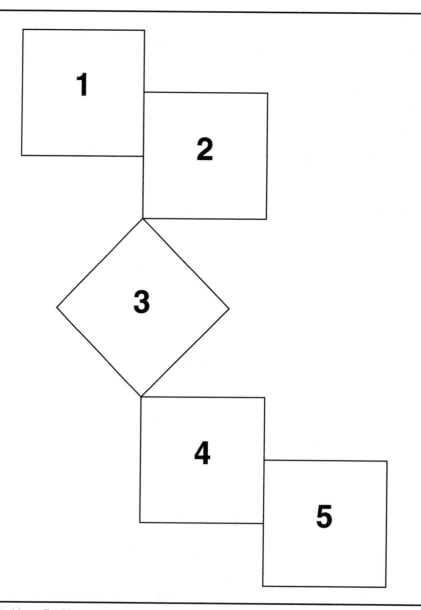

Adapted from: Exhibits 9.6 and 9.7, Directions for Communicator, pp. 205–206. Harris, B. M., Bessent, W., & McIntyre, K. E. (1989). *In-Service Education: A Guide to Better Practice.*

FIGURE A.2 *Communication Diagram #2*

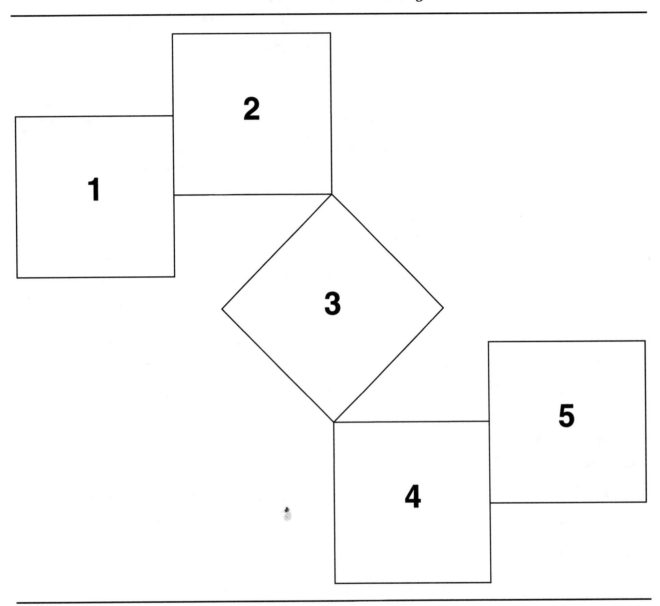

Adapted from: Exhibits 9.6 and 9.7, Directions for Communicator, pp. 205–206. Harris, B. M., Bessent, W., & McIntyre, K. E. (1989). *In-Service Education: A Guide to Better Practice.*

CHAPTER 6 FOCUS ONE:
COOPERATIVE GROUP APPROACH
A Teacher's Story: A Process

Action Plan

What action plan will encourage and support you in the classroom this week toward becoming that teacher who matches your ideal? Use the scribble space below for jotting down your ideas and share these with your group. What will help you be accountable in carrying out the action plan?

The cooperative learning group activity concludes with:

- summarizer writing the group's action plan
- group members signing and agreeing to practice the plan
- observer/encourager returning action plan, individual accountability report, and other materials to designated location

---

EXAMPLE: ACTION PLAN

During the coming week we will look at the characteristics we think the ideal teacher possesses and ask ourselves the following questions: How close am I to becoming this ideal teacher? What is one major weakness I still see in myself? What is one way in which I've improved? We will write our reflections on these questions in our journals.

Example: Response to Action Plan

Ideal Teacher

In control, consistent, confident, "with-it," flexible, sensitive to diverse needs, organized, devoted, motivational to self and students, collaborative, and at times crazy!!!

How Close Am I

Light years away, baby! I feel good about myself and where I stand—but the teachers I work with are seasoned veterans who know this game. They are on top of the game! I will strive to get to this point but for now, I will take it one step at a time.

One Major Weakness

I still have trouble adapting to sudden changes in the classroom. I can handle interruptions, but last second schedule changes and such get me all out of whack. I must learn to be more flexible in these types of situations.

One Area of Progress

I see a marked improvement in my own abilities as a classroom manager. I toughened up and they responded.

CHAPTER 7 FOCUS ONE:
COOPERATIVE GROUP APPROACH
What Do I NOW See?

After all members complete their individual considerations and comparisons, you are ready to begin discussing the questions from **Focus One** with your group.

Action Plan

Where do you go from here? What action will increase your understanding of the teacher role? Use the scribble space below for jotting down your ideas and share these with your group. Include a practical means for being accountable in carrying out the action plan.

Scribble Space for Action Plan Ideas

_____

_____

_____

Did your group reach consensus? Were you surprised by common threads that emerged? Are you prepared to tackle your challenge for the week ahead?

CHAPTER 8 FOCUS ONE:
COOPERATIVE GROUP APPROACH
Teacher as Role Model

Action Plan

What action will help you integrate the idea of teacher as model into your classes in the coming days? Use the scribble space below for writing ideas you will share with your group. What would be a practical way for you to be accountable in carrying out the action plan?

Scribble Space for Action Plan Ideas

_____

_____

_____

EXAMPLES: ACTION PLAN

Try to be open and willing to accept new challenges as they arise. Try to be positive as we move to the second half of the semester. We will journal our feelings about the new surroundings. We will compare how we feel today with how we feel we handle situations in the classroom next week

Facilitator Comments:

Excellent plan—you are anticipating this coming week's reflection! What a positive attitude and attempt to accept what is coming— "come what may."

You seemed to really enjoy sharing with one another even though your responses were similar. Since you stepped away—do the similarities say more to you today than they did a week ago?

Group Member's Follow-Up Comments:

Things have been different but we have tried to be positive everyday. Although it's sometimes difficult to be positive, to let ourselves be negative would only be self-defeating.

Sample: Implementing Action Plan

For my action plan, I believe I have been VERY flexible and will be all this week. Today also could have been quite discouraging, but I am even surprised at how well I am handling negative attitudes (toward me and the class, etc.) and poor behavior. I think at the beginning some of these challenges would have gotten me down. Now, however, I take it with a grain of salt and learn what I can from it!

CHAPTER 9 FOCUS ONE: COOPERATIVE GROUP APPROACH

Monumental Design

Action Plan

What might you take back to the school setting from your group? How will you remember your plan while you are in the school? In the space below write you ideas for an action plan and share these with your group members.

Scribble Space for Action Plan Ideas

_____

_____

_____

Are your ideas similar to others in the group? Did others' comments help you clarify your own thoughts and feelings? Do you feel connected with the plan your group adopted?

CHAPTER 10 FOCUS ONE: COOPERATIVE GROUP APPROACH

I'm Feeling Proud of . . .

Inventory of Cooperative Group Process

You've been a cooperative learning group member for a number of weeks. This experience increases your understanding of being involved as a group member. This may be an area in which you feel proud of your accomplishments. How do you respond to the following checklist for effective management of cooperative learning groups?

Checklist for Managing Effective Cooperative Groups

• *A* Accomplished   • *IP* In Progress   • *HT* Having Trouble

_____ I teach and monitor group roles.
_____ I promote and observe cooperative skills, social skills, and positive interdependence.
_____ I state learning objectives connected with activities assigned.
_____ I design activities appropriate to the group process.
_____ I assign groups, including a mix of students with different learning styles.
_____ I provide and monitor individual accountability.
_____ I provide and monitor group accountability
_____ I arrange the environment: face-to-face, knee-to-knee.

Action Plan

What might you take back to the school setting from your group? How will you remember your plan while you are in the school? In the space below, write your ideas for an action plan and share these with your group members.

Scribble Space for Action Plan Ideas

_____

_____

_____

Are your ideas similar to others in the group? Did others' comments help you clarify your own thoughts and feelings? Do you feel connected with the plan your group adopted?

CHAPTER 11 FOCUS ONE: COOPERATIVE GROUP APPROACH
Look Where I Am!
Action Plan

Has the discussion stimulated new insights about your understanding of what being a teacher means for you at this time? Were you able to build on others' comments? Did you get new ideas that you want to recall during the coming week? Did you feel "heard" by others? Did you recognize different phases you have experienced as a student/intern teacher? Were you able to connect these with your vision of the competent, caring, effective teacher? What suggestions do you have for an action plan that will help you recall a motivating idea or activity during the coming week? Use the scribble space below for writing your ideas and practical means for carrying out a plan.

Scribble Space for Action Plan Ideas

_____

_____

_____

CHAPTER 12 FOCUS ONE: COOPERATIVE GROUP APPROACH
Am I a Collaborator, a Team Player?
Action Plan

What were some common threads you heard from the group discussion about the puzzle activity (see Figure A.3)? Do you have new insights about the collaborative experiences you are now having? In the scribble space below, write your ideas for an action plan that includes these insights and allows you to reflect on your current experiences of teamwork in the school.

Scribble Space for Action Plan Ideas

_____

_____

_____

FIGURE A.3

Puzzle Activity

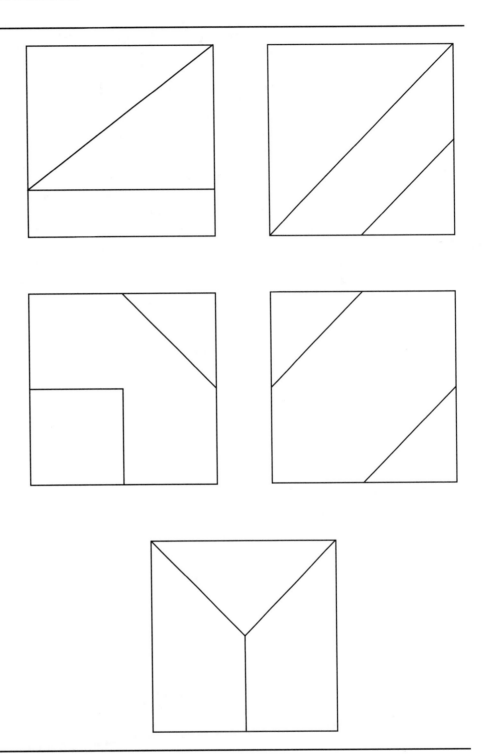

Goethals, M. S., & Howard, R. A. (1985). *Handbook of skills essential to beginning teachers.* Lanham, MD: University Press of America.

Chapter 13 Focus One:
Cooperative Group Approach
For Who I Am and What I Have, Thanks!
Action Plan

As your last opportunity for adopting an action with your cohorts, you may want to consider a plan that extends beyond the coming week. As a professional teacher, how will you approach challenges you encounter during the following weeks? What are the support sources available to you that would benefit you in transitioning to TEACHER? Which of your talents and abilities do the multiple aspects of teaching call forth from you? In future situations, how might you take advantage of support and resources available to you? Use the scribble space below for writing your ideas and practical means for carrying out a plan. As directed in chapter 13, celebrate one of your gifts in the monument provided in Figure A.4.

Scribble Space for Action Plan Ideas

_____

_____

_____

FIGURE A.4 *Monument to Your Special Gifts*

New Teacher Standards

INTERSTATE NEW TEACHER ASSESSMENT AND SUPPORT CONSORTIUM (INTASC) STANDARDS FOR BEGINNING TEACHER LICENSING

1. The teacher understands the central concepts, tools of inquiry, and structures of the discipline(s) he or she teaches and can create learning experiences that make these aspects of subject matter meaningful for students.
2. The teacher understands how children learn and develop, and can provide learning opportunities that support their intellectual, social, and personal development.
3. The teacher understands how students differ in their approaches to learning and creates instructional opportunities that are adapted to diverse learners.
4. The teacher understands and uses a variety of instructional strategies to encourage students' development of critical thinking, problem solving, and performance skills.
5. The teacher uses an understanding of individual and group motivation and behavior to create a learning environment that encourages positive social interaction, active engagement in learning, and self-motivation.
6. The teacher uses knowledge of effective verbal, nonverbal, and media communication techniques to foster active inquiry, collaboration, and supportive interaction in the classroom.
7. The teacher plans instruction based upon knowledge of subject matter, students, the community, and curriculum goals.
8. The teacher understands and uses formal and informal assessment strategies to evaluate and ensure the continuous intellectual, social, and physical development of the learner.
9. The teacher is a reflective practitioner who continually evaluates the effects of his/her choices and actions on others (students, parents, and other professionals in the learning community) and who actively seeks out opportunities to grow professionally.
10. The teacher fosters relationships with school colleagues, parents, and agencies in the larger community to support students' learning and well-being.

New Teacher Standards for Preparation and Certification

Adopted June 1993, Revised November 1994
The Kentucky Education Professional Standards Board

New Teacher Standard I: Designs and Plans Instruction

Standard Statement I: The teacher designs/plans instruction and learning climates that develop student abilities to use communication skills, apply core concepts, become self-sufficient individuals, become responsible team members, think and solve problems, and integrate knowledge.

New Teacher Standard II: Creates/Maintains Learning Climates

Standard Statement II: The teacher creates a learning climate that supports the development of student abilities to use communication skills, apply core concepts, become self-sufficient individuals, become responsible team members, think and solve problems, and integrate knowledge.

New Teacher Standard III: Implements/Manages Instruction

Standard Statement III: The teacher introduces/implements/manages instruction that develops student abilities to use communication skills, apply core concepts, become self-sufficient individuals, become responsible team members, think and solve problems, and integrate knowledge.

New Teacher Standard IV: Assesses and Communicates Learning Results

Standard Statement IV: The teacher assesses learning and communicates results to students and others with respect to student abilities to use communication skills, apply core concepts, become self-sufficient individuals, become responsible team members, think and solve problems, and integrate knowledge.

New Teacher Standard V: Reflects/Evaluates Teaching/Learning

Standard Statement V: The teacher reflects on and evaluates specific teaching/learning situations and/or programs.

New Teacher Standard VI: Collaborates with Colleagues, Parents, and Others

Standard Statement VI: The teacher collaborates with colleagues, parents, and other agencies to design, implement, and support learning programs that develop student abilities to use communication skills, apply core concepts, become self-sufficient individuals, become responsible team members, think and solve problems, and integrate knowledge.

New Teacher Standard VII: Engages in Professional Development

Standard Statement VII: The teacher evaluates his/her overall performance with respect to modeling and teaching Kentucky's learning goals, refines the skills and processes necessary, and implements a professional development plan.

New Teacher Standard VIII: Knowledge of Content

Standard Statement VIII: The teacher demonstrates a current and sufficient academic knowledge of certified content areas to develop student knowledge and performance in those areas.

Getting Organized

BEGINNING TEACHER CHECKLIST

Are you concerned about how to get started? To facilitate organization and planning for this important venture, the following list is provided for you to consider.

1. Call the principal and cooperating teacher of your school prior to appearing at the school. Introduce yourself as a student/intern teacher. Let the principal know you would like to be present for any meetings held prior to the first day of class. Ask that you be informed of dates and times. These meetings can be essential to your becoming partner teacher and member of the faculty in the school setting.
2. Keep a schedule of all important dates to remember. Be on time and appear in professional dress for any meetings.
3. Work as partner with your supervising or team teacher in such activities as:
   arranging the classroom
   scheduling classes
   preparing and organizing materials
   designing bulletin boards
4. Examine the Student/Intern Teacher Handbook from your college/university. You may have questions regarding the required competencies, legal status of your role, or personnel involved in the student/intern teacher experience.
5. Record the actual time spent in observation, participation, and actual teaching experience. You will find a chart for recording the Log of Hours in this appendix.
6. Enter the observations, reflections, activities, and suggestions made each day in a separate journal or log of experience.

STUDENT TEACHER OBSERVATION GUIDE

This outline has been prepared to help you become perceptive observers. You are encouraged to use any part or all of the outline when observing teaching activities. The questions may be used following an observation as you reflect on what is recalled and examined.

I. Planning Procedures

- Can you tell by listening to and observing the teacher what the student learning outcomes are for this lesson?
- Is the purpose of this lesson to develop skills, convey information, or help the students develop attitudes and values?
- Can you write the objectives/outcomes of this lesson, using the criteria for complete instructional objectives?
- Is there evidence that the students were involved in planning the lesson? Were motivating activities planned and used? Culminating activities?
- Can the specific objectives/outcomes of this lesson be synchronized with the goals of the unit?

II. Content

- Is the subject matter adapted to the abilities of the students? Appropriate to ensure achievement of the lesson's objectives? Is the subject matter important?
- What is the source of subject matter: textbooks, other books, films, handouts, others?
- Is the subject content used as an end in itself or as a vehicle for achieving desired learning outcomes?

III. Teaching Strategies

- What teaching strategies are used? Does the teacher lecture, lead class discussion, ask questions, use technology or webbing, or use small group procedures? Is one strategy used exclusively or is there a variety of techniques?
- How are students motivated? Does the teacher gain interest and maintain it? Are the procedures appropriate for the attention span of the students?
- Are reinforcement techniques used? In what ways? What is reinforced?
- Is the text used? What other materials would be effective?
- Was momentum established and maintained? Are transitions accomplished smoothly?

IV. Student Activities

- Are students interested, involved, active, and challenged?
- What percentage of the time is used in student-centered activities?
- Is appropriate student behavior rewarded? How? Are students praised?
- Do students initiate responses? Are students' ideas accepted? Must students be prodded for answers?
- Are students interacting with one another? Positively? Negatively?

V. Evaluation of Teaching-Learning

- Did the evaluation of today's lesson set the stage for the next lesson?
- Was evaluation done in terms of the skills, knowledge, and attitudes developed?
- Was evaluation done by the teacher? Students?

TELL ME ABOUT YOUR CHILD

(Parent/Guardian Survey of Students)

Dear Parents,

Greetings to you from your child's teacher, _____. It is especially exciting for me to begin this school year. To learn more about my students so I can best meet their needs, I am asking you to fill out the following short survey for me. Please return it as soon as possible by September ___. I look forward to meeting you at our first parent gathering. Thank you for your support and encouragement.

1. Which subject does your child enjoy the most?

2. Which subject does your child find the most difficult?

3. What are your child's favorite books?

4. Are there special activities or interests s/he has?

5. Are there any circumstances that would allow me to better meet the needs of your child?

6. Tell me other information you want me to better know your child.

LOG OF HOURS

Month_____   Name_____

	Monday	**Tuesday**	**Wednesday**	**Thursday**	**Friday**
observed:	o:___	o:___	o:___	o:___	o:___
participated:	p:___	p:___	p:___	p:___	p:___
taught:	t:___	t:___	t:___	t:___	t:___

other activities: _____

_____

observed:	o:___	o:___	o:___	o:___	o:___
participated:	p:___	p:___	p:___	p:___	p:___
taught:	t:___	t:___	t:___	t:___	t:___

other activities: _____

_____

observed:	o:___	o:___	o:___	o:___	o:___
participated:	p:___	p:___	p:___	p:___	p:___
taught:	t:___	t:___	t:___	t:___	t:___

other activities: _____

_____

observed:	o:___	o:___	o:___	o:___	o:___
participated:	p:___	p:___	p:___	p:___	p:___
taught:	t:___	t:___	t:___	t:___	t:___

other activities: _____

_____

Totals   OBSERVED   ____ hours

PARTICIPATED   ____ hours

TAUGHT   ____ hours

Lesson Plan Guide

Guiding/Essential Questions:

Instructional Objective(s):

Materials/Strategies:

Instructional Sequence *
    A. Lesson Initiation (Motivation/Set Induction/Overview of Class):

    B. Lesson Development (Demonstrating/Modeling/Activities engaging students in group work, laboratory, etc.):

    C. Guided Practice (Account for Diversity):

    D. Independent Practice:

    E. Assessment of Instruction (Multiple Measures; Scoring Guides/Rubrics):

    F. Reflection:

Accessing Sources of Info		
Reading		
Observing		
Listening		
Quantifying		
Computing		
Visualizing	Goal 1	
Measuring		
Mathematical Reasoning		
Classifying		
Writing		
Speaking, Visual Arts		
Music		
Movement		
Using Electronic Technology		
Nature of Scientific Activity		
Patterns		
Systems and Interactions		
Models and Scale		
Constancy		
Evolutionary Change		
Number		
Mathematical Procedures		
Space and Dimensionality		
Measurement		
Change		
Mathematical Structure		
Data		
Democratic Principles		
Political Systems		
Social Systems		
Cultural Diversity		
Economic Systems		
Geography & Human Activity	Goal 2	
Historical Perspective		
Interpersonal Relationships		
Production		
Analysis of Forms		
Asthetics		
Cultural Heritage		
Cultural Diversity		
Language		
Second Language		
Family Life/Parenting		
Consumerism		
Physical Wellness		
Mental/Emotional Wellness		
Community Health Systems		
Psychomotor Skills		
Lifetime Physical Activities		
Career Path		
Employability Attributes		
Post-Secondary Options		
Positive Self-Concept		
Healthy Lifestyle		
Adaptability/Flexibility		
Resourcefulness/Creativity	Goal 3	
Self Control/Self-Discipline		
Ethical Values		
Independent Learning		
Interpersonal Skills		
Team Membership		
Consistent, Caring Behavior	Goal 4	
Rights & Responsibilities		
Multicultural/World View		
Open Mind		
Critical Thinking		
Critical Thinking		
Creative Thinking	Goal 5	
Conceptualizing		
Decision Making		
Problem Solving		
Multiple Perspective		
Developing New Knowledge	Goal 6	
Expanding Knowledge		

LESSON PLAN (EXAMPLES)
LANGUAGE ARTS—ELEMENTARY

Course Level: Third or Fourth grade

Period of Day: 10:00 A.M.

Type of Lesson: Language Arts integrated with Science

Guiding/Essential Questions:

- How can I get students involved in the story *Peter's Place?*
- After observing an oil spill experiment, will the students be able to write their observations?

Objectives: After completing this lesson the students will be able to:

1. Identify unfamiliar vocabulary words.
2. Listen to the story, *Peter's Place,* and answer specific questions.
3. Observe and participate in an oil spill experiment.
4. Write about what they observed during the experiment and what was learned about oil spills during the lesson.
5. Reflect on their participation and complete a self-assessment form.

Multiple Intelligences Challenged:

Verbal/Linguistic, Visual/Spatial, Intrapersonal, Interpersonal

Materials Needed:

Peter's Place by Sally Grindley, pocket chart, sentence strips, oil, paprika, dish detergent, 2 bowls, water, spatula, feathers, cotton balls, copies of self-assessment form, pencils, and paper.

Modification for Special Needs

I will have the students in cooperative groups actually involved in an oil spill experiment. All special needs students will be actively participating with a particular group responsibility. The oral discussion allows the students' individual responses to be heard. I will choose responders from cards which I shuffle after every class period.

Procedure: Lesson Initiation

Overview: Brief synopsis of the story, reading of the story, discussion, culminating activity is an exciting experiment based on the story. Closure will include questions and completion of their written observation and self-assessment.

Lesson Development

Before reading discuss unfamiliar words with students. Words will be displayed on sentence strips for the students to identify and learn the meanings (ravaged, turbulent, haven, crevice, and names of birds). Story is read to the students.

   Questions to generate a discussion of the story:

How do you think Peter feels about his place at the beginning? After the spill? Why did Peter help with the cleanup effort and rescue? What would you have done? What were your feelings at the end of the story?

* Highlight: Higher Level Questioning (yellow), Real-Life Application (Pink), Concrete Experience (Blue), and Cross Discipline Integration (Green)

Guided Practice

Discuss oil spills with the students, including how oil is transported, spilled, the damage a spill causes, how it is cleaned and removed. Allow for their questions to surface.

Students will observe and participate in the model experiment. I will create a miniature oil spill and try different methods of cleaning it up. Colored cooking oil will be placed in a bowl of water, and several objects will be placed in it so students may see the damage a spill can cause. Students will then create their own in their cooperative groups. I will demonstrate three methods of cleaning up an oil spill—skimming the surface of the water, absorbing the oil around the edges, and adding detergents. After the students have completed their experiment, we will discuss the effectiveness of each method.

Independent Practice

Explain the writing activity to students. They will write about what they observed during the experiment and what they learned about oil spills. For those who may complete before others, they may write about any feelings they have about what they observed and learned.

Closure

Pass out self-assessments for students to complete independently. Explain the directions, and remind students to be honest in their responses. If time permits, have students share something they learned today.

Performance Criteria/Rubric

4—Student participated in the discussion of the story. The student participated in discussion of and experiment demonstrating oil spills. The student demonstrated an understanding of the experiment by writing 3–4 paragraphs discussing their observations. Student completed self-assessment.

3—Student participated in the discussion of the story and oil spills. Student demonstrated an understanding of the experiment by writing 2–3 paragraphs discussing their observations. Students completed self-assessment.

2—Student participated, although very little, to the discussion. Student demonstrated some difficulty in understanding the experiment, and the 1–2 paragraphs about the experiment were sketchy. Student completed assessment with assistance.

1—Student did not participate in discussion of story or oil spills. Student demonstrated much difficulty in understanding the experiment, and was only able to write a few sentences about his or her observations. Student did not complete self-assessment even though assistance was offered.

Art—Intermediate

Type of Lesson: Quilt Design

Time: 35 minutes

Type of Lesson: Introductory Lesson to Designing Quilt Pieces

Instructional Objectives: The students will create one diagram (or plan) using folding, drawing lines to form a pattern combining construction paper and/or wallpaper design.

Materials to be used:

> Pencils
> Rulers
> Examples of quilts
> Glue
> Scissors
> 12″ × 12″ manila paper
> construction and wallpaper pieces
> 12″ × 12″ multipurpose paper

Motivation: Show my own examples of what will be done with their designs.
Examples of quilts (on our walls), point out these.

Procedure

Teacher Activity	Student Activity
Today we will be creating a quilt design. As you may remember we discussed quilting as a craft at the beginning of our year. Do you remember something about quilt designs?	Listening and responding to questions
We will create the design by folding the 12″ × 12″ paper in a variety of ways. (Show the students the example. Discuss patterns.)	Listening
After the paper is folded we will go over the folds with a pencil and ruler. This will be your plan to go by. When your plan is finished, you will need to reproduce the plan on the 12″ × 12″ manila paper. We will do this by cutting out the shapes from our plan design. You will then trace these shapes on the construction paper or wallpaper pieces and then glue them onto the 12″ × 12″ manila paper.	
Show the students the examples. Can you see the different designs that I have make on this model?	Listening, responding to/asking questions
Who can tell the class one of the four steps you need to follow in order to produce a good design?	Variety of students respond
Do you have questions about what you will be designing? Call the table captains to get the table folders and the materials for the tables. They may work on their quilt design or they may finish coloring their self-portraits or work on their loom weaving or stitchery (according to the grades).	Assemble their materials and begin working
The teacher will walk around among students' tables and assist students working, question, and offer suggestions about their designs.	Students work on their designs
Normal cleanup procedures 5 minutes before class ends, then line up to get ready to leave.	Students will clean up

Evaluation

The students fold, use rulers for drawing lines, plan what their design will look like, and complete the quilt designs they planned. (They will continue to work the next week.)

Reflections on Teaching

Some things I will do next time I teach the lesson:

- Write the steps on the board for students to refer to.
- Demonstrate tracing shapes.
- Discuss how and why they follow their plans.
- Remind students to put their initials on the back of all shapes and plans.
- Discuss tracing on the back of the wallpaper and pasting the construction paper so their lines don't show.

ENGLISH—HIGH SCHOOL

Type of Lesson:	Introduction to Short Story Unit—Characterization and Plot
Level:	9th Grade
Materials:	Overhead or Board, Copies of Elements worksheet
Time:	50 minutes
Objectives:	Given teacher's explanation students will:

    1. Identify at least three characteristics of the short story genre and the seven methods of characterization.
    2. Define the terms *setting, tone, antagonist,* and *protagonist.*
    3. List three different forms of conflict.

Motivation: Use dramas and sitcoms on TV to introduce short stories.

Procedure

Teacher Activity	**Student Response**
Short stories are like dramas and sitcoms in that their primary *purpose is to entertain.* What TV programs fit this description?	Take notes and respond to questions relating to analogy.
Secondly, they usually *focus on one theme* or event (everything contributes to one outcome).	"Ally McBeal" "Dawson Creek"
Thirdly, there are a limited number of characters.	
Fourthly, they have a tightly structured plot (introduction exposition, rising action, climax, falling action, denouement).	Write characteristics on board for students to copy into notes.
Finally, they are short and complete in themselves. (Even "Cheers," etc., has a story told each episode.)	
What is one of the first things you need when you write?	
Characters must be developed by authors (don't just happen). They can be developed at different levels, from simple to complex, flat to round.	Listen and respond to questions.

List Seven Methods of Characterization:

1. What does the character look like?
2. Where does the character live, work, and play?
3. What does the character think about?
4. How does the character speak?
5. How does the character react to people, places, and things?
6. How do other characters react to this character?
7. What does the author think about the character?

Take notes on methods of characterization.

Walk to empty chair and announce that Stanley Realbozo (or
   some other character) is seated there. Explain that we as a class
   will bring him to life.

Lead discussion in which all previous questions are answered in   Answer questions on the board to develop
   order to flesh out Stanley.   this character.

Assemble a composite picture of Stanley and "decide what to do
   with him." We will write a story with Stanley as our main
   character. He is now a now a member of our class. We have
   enrolled him in Freshman English.

Explain: stories have to be planned like a blueprint of a house. In
   a short story, the plot is the blueprint in the writer's plan for
   writing the story. Point of view: We will be third person
   omniscient; i.e., we will know everything about the character.
   (Other options: first person or third person objective.)

Write out the five stages of plot in question form:

1. What is the situation of the story? (Discuss the terms *setting*   Take notes in class
   and *mood*.)

2. What is the main conflict of the story? What are the generating
   circumstances and what gets the actions going? (Discuss the
   different forms of conflict (person vs. person, person vs. self,
   and person vs. god, nature, or mankind). Also, discuss the
   terms *protagonist* (main character) and *antagonist* (one or ones
   who try to thwart the main character). What events in the
   story increase the conflict and push forward action?

3. What is the climax or highest point of the story?

4. How is the conflict resolved?

5. How does the story end?

Discuss these five questions in terms of the Stanley Realbozo
   story. Completion of questions will result in a full-blown short
   story.

What is the theme/purpose?

Assessment

Student responses to oral question, written notes, and writer response on in-
class activity

Reflection

Students seemed to listen more to each other after I began writing their comments on the board. I still need to allow more wait time after asking higher level
questions.

Mathematics—High School
Box and Whisker Plots

Course Level:	Algebra I
Type of Lesson:	Reinforcement of concept/enrichment
Behavioral Objectives:	Given a set of data, the student will identify meaning of points; describe and state interpretations that can be made from examining data when asked by teacher.
Materials to be used:	Box and Whisker Graph
	Overhead Projector
	TI-81 and TI-82 overhead models
	Prepared overhead transparencies (6)
	Prepared transparency guides (6)
	Overhead markers (6)
	Yard/meter stick (optional)
	Ruler (6) (optional)
Motivation:	Classwork is always used to orient the student to working with math. Using classwork to tie into the lesson will make the student feel classwork truly is necessary and also wonder how it will be used during class.

Procedure

Teacher Activity

Put on board:

CLASSWORK: Arrange the following quiz scores in rank order (sort):

2, 5, 7, 7, 9, 10, 5, 4, 2, 8, 8, 9, 5, 3

(Allow approximately 5 minutes)

Draw on board:

```
├──┼──┼──┼──┼──┼──┼──┼──┼──┼──┤
0  1  2  3  4  5  6  7  8  9  10
```

"Can anybody tell me how to find the median of this data so we can draw the box plot for it?

"Great! So I'll mark that on my graph."

Draw:

0 1 2 3 4 5 6 7 8 9 10

"Now what two points do I need?"

"Very good! How do I get the 1*st* quartile point?"

"You're exactly right! And what is the 1*st* quartile value?

Draw:

0 1 2 3 4 5 6 7 8 9 10

"Very good! What is the 2*nd* quartile value?

Student Activity

Sort the data (either in ascending or descending order). Find the middle number. Since there are an even number of pieces of data in this example, add together the 7th and 8th piece of data and divide their sum by 2. The median is 6.

"The 1st and 3rd quartile points."

"Find the median of the lowest half of data."

"4"

"8"

Teacher Activity   **Student Activity**

Draw:

"So now all we have to do to complete our box and whisker plot is to draw our box like so:"

Draw:

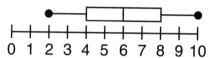

"Are there any questions?"   (Yes or No)

"Let's go over how to graph this data on the calculator."

"What is the first thing we must do?"   "Enter data in a list."

"Exactly! To do that we push STAT and then ENTER because we want to edit a list." (demo)

"Then just enter each number in the list by pushing ENTER after each entry."

"Now we have to tell the calculator we want to graph this data using the box and whiskers plot."

"Does anyone remember how to do that?"   Yes or No

"Push 2ND Y= (or STAT PLOT) and push ENTER to turn on Plot 1. Push ENTER again to highlight the word "ON," then push the down arrow key and go over to the little picture that looks like a box plot and push ENTER. Since the L1 list is highlighted, and that's where our data is, go ahead and push GRAPH."

"Our two graphs look similar. Do they?"   "Yes."

Now graph this data and draw it above the first one on your paper."

Put on board (or point to it):

7, 7, 8, 6, 6, 5, 4, 7, 5, 6, 7, 5, 5, 6

Turn off the overhead.

Graph using the calculator.

Turn overhead on.

"Your two graphs should look similar to these."

"What can we tell about the quiz grades of the two classes by looking at the graphs?"

"Grades are scattered in one class and bunched in the other."
"Median grade is the same in both classes."

"If you were a teacher, which class would you rather teach?"   "The second class."

"Why is that?"

"All students in that class perform at approximately the same level."

"That's exactly right! Even though there are no real high achievers in the class, everyone seems to be on the same level."

Pass out ditto.

"As you can see, there are 6 sets of data on this ditto. Each number represents the percentage of ineligible students a given high school has for a particular sport. What do you think a blank means on this worksheet?"

"School doesn't offer that activity."

"You're exactly right!"

"What I want you to do for this activity is to get into groups, which I will assign, and find the box plot for the list of data I assign your group. I then want you to draw your box plot on an overhead transparency I will give your group."

"When you draw your box plot, draw it in the area I have marked off for you on the sheet of paper you will get. On the paper is also the scale you are to use. *Remember* to draw your graph on the transparency."

"We are not going to take much time to do this, so when your group is done, put your desks back in order and elect someone in your group to put the transparency on the overhead. So there will end up being 6 transparencies on the overhead at once.

"Are there any questions?"

Yes or No.

Group 1—first person in each row—Band
Group 2—first row—Drama
Group 3—second row—Yearbook
Group 4—third row—Baseball
Group 5—fourth row—Boys Track
Group 6—fifth row—Girls Track

Work in group on activity.

Turn on overhead.

Place transparencies on overhead.

"Okay. From our graphs, does it appear that band members or baseball players tend to have higher rates of ineligibility?"

"Band members."

"How can you tell?"

Bigger box

"Very good. Why is there no lower whisker on the yearbook box plot?"

"First quartile value was 0. 1/4 of data was 0."

"Excellent! Now write five sentences that summarize what you can tell from these graphs."

Have students read responses aloud in class.

Various responses.

Assessment: By means of questioning, observation, and guided practice.

Assignment: Application 13—Roller Skating Clubs data (box plots)

Rubric for Designing Lessons and Instructional Materials

Distinguished	Proficient	Apprentice	Novice
Learner Goals			
1. Focuses instruction on one or more learning goals and outcomes.	1. Learning outcomes are well developed according to the concept being taught.	1. Learning outcomes are limited and lack sources.	1. Learning outcomes are unrelated to procedure.
Integration of Curriculum			
2. Integrate skills, thinking processes, and content across the disciplines.	2. Evidence of integration of skills, thinking processes, and content across disciplines.	2. An attempt to integrate skills.	2. Minimal attention to integrate across disciplines.
Instructional Materials			
3. Proposes learning experiences that challenge, motivate, and actively involve the learners.	3. Proposes learning experiences that involve the learner.	3. Random learning experience that involve the learner.	3. Random and/or weak organization or plan involving the learner.
4. Proposes learning experiences that are developmentally appropriate for learners.	4. Proposes learning experiences that are appropriate for learners on the level being taught.	4. Unelaborated development of ideas and details of learning experiences for learners on the level being taught.	4. Minimal development of ideas and disciplines of learning experience for learners on the level being taught.
5. Incorporates strategies that address physical, social, and cultural diversity.	5. Demonstrates sensitivity to differences.	5. Little or no attention to cultural diversity.	5. Cultural diversity inclusion is missing.
6. Includes comprehensive and appropriate school and community resources that support learning.	6. Includes appropriate school and community resources that support learning.	6. Few school community resources are included to support learning.	6. No mention of school and community resources to support learning.
7. Includes learning experiences that encourage students to be adaptable, flexible, resourceful, and creative.	7. Includes learning experiences that encourage students to be flexible and resourceful.	7. Learning experiences are controlled and unelaborated.	7. Learning experiences lack focus.
Use of Computers/Technology			
8. Includes creative and appropriate use of technology as a tool to enhance student learning.	8. Illustrates use of technology with learners.	8. Little mention of technology use by learner.	8. No technology is mentioned.
Learner Assessment			
9. Includes appropriate assessment strategies and processes.	9. Includes acceptable assessment strategies and processes.	9. Assessment strategies and processes are simplistic and do not match outcomes.	9. Assessment is inappropriate.

Professional Portfolio Assessment Criteria

The student teaching/intern experience provides you with multiple opportunities to perform and reflect on your progress under the guidance of supervising teachers from the school and college setting. Professional portfolio development tasks and the rubric are designed to assist you in becoming an excellent teacher candidate who can compile an outstanding teaching portfolio.

Performance of the criteria stated after each of the standards is rated using code numbers 1 through 4. An explanation of the code numbers is given below.

CODE 4—Outstanding

The portfolio contains all important components and communicates ideas clearly.

The portfolio samples and narratives demonstrate in-depth understanding of the relevant concepts and/or processes needed in teaching and learning.

Where appropriate, the student offers insightful interpretations or extensions (generalizations, applications, analogies) of effective teaching and assessment.

CODE 3—Competent

The portfolio contains most important components and communicates ideas clearly.

The portfolio samples and narratives demonstrate understanding of major concepts of teaching; omits or misrepresents some less important ideas or details.

CODE 2—Developing

The portfolio contains some important components and communicates these clearly.

The portfolio samples and narratives demonstrate that there are gaps in his/her conceptual understanding of teaching and learning.

CODE 1—Beginning

The portfolio shows minimal understanding of necessary components.

The portfolio samples lack evidence of concepts/processes necessary in effective teaching and learning.

Example: Portfolio Response

(Eighth Grade Social Studies and Language Arts)

Standard: Creating and Maintaining a Learning Climate

In creating and maintaining a learning climate, teachers are faced with a tough task. To be an effective classroom manager, a teacher must be well prepared and exhibit good planning techniques. As an educator, I must first be in touch with my own feelings about life, culture, children, and the educational process. I bring with me to the table a set of values and beliefs shaped by my own background, upbringing, and experiences. I must first see myself as a person, as someone with feelings, emotions, and beliefs. It is imperative that I am aware of these factors and how they influence my teaching. Students are going to have a whole different set of backgrounds and experiences of their own. This fact shouldn't be taken lightly.

I am able to effectively communicate with my students; therefore, I must understand from where they come. Communication is key. It is the essential component of teaching and learning, and without it neither can occur. I must communicate what is and isn't acceptable in my classroom, and I also have to set and enforce rules (via consequences). My goal as classroom manager is to maximize the amount of student learning time, and unacceptable behavior jeopardizes this goal. Therefore, my expectations of student behavior must be clear and firm. It is vital that I create an atmosphere conducive to learning and immediately discourage any behavior that threatens that atmosphere.

I use preventive disciplinary approaches and have found that the best way to deal with a problem is to identify it immediately, label it as unacceptable, and implement subsequent consequences. During the first days of classes, I post a set of classroom rules and make sure that students know and understand these and the consequences. This process helps them realize that they are accountable for their actions. I have also discovered that establishing daily routines is helpful in minimizing distractions. Clearly stating to students that they are expected to come into the class, sit down, take out a pen and some paper, and begin quietly writing a response to a question displayed on the overhead has worked beautifully for me. If the students aren't awarded opportunities to misbehave at the beginning of class, it will be much easier to hold their attention for an extended period of time. As I've been told and have learned through my own experience, "once you've lost them, it's very difficult to get them back!"

During my student teaching experience I have taught several special needs students. I have students who have impaired hearing, muscular dystrophy, and cerebral palsy. I wear a highly sensitive microphone attachment so the one student can listen as I speak and I make sure he can see the TV captions and writing on the board. The student in the wheelchair needs other physical arrangements and special books with enlarged print. I am grateful to have had the opportunity to teach these special needs kids. I am inspired by their determination and work ethic. They will not be denied anything! They believe in themselves and are determined to achieve whatever they set their minds to.

There are also cultural and social differences among the students I teach. I have students who live in fancy neighborhoods with elaborate homes and those who live in inner-city housing projects. It has been an eye-opening experience observing these students as they develop their cliques and discuss their common experiences. In walking by (in the lunchroom) a group of students from the projects, I heard them discuss their relatives being associated with and being killed by gangs. At the same table the suburban students were discussing what they were planning for the weekend or what happened last night on "The X-Files." It is imperative that I recognize differences among students' experiences and invite students to share these. In a lesson on limericks I encouraged them to write on any topic and use humor, and I found that the freedom to choose actually enhanced the quality of students' work.

I have planned and taught lessons that require students to perform in many different ways. In a mini-lesson about amiable characteristics, I had students create their own epitaphs and include all the amiable characteristics they thought they possessed. When they had finished writing, we began sharing their epitaphs. However, two students were talking and creating a disruption, so I exclaimed in a weeping voice, "Excuse me, Ebony, but it seem that someone is being so rude as to speak during this solemn occasion. Have you no respect? We are paying our respects to the late, great, wonderful Ebony! How rude—and you're not even wearing black!" I then briefly discussed the importance of listening to one another out of respect. It worked wonderfully and I think the students responded well.

Students work individually and within the large group. Each class period begins with a learning log activity in which the students responded to a question related to the day's lesson. I often organize students into small groups and they act as peer editors of each other's written work. When dealing with groups, I think I display an awareness of the on-goings within the classroom ("withitness"—Kounin). It was clear to the students that I would seek out and correct undesirable behaviors. Students were aware of my expectations concerning classroom behavior. They knew that I would circulate, monitor their behavior, and hold them accountable for their work in small groups. I always checked to be certain that each member was contributing to the completion of the task. I sometimes observed them closely and used proximity control to influence their participation. Other times I would observe from a distance and quietly approach individuals and ask that they join in. I would stand there until they cooperated. I also reminded students that working together often results in higher quality work and that each member's participation was essential to the completion of the task (positive interdependence).

Finally, I think I engaged in teacher/student interactions that contributed to establishing a learning environment. I really pushed some students as group members, and being persistent I was able to get each student to contribute. I give students options, ask them to choose, and then circulate to observe how they follow through with their decisions. I have learned that keeping students engaged contributes much to the classroom environment.

Evaluation Forms[*]

EVALUATION OF STUDENT ORAL PRESENTATION

Name _____   Date _____

Type of Presentation

1. Voice is pleasant—natural tonal quality   1 __   2 __   3 __   4 __

Comments _____

2. Voice is projected   1 __   2 __   3 __   4 __

Comments _____

3. Speech is at conversational speed   1 __   2 __   3 __   4 __

Comments _____

4. Words are clearly enunciated   1 __   2 __   3 __   4 __

Comments _____

5. Fillers are avoided (ah, like, you know . . .)   1 __   2 __   3 __   4 __

Comments _____

6. Vocal emphasis used for key words, sentences   1 __   2 __   3 __   4 __

Comments _____

7. Enthusiastic, vibrant   1 __   2 __   3 __   4 __

Comments _____

8. Volume and rate of speed varied to show emotion   1 __   2 __   3 __   4 __

Comments _____

9. Able to hold audience's attention   1 __   2 __   3 __   4 __

Comments _____

10. Appropriate gestures and facial expressions   1 __   2 __   3 __   4 __

Comments _____

11. Posture is erect, comfortable, appropriate   1 __   2 __   3 __   4 __

Comments _____

12. Eye contact with audience is maintained   1 __   2 __   3 __   4 __

Comments _____

*Adapted from unpublished materials—Marie Sanders

Student Form

Student Name _____ Language Arts Teacher _____

Date _____ Class _____

We have been reading the book _____ by _____

It is _____ fiction, written in _____ style.

While reading this book, I learned _____

_____

We have kept a reader response journal while reading the novel. A good reader response entry includes _____

_____

Parent-Teacher-Student Conference Notes

My reader response journal is interesting to read. The entry dated _____ is my best entry

because _____

The entry dated _____ needs more reflection because _____

My writing portfolio includes _____

from _____ grade. To date, _____ grade pieces include: _____

_____

At this point, I think my strength in written communication is _____

_____

As a writer, I would like to be able to _____

_____

In order to reach this goal, I will _____

_____

I could rework this entry as a _____

The entry dated _____ needs more work because _____

_____

I could make this more interesting by _____

_____

I have participated by _____

One way I could improve my participation is to _____

As an independent reader, I would rate myself as

 Outstanding _____   Satisfactory _____   Needs Improvement _____ .

I have read the following books and selected one for a book talk, book review, or presentation in class.

Title _____ Author _____ No. of Pages _____ Rating _____

WRITING

Student and Teacher Evaluation

Student Evaluation

Date _____ Title of Piece _____

Name_____ Grade _____ Section _____

1	2	3	4	The idea for my writing is creative. I have brainstormed and selected my best ideas to write an original piece.
1	2	3	4	This piece of writing "sounds" like me. It has style!
1	2	3	4	My writing makes sense. There is an introduction, a middle, and an ending.
1	2	3	4	Events happen in a logical and sequential order.
1	2	3	4	Each paragraph is indented.
1	2	3	4	Each paragraph has a topic sentence and supporting details.
1	2	3	4	Each sentence is interesting to read. The length is varied, and the thought is complete.
1	2	3	4	My choice of vocabulary is perfect for my piece of writing. The words are exciting and colorful I have used a thesaurus.
1	2	3	4	I have reread my piece and added details, explanations, adjectives, and/or dialogue to make my writing electric.
1	2	3	4	I have checked: possessives, plurals, subject/verb, and person.
1	2	3	4	I have capitalized proper nouns and adjectives.
1	2	3	4	I have checked my writing for punctuation. [., ?, !," ", ( ) ____].
1	2	3	4	I have checked my writing thoroughly for misspelled words.
1	2	3	4	I have rewritten my final draft using my best handwriting.
1	2	3	4	I think this piece is my best work yet, and I am ready to publish.

I am (satisfied/not satisfied) with this piece of writing because _____

_____

_____

_____

Teacher Evaluation

1	2	3	4	Idea: _____
1	2	3	4	Voice: _____
1	2	3	4	Content: _____
1	2	3	4	Organization: _____
1	2	3	4	Sentences: _____
1	2	3	4	Vocabulary: _____
1	2	3	4	Grammar: _____
1	2	3	4	Punctuation: _____
1	2	3	4	Spelling: _____

MIDDLE GRADES INDEPENDENT
READER RESPONSE QUESTIONS

Independent Reading Log

Daily Minimum Requirement

20 Minutes Reading + A written response to the literature = a healthy lifelong habit that is fun!

Select an appropriate question and respond to what you have read by writing a reader response in your independent reading notebook. (If you would like to respond to the story on your own, that is acceptable.)

The questions are designed to help you get started writing and focus your thinking. Have fun! I am very interested in what you have to say. Remember to write the date at the top of each entry and the pages you have read. Example: April 16 (Pages 1–22)

1. Based on the title, what do you think the book will be about?
2. After scanning the chapter titles, what are some things you noticed?
3. What comes to mind (image or idea, feeling, sensation, memory) now that you have read the title and opening paragraphs?
4. What questions might you have after reading the first few pages or the first chapter?
5. What are you expecting from this writer now that you have read the first couple of chapters?
6. As you read, what caught your attention?
7. As you read, what new images did you form?
8. Were there words you did not understand or parts that did not make sense?
9. What is in your mind (image, idea, feeling, sensation, memory) now that you have read further.
10. As you read, what happened to your first impression of a character?
11. Now that you have completed the entire novel (story), what realizations do you have?
12. What interpretations and ideas have you gotten from the book?
13. Now that you have completed the entire book, what do you think about a character's actions? About his/her decisions?
15. If you were to write the author of this text (book, story, poem), what would you say to him/her?
16. What tips would you give to readers who are just starting to read this story or novel?

Additional Response Suggestions

1. Design a character map—illustrate the relationship between the main character and minor characters.
2. Illustrate how a character changes over time or responds to events in the story or book.
3. Trace the plot of the book or story by creating a story ladder. (The above suggestions will need to be added to as the story unfolds.
4. Illustrate a favorite scene and write the book's description beneath your drawing.
5. Select favorite quotes from the book or story and tell why they were interesting to you.
6. Select phrases or passages from the book that you would like to imitate in your own writing.
7. Write a new ending to the book.

8. Write a dialogue between two characters that could have taken place. Be sure to use quotation marks.
9. Jot down anything you noticed about the author's style of writing: adjectives, a special theme, use of odd words, suspense, etc.
10. Compare the book to another you have read by the same author or a different author.

Still Stuck?

1. I began to think of . . .
2. I wonder why . . .
3. I know the feeling . . .
4. I noticed . . .

Index